Navigational Selling

Piloting the Client Decision Journey

A Guide to Selling Service-Intense B2B Offerings

by Jerry Vieira, CMC

D1706265

Navigational Selling™

Piloting the Client Decision Journey

A Guide to Selling Service-Intense B2B Offerings

Jerry Vieira, CMC

Copyright

Navigational Selling™

Piloting the Client Decision Journey

A Guide to Selling Service-Intense B2B Offerings

Published by The QMP Group, Inc.

Hillsboro, Oregon

Dedication

To those who have found great success, personal satisfaction, and joy by embracing the enlightenment-of-purpose called "Navigational Selling".

*****

"You will get all you want in life, if you help enough other people get what they want."

Zig Ziglar

Acknowledgements

I would like to thank a number of clients, colleagues and individuals for their support, guidance, consultation, and willingness to review draft manuscripts during the creation and publication of this book.

To my SMB2B clients, their sales training program participants, and my individual mentoring & coaching clients: Thank you for placing your trust in me, the QMP methodology, and its insights, techniques, and tools. Your personal commitment and hard work created the most memorable successes of my management consulting career.

Thank you also, for your personal friendship. I am continually delighted when we meet again, sometimes many years after a training session, and you mention some technique, story or memorable word or phrase, stored in the rapid access vault of your memory, that has stood the test of time. It is good to know you value them and that they have real stickiness.

To my Vistage Trusted Advisor Group: As with my first book, The Consultancy Navigator®, thank you for your support and encouragement with Navigational Selling™.

To Mr. Roy Serpa, my personal coach and mentor: Thank you for suggesting this title as the next offering in the QMP Marketing & Sales Navigational Series and for your perceptive critique. I appreciate and value your continued support and guidance.

To Messrs. Bob Phillips & Larry Johnson: For use of their management styles matrix and trademarked word, "Lipotage™".

To Mr. Joe Connors: For your determination, dedication to and adoption of Navigational Selling™ techniques and tools. You are a prime example of its power when wielded by a sincere, dedicated sales professional.

To Mr. Peter Adams: A successful SMB2B business owner, U.S. Coast Guard Certified Coxswain, friend, experienced Navigator, and talented salesperson in his own right, for his help on the role of sea-faring Navigators.

To Mr. Steve Bohnenkamp: Whose enormous depth of experience in the-field as a front-line salesman, sales manager, and management consultant, helped assure appropriate emphasis was placed on the proven and most effective concepts, principles, and behaviors in Navigational Selling™. Steve, you were a true Master Sales Manager and Salesperson – and a good man. You left us way too soon. May you Rest in Peace, my friend.

To Ms. Diane Gibson: My ideal reader and line editor who patiently navigates my manuscripts and provides extraordinary and constructive editorial guidance.

To Mr. T. J. Romano, Esq: For his excellent and wise counsel.

Table of Contents

A Note to Readers

Visitors who elect to wander through the Crater of Diamonds State Park in Arkansas, are driven by the real potential of discovering its namesake gems without much digging – and some do. Inspired by that thought and recognizing that businesspeople don't have a lot of time, I have attempted to stock this book with valuable sales and marketing gems - and make them easy to find. My hope is, that like discovered diamonds, they will be stuffed into the reader's mental pocket, taken home, and kept in a safe place for quick access.

This is a large book. So, to facilitate gem discovery, I have attempted to assure that a scan of the detailed Table of Contents, Table of Figures, Index and Glossary of Terms will enable the time-constrained executive to quickly focus in on topics of their highest interest and most urgent need.

What is Navigational Selling™ ?

Navigational Selling™ (NavSell) is a _method for selling tailorable, technology-oriented, service-intense_ offerings (products, services, or both) to business-to-business (B2B) clients. Moreover, NavSell is applicable to the sale of any product or service offering that, to be sold successfully, will involve some combination of the following:

- a detailed pre-sale understanding of the client's situation,
- a multi-step client decision making process,
- a multi-stage seller's sales process,
- the involvement of several levels of decision makers, decision influencers, and specialists within the client's organization, and
- the customization of the solution to a client's unique situation and needs.

If any combination of those requirements exists, a salesperson can expect a complex selling journey that needs to be carefully navigated.

Navigational Selling™ is Intended for Several Constituencies

One of the primary objectives of Navigational Selling™ is to educate and improve the effectiveness of the individual salesperson. Yet, there are three additional constituencies for whom this book will provide meaningful value: *Executives-in-Charge* (EICs), *Sales Draftees*, and *Solo Service Practitioners.*

Navigational Selling™ recognizes that the members of each group, by the varied nature of their business responsibilities, experience levels, and objectives, will likely have different needs, challenges, and degrees of sales process understanding. Moreover, the connectedness, challenges, and implications of embracing a disciplined sales process, impact each constituency differently.

Consistent with the intent to provide value to such a breadth of readership, Navigational Selling™ encompasses a wider range of topics than would normally be the scope of a book solely dedicated to sales skills, techniques, and process disciplines.

Given the different constituencies and range of topics, this book is divided into four parts.

Part 1 - *A Framework for Sales Success:* It is essential that EICs, CEOs, Business Owners, Entrepreneurs, and Marketing & Sales Executives understand the impacts that corporate culture, organizational framework, and process interconnectedness have on the successful implementation of any new sales methodology. Part 1 covers those topics.

Part 2 - *The Navigational Selling™ Process:* Part 2 is written for salespeople, mid-level marketing & sales managers and anyone circumstantially "drafted" onto the sales team. For this group, a common understanding of sales process dynamics and vocabulary will assure everyone is on the same page in any sales situation.

Part 3 - *Adoption and Evolution:* Part 3 has two chapters. The first, Chapter 12, is written for the individual salesperson, who may wish to embrace NavSell methodology techniques - independent of a corporate-wide implementation. Chapter 13 is written for EICs, CEOs, Entrepreneurs, Business Owners, and Marketing & Sales Managers. It covers how to achieve rapid success from a gap-driven implementation of the techniques in this book.

Part 4 - *Appendices:* Part 4 is intended for anyone who wishes to delve into the deeper details of NavSell tools and techniques, and the two other key business processes to which any selling process must be wed, namely, Market Strategy and New Business Development.

Some readers will find value in reading the complete manuscript. Others, those seeking insight within the narrower scope of their roles, will likely want to focus only on those parts that relate to their specific and more immediate needs and challenges.

Given the breadth of roles and content, I offer the following content guidelines for each group of readers.

To Executives-in-Charge (EICs) and SMB2B Business Owners

EICs have a major impact on a sales team's effectiveness. Through their personal example and uncompromising insistence on adherence to process discipline, training, continuous improvement, and individual accountability, their organizational journey to higher sales performance is achieved. Yet, many SMB2B EICs have never had to personally make a living by selling, or in the street vernacular of sales, never had to "carry a bag".

If you are an EIC, an understanding of the complete Marketing & Sales Engine will be important. To implant that important understanding, I strongly recommend you begin your journey at the beginning of Part 1, *A Framework for Sales Success*, before embracing Part 2, *The Navigational Selling™ Process*. Proceeding to Part 3, Chapter 13, *Organizational Level Process Adoption* will assist greatly if you want to consider a Navigational Selling™ corporate-level implementation. Part 4, *Appendices*, provides valuable supplemental material regarding assessing your organizational needs, the importance of a sound Market Strategy, and the role of New Business Development.

To Professional Salespeople

If you are a salesperson or a sales & marketing manager in an SMB2B enterprise and are primarily interested in improving your own or your team's sales skill set, you may elect to jump directly to Part 2, *The Navigational Selling™ Process*, and work from that point through Part 3, Chapter 12, *Individual NavSell Process Adoption*. Appendix D, New Business Development, will also be of high value. If you are on a career path to Vice President or General Management, I suggest you begin with Part 1 and run through the complete book.

To "Draftees" - Support Specialists without Sales Experience who Need to Support a Selling Effort

A co-equal intent of Navigational Selling™ is to inform and educate the technical and operational specialists employed within SMB2B firms, who are periodically "*drafted*" into supporting the sales effort in the field. If you are a technical specialist or hold another important role in an SMB2B firm (roles like operations, marketing, quality, finance, engineering, customer service) and are occasionally called upon to support a specific sales effort, you will likely find Part 2, _The Navigational Selling™ Process_, most immediately helpful. The option of engaging with the complete Marketing & Sales Engine model, by beginning in Part 1, _A Framework for Sales Success_, remains available for the ambitious student of Marketing & Sales or the merely curious.

To Solo Consultants or Solo Service Practitioners

The final group of non-salesperson readers this book hopes to influence, are professionals employed as Solo Practitioners or Consultants. Members of this group may not have a track record in sales or may harbor insecurities about their sales abilities, instead relying almost completely on their technical skill and reputation to generate business. Yet, they do need to be effective at sales to eat.

If you are a consultant or independent service solo practitioner, I recommend you start at Part 1: _A Framework for Sales Success_, or even better, consider reading the first book in the QMP Marketing & Sales Navigator Series, _The Consultancy Navigator®_, currently available on Amazon in both Kindle and paperback formats.

That book provides a more specific and comprehensive tutorial and roadmap for starting, managing, and growing a successful management consulting practice. Its examples, stories, and tools are tailored for that specific journey.

An Invocation to All Readers:

I sincerely hope that you come away from these pages saying, "_Gee, I never thought about our marketing & sales function that way before – but that makes a lot of sense._" For the sakes of all the stakeholders in your firm, your colleagues, business owners, family, and community, the leverage generated from what you learn, implement, and exemplify will enable and fuel success for all.

Conventions

Standard conventions used throughout this book:

Gender Use: The use of the pronouns he and she, when not associated with specific stories or individuals, will be referred to as "they" or "their". For example, when the word salesperson is used, the words they or their will be used as appropriate to the context of the idea. An example: "A salesperson must monitor their time allocation closely."

Navigational Selling

Products vs. Service: Except in specific illustrative stories, we will try to use the generic term "Offering" instead of "Products", or "Services". An Offering may be a Product, a Service, or combination of both.

Customers vs. Clients: The word Client typically denotes the recipient of a service offering, while Customer denotes the recipient of a product-oriented business. Lawyers have clients. Supermarkets have customers. Since Navigational Selling™ embodies an expansive view of what a business delivers, namely an expanded concept of received value, all receivers of a firm's offerings (product or service) will be referred to as Clients.

Storytime: Stories are used throughout this book to illustrate specific important points. They are clearly denoted within the text with the word *Storytime* followed by the title of the story. Almost all stories are from real life, keeping names unidentified and occasionally changing genders for privacy reasons. A few stories are not from our experience archives. They are offered to illustrate key concepts and are noted as such. Each story will contain an explicit *Moral of the Story* at the end.

The Use of Assessments: The implementation of Navigational Selling™ is assessment driven. Four different assessments are offered to assist implementers understand and focus on the highest leverage and processes and behaviors to improve. Those assessments are:

- *The Marketing & Sales Organizational Effectiveness Assessment*
- *Organizational-Level Sales Process and Skills Effectiveness Assessment*
- *Individual Sales Skills Effectiveness Assessment*
- *Organizational Culture Assessment*

Military Analogies and Examples: The Navigational Selling™ manuscript includes a few military examples. Not everyone appreciates the use of military analogies and examples. Yet, there are many similarities between military science and market strategy and sales. The lessons to be learned are valuable and applicable. As an example, the Battle of Stalingrad example at the beginning of Chapter 1 will sear an image in the psyche of some readers and hopefully teach a valuable lesson for a lifetime.

Emphasis: Navigational Selling™ is a methodology that uses a specific vocabulary. Throughout the book I have elected to frequently capitalize and underline the key concepts and vocabulary for the sake of establishing, through repetition, their importance. The reader will find words and phrases such as, *Value Quotient*, *Discovery*, *Discussion Summary*, *Management Style*, *Qualification Factors* frequently displaying such a font style.

Repetition: As you read through the manuscript, you may notice concepts and ideas that are repeated. Such repetitions are intended.

In consideration of the reader's time availability, objectives, and situation, each may elect different routes through the book. In selecting some paths, important examples, and concepts from the skipped over chapters may be missed. Repetition is intended to assure important examples and concepts are captured along any individual's reading path.

When you encounter those incidents of repetition, please consider:

If it's repeated, it's damned important!

*****

Preface

Evolution

It was near the end of my senior year at engineering school. Graduation was within grasp - if I could just make it through last semester final exams.

Corporate, Government and Military recruiters were arriving on campus. Interviews were imminent - as was a haircut, a shave, and a tie. It would soon be time to make a career decision. Would it be electrical power generation or electronics? I was flexible, but harbored one strong conviction; I could never, ever be a salesperson.

I would prefer a life as a carpenter's helper, lugging 80-pound packs of asphalt shingles on my shoulders, across the steep roofs of two-story New England colonials in the heat and humidity of August, before I would ever be a salesperson. As a low-wage grunt on a small construction crew, I had done that very job one summer between high-school and college. I absolutely hated it. It was too much like work – and I was too young for a cold beer afterwards.

I imagined that even with a company-paid air-conditioned car, and with enough money for multiple cold beers, a career in sales still seemed a scary post-graduation option. Call me chicken, ignorant and short-sighted. I plead guilty.

I envisioned relentless ever-increasing sales quotas and loud high-pressure sales managers. I harbored images of having to jump up from my desk and ring a bell every time a customer said yes. I saw a future of extensive travel away from a family I did not yet have.

It all seemed like an existence of perpetual stress, an emotional roller coaster that ramped from sales pressure to customer crisis, and back again to sales pressure. Rinse and repeat. And all would be exacerbated by the fickle roller-coaster of the economy.

Moreover, being a salesperson after four years of rigorous engineering study would have been, in my mind, an admission of failure, a violation of some unwritten honor code, a sell-out. After all, I was an Electrical Engineer, an academic veteran of partial differential equations, vectors and matrices, semiconductor physics and the

EE's nightmare of thermodynamics. I had the GPA battle scars, sans medals and Dean's list acknowledgements, to prove it.

My dream was to nobly wear a white lab coat, with a pocket protector of course, and invent stuff to make the world a better place. My inventions would be recorded scrupulously in my lab notebook, patented, and I would be proud to look back at the end of my career and know I had contributed something meaningful to society.

The quiet life of an engineer, a lab rat, was more to my liking. Selling simply wasn't me.

And so, right out of college, through more luck than deserved reward (considering my GPA) my dream of becoming an electronics design engineer became a reality. I felt like I had drawn an inside straight on a big pot.

During the subsequent 25 years, as my career progressed from inventor, to engineering manager, to marketing manager, I slowly began to realize that I had been selling to some extent throughout my whole working life.

As an engineer and manager in a Fortune 500 high-tech company, I was frequently required to make appeals - affectionately known as "pitches" - to executives at the highest levels of our firm. When investment funding was needed for a project, when approval was required to recruit new members of a project team, or cash committed to acquire and implement new automation and testing equipment, I had to sell.

I had to convince our experienced and scary-smart corporate executives, most of whom were accomplished engineers in their own right, that my technical judgment was sound, my management skills could be trusted to direct the resources required to achieve the needed results, and the schedule I was promising could be met.

I was required to credibly project financial returns on those investments, demonstrate how the investment was going to be made, evaluate alternatives, negotiate equipment acquisition and deployment costs, convince technically talented job candidates to come and work with us, and make convincing arguments to our management team about precisely how the outcomes would be achieved.

It was all selling.

If while reading this, any of you recall your own experience in selling to engineers, you will perhaps relate to the particularly challenging task it can be. Some say that engineers are the toughest customers of all, no matter what you are selling them – from life insurance to life-sciences equipment. They are a tough, skeptical, data-driven, methodical, unemotional, and hugely analytical audience.

When, after 25 years, I launched my management consulting firm, I was pleasantly surprised at how relatively smooth the transition to selling market strategy consulting services to SMB2B executives seemed to be.

I pondered that epiphany and concluded that it was primarily because as an engineer, solving challenging problems had always been the primary focus of all my career assignments. Moreover, I had always been intensely driven to solve problems in a way that was clearly in the best interest of the business. In fact, the first tag line of my consulting practice was, "*Dedicated to client success*™". And while it is no longer my tag line, it remains the primary operating principle of my practice.

As a management consultant selling to C-level executives, I first assess, analyze, and diagnose client situations. I then explain the implications of any problems discovered and make recommendations about which alternative direction the client might take to resolve their issues and achieve their objectives.

If that sounds like selling, it is.

In the beginning, logic and creative problem solving were my dual sales superpowers.

Logic was effective in analyzing data, advising clients of the root problem, explaining its implications, and charting a course to improve the situation. My creative problem-solving skills would often seal the deal, often eliciting the comment, "*Gee! We had never thought of things that way before.*"

Logic and creative problem solving were the only capabilities I needed.

Or so I thought.

Over time I discovered that client emotions were too significant a factor in sales success to be ignored. Selling to engineer-executives was tough, but logic was a useful tool – like the "go-to" golf club in your bag. In contrast, selling to "normal" non-engineering people, that exhibited and often hid a full range of emotions, was foreign to me.

Adding emotional awareness to my sales approach was not without challenge. But I realized that when my logic-driven approach would fail, it was often because client emotions had transformed my smooth, logic-and-creative-problem-solving sales process into a scree-littered mountain climb during an earthquake. I had slipped on this scree more than once, resulting in painful failure to win important engagements.

Something needed changing – and it was me.

Though it took some time, I embarked on a growth journey to understand and integrate client emotions, personality types, motivations, and management styles, into my client communications, sales processes, and consulting engagements. Those added ingredients became high-value support pillars of my business, executive consulting engagements, and training programs. In effect, reading people emerged as a third essential ingredient of success, taking a co-equal seat alongside logic and creative problem solving.

Truth is, my personal ability to read people and discover their true feelings during a selling opportunity, falls short of the level of a super-power. But people tell me I've become fairly good at it. And it has become immensely helpful.

Over time, I became confident and skilled enough in an emotion + logic + creative problem-solving sales process, to blend these components it into a sales methodology. I have used it for more than 25 years to train and coach SMB2B salespeople and consultants in hundreds of SMB2B firms. Now, in training-session attendee comments, the Reading People content gets the highest positive rating scores. We will cover this topic in Chapter 8, Reading People.

The Birth of a Book

In late 2019, I received a message from a friend who wanted to discuss a periodic problem he was having selling finance and accounting support services to SMB2B owners and EICs. As an owner-partner with a regional new business development role in his firm, it was his responsibility to discover clients with Finance or Accounting challenges, identify appropriately experienced finance and accounting specialists from his bullpen of resources, then craft and win a support agreement.

He was an accomplished salesperson in his own right – a successful graduate of my sales coaching program. So, I was curious about what his sales challenge might be.

He revealed that "closing" meetings did not always work out the way he had intended. Occasionally, a meeting in which the skilled resource from his bullpen met the client for the first time, would crash the deal rather than seal it. The problem was never a technical or skills-match. Some of his stable of finance and accounting specialists were simply lacking some basic customer communications and sales skills. He asked if there was anything I might suggest.

At that time, I had just published my book The Consultancy Navigator® and had included a long chapter on selling professional services to SMB2B clients. I offered to put together a mini coaching/training program based on that chapter to provide guidance to those resources-in-need. That program, adjusted to include product as well as service-based businesses, and expanded for a broader audience of EICs, sales support specialists, and journeyman salespeople, became this book.

The concepts in Navigational Selling™ have been proven effective. But like any other tool or method – it depends largely on the skill of the user. Let's face it, Tiger Woods would beat me in a head-to-head golf match using my set of golf clubs or his. Yet, even the unskilled, through consistency, discipline, practice, and process adherence have used Navigational Selling™ techniques to achieve great success.

One of the most successful individual adopters and adherents to the principles of Navigational Selling™ is a CPA/banker, who was assigned to a new client business development role, never having sold before in his decades-long professional career. In a relatively short time, he was receiving awards for his sales results.

Another was an Information Technology specialist for a Hospital, who also had never sold before. Through a strange twist of fate, he found himself assigned as a Regional Sales Manager for a wholesale distributor of construction materials. Based on adoption of the principles of Navigational Selling™, this "novice" quickly turned around his region of 12 sales reps from last to first place in performance - out of a group of 14 regions.

In both these successes, the principles of Navigational Selling™ equipped those two individuals with an effective framework, tools, and knowledge through which to focus their natural skills, abilities, and experience.

Which natural skills and abilities, you might ask? Both the successful individuals mentioned have a great way with people, are not afraid to work hard, think before they act, and are disciplined.

The concepts, behaviors, and tools offered through Navigational Selling™ have helped both official salespeople (those with the title of Sales) and unofficial salespeople (those with non-sales support roles that are periodically drafted in to assist a salesperson) succeed.

Moreover, Navigational Selling™ has assisted salespeople improve their performance over a wide range of industries: banking, software, plastics, capital equipment, metal fabrication, renewable energy, healthcare products, information technology, manufacturing, consulting, executive recruiting, wholesale distribution, professional services, and medical equipment.

Navigational Selling™ offers a robust combination of tailorable process steps, methods, tools, concepts, script dialogues, checklists, and easy-to-remember mental triggers. It is intended for anyone who finds themselves in a situation, some time in their career, where they want or need to improve their sales skills.

No matter the need or personal motivation, Navigational Selling™ will provide the foundation for how to build trust with clients, by discovering and navigating *their* paths to achieve *their* objectives – with a focus on *their* needs first.

Navigational Selling™ will dissolve commonly held stereotypical, and sometimes unflattering ideas about what a salesperson should be, how they should behave, and what they need to do to succeed. It will dissolve beliefs about the perceived effectiveness of the darker side of selling – pushing, hustling, hyping, closing tricks, and the self-inflicted poison pill of "dropping the price". Those behaviors give the sales profession a bad reputation.

Navigational Selling™ lays the foundational imperative that successful, non-manipulative selling, must be built on client Trust. It repetitively pounds the principle that building Trust requires that the client never doubt, even for a moment, that you are working primarily in *their* best interest, to solve *their* problem, overcome *their* barriers, to help them meet *their* needs and achieve *their* goals.

If you can embed that single word, "*their*", within your sales psyche and behaviors, you will succeed – no matter your pre-conceived notions, current skill, or fears about selling. If you are employed in a small-to-midsize business and need to contribute in any way to a selling effort for your livelihood, this book is written and designed to help you.

As Zig Ziglar, famous author, salesperson and motivational speaker said,

---

"You can get everything in life you want, if you will just help enough other people get what they want."

Jerry Vieira, CMC

Hillsboro, Oregon

July 2021

Introduction

In this Chapter …

Another Book About Sales?

The Birth of Navigational Selling™

Why Navigational?

Navigation: More Than Just Plotting and Planning

The Trusted Navigator

Building Trust: Essential but not Sufficient

The Fallacy of a Sales-Process-Only Solution to Sales Improvement

Navigational Selling™: *More than Just a Process*

Process Discipline: A Restriction on Sales Flexibility and Creativity?

Sales: Just One Gear in Your Marketing & Sales Engine

Service Also Plays an Important Role

Navigational Selling is for SMB2B

Another Book About Sales?

According to the Bureau of Labor Statistics (2019), there are just under 16 million people in the U.S. workforce classified within some sales or sales support role. If retail salespeople (cashiers, counter people, etc.), and some consumer sales (door-to-door and other non-B2B sales-types) are extracted, there remain roughly 6 million product and services B2B salespeople.

If we stipulated any measure of sales success, such as sales productivity, and ranked all those salespeople from top to bottom, we would recognize that one half of that total population, the poorer-performing half, is less effective than the better performing half. That means three million or so salespeople could benefit from improving their sales game.

Having worked with sales teams of more than 100 people, I can attest that there always exists a wide range of individual sales skills and success levels among any team. Even among those salespeople with decades of experience, significant underperformance existed.

At minimum, with a dedicated and committed effort to improve, good individual performers and organizations have the potential for achieving excellence, and poorly performing individuals and organizations can significantly improve.

Such individual and organizational improvements are the Holy Grail pursued by every SMB2B business owner and EIC with whom I have worked. And until improvement is ultimately realized, with the repetitive assurance and predictability of the ocean tides, salespeople and sales managers will continue their quest. Sales books of all varieties, formats and approaches will continue to be written and bought. Those books, whether paperback, eBook or Audible, will arrive and take their place on nightstands, in cellphones, and on office bookshelves worldwide.

Moreover, if one agrees that, at minimum, half of the SMB2B salespeople are underperforming and need improvement, how about the sales skill levels of those non-salespeople within an SMB2B business who are periodically "drafted" to support the sales effort? These comprise business owners, executives, managers, technical, and operations specialists, who are pulled into the sales activity by the salesperson, as needed, to reinforce the prospective client's perception of expertise and credibility.

The Drafting of a support specialist commonly occurs without warning, and regardless of the likelihood that the specialist has not been educated, trained, or experienced in effective sales process disciplines and behaviors. It is not uncommon for the salesperson to sit nervously during such client-to-specialist interactions, fearing the specialist or executive might say or do something inappropriate, go off on a tangent, or crash the deal completely. The unpredictable results of these drafts should be no surprise.

During a sales meeting with a client, untrained draftees may say inappropriate things, be too cautious, delve into too much irrelevant detail, hedge, or never know when to simply stay quiet. Familiarity with sales process subtleties revealed in this book, will help draftees contribute immensely to a sales effort.

A final consideration: The US economy comprises millions of unique or near-duplicate products and services, sold into thousands of different markets. Each product and market combination has its own client engagement nuances and sales approach. Given that breadth of offerings and markets, one single hard-wired sales process will not be able to fit all product, service, and market permutations. Therefore, a good sales process must be flexible, tailorable, easy to understand, and offer value to a wide range of businesses and levels of professional sales experience.

These considerations led me to conclude that there remains ample need for improvement across the population of SMB2B sales and sales support organizations. In SMB2B, there remains plenty of need and opportunity to explore sales process improvement through, at least, one additional book or two. Navigational Selling™ is my contribution to that goal.

The Birth of Navigational Selling™

In 1992, I began my consulting practice as a firm specializing exclusively in Market Strategy. I quickly realized that in order to accomplish my mission, no matter how noble my purpose, I would need to sell. I would need to sell myself, my insights, my strategy development methodology, and my experience and expertise.

Furthermore, I would need to be certain that my Market Strategy development process dove-tailed with whatever legacy sales process a client may already have in place. And if the client did not have a formal sales process, a circumstance I discovered was not uncommon, I would need to offer a sound, tailorable sales process that fit the products, services, markets, and industry mechanics of the client's business.

I needed to create or find a sales gear. I had to integrate a flexible sales process that I could use myself to qualify and win new clients, and one that would also serve as a process I could tailor and implement in my marketing & sales organizational transformation engagements. And, since I would be consulting with many different types of business in multiple industries, the sales gear would need to be flexible and highly configurable. It would need to handle both products and services, manufacturing to accounting, software to medical equipment, and law firms to information technology.

I read a lot of sales books in my search. Some were insightful – their conclusions and recommendations based on extensive and extremely well-done research. Others were narrowly focused and more applicable to large corporate organizations rather than SMB2B. Some were self-motivational, ego-centric, rah-rah, "go-get-'em". Yet others encouraged sound process discipline but seemed to have a narrow perspective, treating sales as a stand-alone business process - apparently assuming that the antecedents for success in sales were handled somewhere else within the organization. But in real-world SMB2B, Market Strategy, New Business Development, and Sales activities are so tightly co-dependent, that to enable wise SMB2B EIC decision making, any discussion of sales needed to include those other gears.

So, I developed Navigational Selling™, a holistic approach which recognizes the interdependence and connectivity of a high performing Marketing & Sales Engine.

Navigational Selling™ is Driven by Two Basic Principles

First: The primary objective of an ethical, skilled, and effective salesperson is to help the client achieve their objectives, by analyzing, diagnosing, and advising as to the best approach to overcoming the client's problem, challenge, or barrier-to-success. The salesperson's reward ultimately derives from achieving that objective.

Second: A client's decision is driven by their perception of the Value-Quotient of the offering, as it applies specifically to their situation. That Value Quotient comprises economic, emotional, physical, social, and political considerations (benefits vs. costs), at both the client's conscious and subconscious levels.

If a salesperson wants to achieve a complete, leverageable win-win, the client must win first. They win by receiving meaningful value in all relevant dimensions of the offering they receive.

Achieving the client's objective leads directly to achieving the salesperson's objective – in that order.

Why "Navigational"?

The primary responsibility of a Navigator is to plan and pilot a ship's journey from port of origin to the destination. Because so much depends on the skills, experience and vigilance of the Navigator, a ship's Captain must unequivocally trust their Navigator to wisely advise them and guide their ships safely through both calm and rough seas.

Before a voyage, the Navigator develops and communicates a passage plan to the Captain. That plan is a detailed description and recommendation of how the entire voyage should proceed. Formulating the plan requires course charting, assessment of weather forecasts, adjustments for tides and currents, identification of narrow passages, shoals, and submerged objects, planning for the timing and location of course changes that will be required during the voyage, and anticipating any potentially dangerous, low probability events.

The Navigator must consider tides, the laws of physics, weather, ship speed, barometric pressure, and much more. A Navigator would never recommend a plan or course that violated or ran contrary to the data processed through proven nautical scientific principles, just to make their job easier. The risks and consequences would be too dear.

In Navigational Selling™ the client EIC is the Captain. The trusted salesperson is the Navigator. The "passage" is the best route to achieve the client's goals. As a salesperson, you have no authority or decision-making power. You cannot grab the helm. You can only plot a course for the Captain to follow and advise of any necessary course changes along the decision-making journey.

As the salesperson for your offering, you are the expert. You have been through the buyer journey many times – a lot more than any one client. You know the path to the most appropriate solution, where the challenges commonly arise, and how best to overcome them. To help the EIC sail through the decision process, your expertise and Navigational advice has value.

Navigation is More than Just Plotting and Planning, It's About Trust Too

During a voyage, the Navigator must remain aware of the ship's position, current sea and weather conditions, ship speed, draft (based on cargo tonnage and ballast), as well as the condition of the crew. The Navigator must advise the ship's Captain in real time of the course to be steered and hazards to be avoided.

This real-time situational adjustment and delivery of advice is called Piloting.

The Navigator must continually think and process current information before making recommendations to the Captain. Because of the many variables that need consideration, each plan, and its adjustments, even for repeat journeys from the same port to a repeat destination, are unique. Effective Navigation is the uncompromising process and skill set required to repeatedly achieve the goal of a safe and efficient journey.

As a result:

Navigation = Planning + Piloting

In Navigational Selling™, your client EIC is the Captain. The trusted salesperson is the Navigator. The Captain in sailing, and your client EIC in business, make all the ultimate decisions. The salesperson's role is to plan a "decision voyage" and pilot the EIC's decision process. Along the client's decision journey, the Navigator salesperson must continually provide essential, current, and relevant information to the client along the way.

The Trusted Navigator

Establishing trust is essential to both seafaring navigators and salespeople. Just as the expert Navigator must build a bond of trust with the Captain, the salesperson must build an unquestioned bond of trust with the client EIC.

At all times in your sales journey, you must leave no doubt in the mind of EICs that you are, first and foremost, unselfishly guiding and advising them in the best interest of their business, not your own. In emergency or critical situations requiring rapid action, a lack of unquestioned trust will slow a Captain's response to a Navigator's piloting advice.

Trust enables the salesperson to advise and guide their client EIC safely and quickly through a decision journey. The salesperson must enable the wisest, best informed decision-making by the EIC, to enable them to reach their objectives quickly and efficiently. Without direct access to the helm, the salesperson can only advise.

By consistently behaving in such a way as to continually build this growing level of trust, and reminding yourself of your primary advisory role, both you and your client will find it easier to achieve your mutual goals.

Building Trust: Essential but not Sufficient

Building trust by demonstrating low self-interest with clients, is not the only requisite for success in sales.

To succeed, salespeople must also represent a high-client-value offering. That offering must be well-positioned in its target market, deliver high client-perceived value, and be competitively advantaged. In addition, a sales effort is enabled by a healthy economy, a sound market strategy, the right market focus, and a whole business that is client-centric and committed to delivering a market-leading client experience. Even the purest sales process and client-centric motivations cannot overcome major shortfalls in any of these areas.

While we emphasize Trust, we will also address, in detail, how to recognize and assure the other antecedent factors required for your success in sales are in place and effective. So, do not be frustrated if we don't begin the discussion of sales techniques until we have laid some extensive antecedent groundwork in Part 1.

Navigational Selling™: More Than Just a Process

The Navigational Selling™ methodology emphasizes and provides the techniques, tools, and vocabulary for rigorous situational Qualification and Discovery. Foundational to this method, is the principle that a salesperson's success rate improves markedly, when they dedicate the majority of their selling effort to in-depth client inquiry. Such inquiry includes the client's business-level and technical factors, as well as any personal motivations surrounding any new SMB2B selling opportunity.

A salesperson's ability to craft proposals that will resonate and win, requires much more than simply a technical understanding of the challenge, problem, or barrier the client wishes to overcome. At least equal in importance, the salesperson must develop the skills needed to reveal the personality and motivational drivers (both conscious-explicit and subconscious-implicit) of both the client's EIC ultimate decision maker and the client's decision-influencing team.

Like price, the best technical solution is rarely the sole determining factor for a win. Despite that realization, salespeople spend disproportionate amounts of their sales time focused on the technological requirements of the client. In reality, as long as the basic technical requirements are met, the win most frequently goes to the firm which has crafted the offering that resonates most with the client's personality, their deeper motivations and fears, and their values. Navigational Selling™ is a process, a vocabulary, a tool kit, a set of techniques and best practices, and a way of thinking.

Process Discipline: A Restriction on Sales Flexibility and Creativity?

Some salespeople cringe on hearing the words "process" and "discipline". To them, the words denote rigid adherence and uncompromising obligation to a series of steps that restricts their freedom and creativity, overseen by some out-of-touch administrative authority.

To those so inclined, I suggest they consider the Navigational Selling™ process like the preflight checklist that aircraft pilots and co-pilots use – a way of assuring that nothing important has been overlooked before the plane is committed to the air. Applied to selling, this means assuring that nothing has been overlooked before crafting and delivering your proposal.

The captain of an airplane has a lot of responsibility. Making the time to go through the preflight checklist is a small investment of effort compared to the consequences of overlooking something important that might cause problems during takeoff, flight, or landing.

The benefit of a disciplined process is the consistent framework that helps the salesperson and their firm understand, communicate, and strategize the account or sales opportunity that is entrusted to them.

The tool kit helps the salesperson take specific action on the account or opportunity. Think of the NavSell tools as the flight controls - a plane's ailerons, elevator, and rudder - the primary controls required to fly an aircraft safely, given any specific set of circumstances.

Like any tool kit, you want to select the tool required for the job at hand, as not all tools are required to work on every unique sales challenge. Whether your toolkit is a well-stocked, multi-drawer Craftsman on casters, or a small drawer in your kitchen, you must use the appropriate tool for optimum results.

That doesn't mean you cannot ever use the handle of a screwdriver as a hammer in an emergency situation to affix a picture hanger to the wall – but it doesn't work very well. So, when choosing your tool, do not expect too much from a gizmo used for something other than its original purpose. The same holds true for the Navigational Selling™ toolkit.

In competition, the rules of golf limit the number of clubs a golfer can carry to 14. Yet some golfers find remarkably creative ways to use them. Occasionally a golfer will use a 3-wood, normally used for driving off the tee, as a chipping / putting tool – instead of a putter.

And the music of the western world has only 12 notes in its chromatic scale, and a set of sound-pleasing rules for creating melodies and harmonies with them. Yet the amount of music that has been (and will continue to be) composed from it seems limitless.

Creativity is not limited by either the process, the rules, or the tools, but rather the imagination and skills of the individual using them.

The Fallacy of a Sales-Process-Only Solution to Sales Improvement

Through all my client engagements, there has never been disagreement that a sound Sales Process Discipline was essential to high performance. As a result, it is not surprising that the Sales function is the first place the majority of executives look to fix their revenue generation problems.

However, more often than not, the root cause of revenue generation shortcomings is most commonly discovered as a deficiency within the firm's Market Strategy, not its Sales gear. Furthermore, only after the strategy is fixed, can improvements in sales process achieve their full potential and be sustained.

That is not to imply that the Sales Process should be given a lower level of import or ignored. It means that a low sales level is often a symptom, whose relief can only partially and temporarily be alleviated by addressing sales skills alone. Sound market strategy, based on data, and reflected in good tactical market messaging, assures that an improved sales process is delivering all that it can.

The quest to optimize sales performance is, in essence, a quest to optimize the performance a firm's complete Marketing & Sales Engine. Executives, business owners, and salespeople, hoping to build business and personal wealth, must recognize this reality, or forever be doomed to the frustration of suboptimized business performance, competitive weakness, and ineffective investment.

Sales: Just One Gear in Your Marketing & Sales Engine

For nearly three decades my mission has been to assist individuals and SMB2B firms in their quest to achieve their personal, professional, and business goals. I have advised, coached, mentored, guided, and trained hundreds of businesses and thousands of individuals in the science of Marketing & Sales. And, while my consulting journey began with a singular mission to spread the virtues, principles, and truths of sound *Market Strategy*, it soon evolved into a quest, like that of Johnny Appleseed, to plant the seeds and nurture the growth of complete, powerful *Marketing & Sales Process Engines*, wherever I was engaged.

I realized that both *Market Strategy* and *Sales Process Disciplines* needed to be understood as essential gears within a more complete, closed-loop, Marketing & Sales Engine. What evolved was an aspirational Marketing & Sales Engine model, Figure 1, that embedded several essential and powerful elements:

- the essential truths extracted from extensive published market-strategy research and military science,

- a model and methodology that integrated all the important gears,

- a toolkit of worksheets and techniques that would facilitate its adoption and release the engine's power in practice, and

- stories that related the real-world experiences and lessons-learned to illustrate its practical benefits.

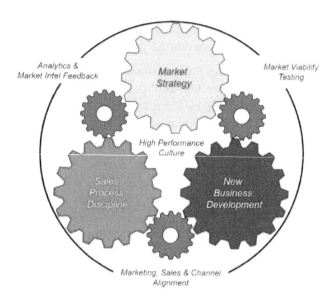

Figure 1: The QMP Marketing & Sales Engine

The complete engine recognizes that a sales function alone is insufficient for an organization to achieve long-term success. Likewise, a stand-alone Market Strategy or a stand-alone New Business Development initiative are also insufficient. An integrated, interdependent, and complete, closed-loop process is required to achieve consistently high performance.

While the tools and techniques embedded within the QMP Marketing & Sales Engine have evolved over time, no client engagement has ever invalidated the model, nor has any engagement ever dis-proven its design.

In SMB2B, to avoid running aground on some unanticipated business reef, EIC decision making should adhere to scientifically proven principles of empirical

Marketing & Sales science. Yet, people and companies that experience marketing and sales challenges repeatedly violate that advice.

Why?

Many times, it is because of ignorance of those core principles. On other occasions, it is the result of mental laziness or an impulse to act only on gut instinct.

The principles of Navigational Selling™ and the Marketing & Sales Engine dissolve ignorance, by revealing, clarifying, and explaining how to embrace those core principles to achieve SMB2B business goals and sustain performance.

What About Service?

Navigational Selling™ recognizes that no B2B business is completely free of the need to provide some form of service to its clients. Service components, explicit and implicit, tangible and intangible, deliver meaningful value to clients. Those service components can encompass the need for client problem assessment, product selection guidance, solution design, planning, coordination, tailoring, delivery, installation, integration, testing, training, environmental or safety assurance, repair service, reliability checks, updates, spare parts, hot-line access, on-time delivery, quality, and post-sale follow-up.

Even the emotional reassurance implied from a brand name, can be considered a value-delivered service. The use of the Intel-inside sticker on computers, implying the most recent levels of performance, reliability, and quality, delivered value to those laptop clients who decided to buy them.

Service considerations are essential ingredients within the client *Value Quotient*. In the QMP Marketing & Sales Engine model, service considerations are designed into the *Market Strategy*, *Channel Alignment*, and *Sales* gears – as well as incorporated into the *Culture* of the firm and the design of the total *Client Experience*.

In today's world, no SMB2B business is selling anything devoid of explicit and implied service.

Navigational Selling™ is for SMB2B

This book is not intended for large Fortune 500 firms with worldwide sales teams of tens of thousands. It is intended for the SMB2B business community and written to provide high value to the following people and circumstances common in that community:

- ✓ SMB2B *EICs, CEOs, or Business Owners* who need to understand how a high-performing marketing and sales function should be designed and managed,

- ✓ SMB2B EICs, CEOs, or Business Owners who have never been salespeople, but find themselves repeatedly thrust into a sales role to support the sales team for "big deals",

- ✓ *marketing people* who need to understand their clients' value-quotients, typical decision-making processes, the journey a salesperson must travel with a prospect to land new business, and how to create *market-leading client experiences*,

- ✓ *technical support professionals* who are periodically drafted to meet with clients in support of a salesperson,

- ✓ *project managers* involved in the selling, deploying, and execution of projects sold by their sales team,

- ✓ solo *professional services practitioners* (consultants) who must sell to eat,

- ✓ professionals who are *service franchise owners* of national firms, but need to sell their own local deals to generate new business,

- ✓ independent, local specialty *subcontractors* who serve as the "bullpen" of resources for a larger franchise and marketing organization, and

- ✓ anyone within an SMB2B who wishes to understand the workings of Marketing and Sales.

As a salesperson or executive within an SMB2B entity, you must have more than just the drive, resourcefulness, and will-to-win. You must have the knowledge of *what* it takes to win, and the discipline to execute those win-generating behaviors. This book will provide that knowledge – if you choose to use it.

*****

Part 1:   A Framework for Sales Success

The chapters within Part 1 of Navigational Selling™ are addressed primarily to EICs. The topics included will enlighten the EIC as to the foundational principles and functions required for any corporate sales function to achieve long-term success. They lay out an overarching framework for a world-class sales function within SMB2B firms.

Part 1 will also help SMB2B support specialists who are not experienced salespeople yet are occasionally compelled by their role within the firm to contribute to the sales effort. They will also help those who fear and dread the thought of having to sell - yet know they will need to sell at some point in their careers or manage a sales function as part of their future general management responsibilities.

Chapter 1: The Essential Ingredients of Sales Success

Chapter 2: Powering Sales Success - Your Marketing & Sales Engine

Chapter 3: Assessing Organizational Sales Effectiveness

Chapter 4: Five Considerations that Influence SMB2B Sales Success

Chapter 1: The Essential Ingredients of Sales Success

In this Chapter …

Enemy at the Gates: A Lesson from War

Common Sales Success Myths

Enemy at the Gates: A Lesson from War

In the 2001 movie, "Enemy at the Gates", about the World War II, tide-turning, eastern-front Battle of Stalingrad, there is a memorable and horrific scene near the beginning of the movie. In this scene, a Russian Army regiment is ordered to make a frontal assault, through the devastation and wreckage of the city, to drive out the well-entrenched, heavily armed, and barricaded German occupiers.

To begin the assault, the Russian commander shouts the command, "*Attack! No retreat!!*". The loyal, brave, but poorly armed Russian soldiers charge forward as ordered. The attack is met with deadly fire from the German lines. There is nothing short of total carnage in the charging line of the attacking Russians. The assault quickly falters. The few surviving and wounded Russian soldiers turn and begin to retreat to the safety of their own lines – even while the Russian Commander continues to scream, "*No Retreat! No Retreat!*"

In frustration and anger at his retreating troops and the faltering attack, the Russian commander orders his machine gunners to open fire on his own returning soldiers. The result of this insane and deadly attempt to convince them to turn around to renew the suicidal attack against the German lines, is complete decimation. After the withering fire from both sides, there is only one survivor, our hero, who cleverly takes shelter in a dried-out fountain in the middle of the city square, pretending to be dead.

Beyond its contribution to the story, the gruesome scene offers a critical lesson to business. When I first saw it, it hit me immediately.

That "Attack-Sans-Strategy" (aka the "ASS" strategy) is exactly what I have witnessed many business managers doing with their sales teams! They send them on virtual suicide missions to sell in a poorly conceived, direct frontal assault against entrenched, powerful competition. With no real market segment focus, a weak non-competitive market strategy, poorly positioned offerings, and a dearth of sales skills and tools, the salespeople are doomed.

When they consistently return to the office devoid of new business, they are challenged, or worse, fired. Then they are replaced by new sales-soldiers with the same low probability of success - because nothing else changes – and the business is doomed to repeat the same strategic insanity in attack after attack.

Those business owners and sales managers might just as well be shouting, "*Attack!! No retreat!*" from the safety of the corporate office.

Shortly after the movie's release, I bought the DVD and incorporated that Stalingrad battle-scene into my sales training programs, to make the point that much of sales success depends on a wise and sound strategy. Of course, we are sensitive to participants, and always provide a warning and opt-out option to viewing this violent film clip.

The lesson is this:

While having dedication, intensity, motivation, energy, and good sales skills are critical, a sound strategy is the foundation of sustained, defensible success. No sales effort can succeed in a strategic vacuum or survive long with an unsound market strategy. In such a situation, even the best soldier becomes a casualty.

This lesson is so important that, while this book is about Sales, and written for SMB2B owners, managers and salespeople, this chapter delves into the key considerations that must be in place to make any business successful. As is too often the case in SMB2B, a great salesperson, just like a great soldier becomes a casualty quickly, if the strategy is non-existent, unclear, or ill-devised.

The good news is, in contrast with large organizations, an SMB2B firm has streamlined communications and decision making. An informed salesperson is better positioned to influence the kinds of strategic decisions and tactical new business development initiatives so essential to their own personal success. And, as you will discover as you read through Navigational Selling™, even if an initial strategy is poorly conceived, it is well within the capabilities of a salesperson to still succeed if they understand some basics about Market Strategy and New Business Development.

All that is to say:

Sales success in any SMB2B business requires a smooth-running Marketing & Sales Engine. That engine must consistently produce offerings of high client-perceived value, formulate wise market strategies, execute cost-effective new business development initiatives, and have a rigorous and disciplined sales process that enables opportunities to flow quickly through to Wins.

Common Sales Success Myths

Many sales process improvement books make assumptions that may not apply to SMB2B businesses. Among those assumptions are:

- Good sales skills and process disciplines are sufficient to assure sales success for all involved: the salesperson, the client, and the firm.
- The market strategy and client-perceived value delivered by the firm and its offerings are valid, proven, and competitively advantaged.
- Salespeople have all the sales tools they need to communicate successfully to prospects.
- Tactical marketing efforts are effective in generating sufficient customer leads and opportunities to achieve sales goals.
- Sales is a numbers game. The more "at-bats", the higher the success rate.
- The salesperson simply, and only, needs to sell. There are other individuals and departments that can handle all the other key ingredients required for success.
- Discovering new customers takes priority over current customers in terms of allocating sales assets.
- All business is relationship-based. Building relationships is Job 1.
- Market focus is ill-advised and crazy. One needs to cast as wide a net as possible.

Remember, I am listing these as myths. There are some statements on the list that you probably don't believe are myths. I will give you that some may be true to a small degree and under certain conditions. However, you are better off to assume they are just as they are offered – myths. Blind adherence to these false assumptions can prevent and delay an SMB2B from achieving its growth objectives.

Throughout this book, Navigational Selling™ will address, qualify, and debunk a number of these assumptions. Navigational Selling™ will challenge conventional beliefs held by many an EIC, salesperson and sales manager, with "Truths", such as:

- In the majority of situations, you do not lose because of "price" and win because of "a good relationship".

- If the marketing team is delinquent, incompetent, or non-existent, it is _not_ beyond the responsibility and capability of the salesperson to formulate an effective market strategy and business development plan themselves.

- In most breakthrough and turn-around situations, a good market strategy and focus can accomplish more than a major investment in marketing automation.

- Client purchase decisions are not solely economic. More than many salespeople recognize - emotions, politics, social pressure, and physical considerations also enter into decision making.

- More leads do not lead to more sales. Fewer leads with a better focus and qualification do.

- Everything a company does becomes part of the _Client Experience_ – from the first time the client sees you and your material, to the time, perhaps many years later, when they no longer need to do business with you, but can still refer others to you. Everything you and your company does must build and reinforce the trust associated with a good client experience. A high-quality customer experience is everyone's job.

- Your brand logo, tagline, website, and fancy marketing promotions do not establish your true brand. Your _Client Experience_ does.

As you read, be prepared to challenge your own mythical beliefs, and replace them with facts.

*****

Chapter 2: Powering Sales Success – Your Marketing & Sales Engine

In this Chapter …

The Marketing & Sales Engine

The Market Strategy Gear

The Market Viability Testing Gear

The New Business Development Gear

The Channel Alignment Gear

The Sales Process Discipline Gear

The Market Intelligence Feedback & Analytics Gear

Corporate Culture: The Lubricant of the Marketing & Sales Engine

Assessing Marketing & Sales Engine Effectiveness

The Marketing & Sales Engine

Sales is just one gear of a more complex and complete engine that drives the top line of any business. Moreover, every for-profit business, independent of size, industry, or employee count, has in effect, a Marketing & Sales (M&S) Engine, within which exists a Sales Process gear.

(This engine graphic was shown previously and is intentionally repeated here for the reader's convenience and to punctuate its importance. As I cautioned in the Note to Readers, there is intentional repetition in this book and if it is repeated, it is critically important.)

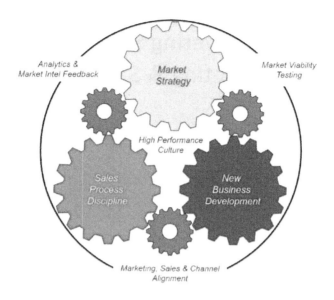

Figure 2: The QMP Marketing & Sales Engine (redux)

In working with and training hundreds of SMB2B clients, I have never seen a company that did not have some marketing and selling activities ongoing. However, I do not recall any that recognized, documented, and memorialized those functions as part of a continuous, rapid-cycle closed-loop process.

Many client businesses had stand-alone gears that were underperforming. Others had gears completely missing. Few understood the long-term implications of not having a closed-loop model, of having disconnected gears, or the lack of a culture-based lubricant for their engine.

Some had great offerings, with the potential of delivering enormous value to clients, but were aimed at the wrong target markets – a common market strategy deficiency. Some had a great strategy, market focus, and high value offerings but were stymied by a blockage in the channel-to-market alignment gear. Others spent a lot of money on new business development (which, for purposes of this engine model includes tactical marketing) for poorly designed, low value-quotient offerings – ultimately gaining no traction. Even some relatively large businesses, with revenues in the hundreds of millions, were operating inefficiently because of a missing or poorly functioning analytics gear.

All clients had the same desire, to increase sales. None found their ultimate answer in solely addressing the *Sales Process* gear. Let me repeat, NONE!

The sales gear is connected and codependent on an integrated system of preceding and proceeding gears. It is dependent on receiving the information and energy transferred from its previous antecedent gears. And while the sales gear is a critical part of the engine, it cannot single-handedly power it.

Assuring that your firm's Marketing & Sales Engine is functioning well in all gears, is akin to assuring that a ship is seaworthy prior to beginning a sea voyage.

I know you are likely reading this book to learn how to improve your organizational and individual sales effectiveness. As such, you might see this Marketing & Sales Engine discussion as an unnecessary detour, that will delay achieving your objective.

Stay with me here. No lasting success will survive a fundamentally weak foundation. No ship will run at maximum efficiency with leaks in the hull. And few soldiers will survive a poorly formulated battle plan.

It is important to remember that a sales process alone is not the solution. By the nature of an SMB2B business, you as a manager, executive, salesperson, or tech support resource, have the power, and in my opinion, the responsibility, to reinforce the Marketing & Sales Engine to make your collective path to success easier and faster.

To effectively contribute to the engine's performance, you first need to understand how the engine should work. With that understanding you will be able to inject your ideas, observations, information, data, and energy at the right place within the engine for maximum impact. Many of the most significant breakthroughs I have experienced with clients, had as their source of insight, people within the organization that were neither field salespeople nor marketing types.

So, let's quickly explore the importance, function and value contributed by each part of the engine.

The Market Strategy Gear

Market Strategy comprises the activities associated with identifying target market segments with sufficient economic momentum, and significant unmet needs, that can be serviced by your offerings. It includes the design and development of high-value-quotient, competitively advantaged, differentiated offerings that will provide meaningful value and benefits to clients, beyond those provided by currently available competitive solutions.

A simple canoe metaphor will help illustrate the impact of selecting the best and most lucrative target market, as the first and most important part of a sound market strategy.

Storytime: The Canoe Race

Assume you want to launch a large canoe into a stream for use by a team of rowers. Your objective is to set the state record for travelling from the stream's headwaters to its mouth, where a flag festooned finish line, cheering crowds, a silver Victory Cup, and cold beer await.

So, you build a strong canoe, train the rowers in a strenuous regimen of physical conditioning, and teach them to row in a highly coordinated way. Completely prepared and confident, you inform them that you believe they are ready to attempt to set the record. You tell them to take the canoe to the stream.

When they reach the bank of the stream, they lower the canoe and jump in, each taking their predetermined seat and gripping their oars. But to their collective consternation, there is so little water in the stream, the loaded canoe grounds itself, wedging into the soft sand and gravel in the streambed!

How much progress will these superbly conditioned rowers make if there is insufficient or no water in the stream?

None. Nada. Zilch.

Even if the canoe is beautifully designed and crafted, with a fantastic logo emblazoned on its hull, and launched with great fanfare before a cheering crowd being entertained by a live rock band - no one is going anywhere.

Even if you change the logo, paint a clever name and tag line on the prow, have a song composed for the team to sing while rowing, optimize the canoe's structural design, and double down on training - no progress will be made. Market strategies and canoes require sufficient water depth and flow to make progress!

Furthermore, even assuming the stream *does* have sufficient water in it at some point during the year, and you plan another attempt, unless you understand the nature of the stream, the classes of its rapids, its varying depths, and bends, as it courses toward its mouth, you cannot possibly design the canoe appropriately for your journey.

On the other hand, if the stream is filled with deep, rapidly flowing water, the task of rowing will be much easier. In such a case, even a crash-test dummy, propped up on a seat in the canoe without an oar, will make progress - if the stream's current has sufficient momentum and the canoe can float at all.

Moral of the Story: Like picking a stream with the strongest flowing water, selecting the most lucrative target market segment for your offering, the segment with strongest economic, demographic, or regulatory momentum, is the first order of market strategy. It simply makes success a lot easier.

End of Story

But market momentum alone isn't enough. You also need an offering (a canoe) that can succeed in that specific market (stream) and compete successfully against the offerings of other firms (other canoe teams).

As a key resource in your SMB2B firm, it is crucial that you and your management team select the best market segment to target - one that will boost your sales efforts. You must then design your offerings and train yourself and your team, to deliver the highest client-value and differentiated client experience of all your competitors.

Too often the salesperson is left undirected. Flailing about they spend valuable time and resources trying to find a lucrative target market on their own. As a salesperson, if success is slow to arrive, it *may* be your sales process, but more likely it is a market strategy problem. You can read more detail about Market Strategy in Appendix C.

The Market Viability Testing Gear

Market Viability Testing comprises the efforts of the firm, *prior* to launching a new offering, to validate the target market momentum and the customer-perceived value-quotient. It also includes ongoing efforts to repeatedly validate the relevance and magnitude of the firm's value quotient, differentiation and quality of the client experience as perceived by both current and prospective clients.

The New Business Development Gear

New Business Development comprises the activities associated with selecting the optimum channel-to-market, designing a market-leading client experience, building an effective market communications infrastructure, and understanding the target market's system of client peer-to-peer influence. It also includes formulating relevant messages and + them through efficient and effective communications and delivery channels. It incorporates what many call tactical marketing activities, marketing communications, publicity and thought leadership.

Sounds simple enough, but this gear can become a huge sinkhole for cash – particularly if the firm believes it should launch a frontal assault marketing campaign, to "get the word out there", devoid of a focused market strategy.

More effective approaches that leverage the target market's intra-market network have been shown to be *13 times more effective* than mass communication efforts and direct assaults. In short, it's a much better bang for the buck. More about this in Appendix D, New Business Development.

The Sales & Channel Alignment Gear

Key selling points regarding the offering's value quotient, benefits, and competitive differentiation, travel a complex but typical route. From the design & development team to the marketing team, through the salesperson, to the distribution and sales channel and ultimately to the client. Are your messages from the home office to the ultimate client crisp and clear or garbled or misunderstood?

Do you remember the "telephone" game? In the game, one person whispers a message to another, who in turn whispers it to another and another and another, until it reaches the last person in the group. That person announces the message to the group. The final recitation of the message usually resembles nothing like the original.

In the space and time between the formulation of the initial strategy and the market launch, relevant messages about value, targets and competitive strengths and weaknesses can become garbled, mis-construed, forgotten, or even ignored. What marketing wants to communicate, what is meaningful from the perception of the client, what the salesperson actually promotes, and the message the distribution channel delivers to the client, can easily fall out of alignment.

Message modifications and distortions can be both honest mistakes and intentional.

Storytime: He Just Didn't Believe It

> A client of mine was flummoxed by the slow market adoption of one of his truly innovative new product offerings. Case studies and testimonials validating the economic returns on adoption of the product by clients were compelling. Moreover, market research showed that there was a large population of target-market client-prospect businesses across the country that could benefit significantly from the innovation. Competitors had nothing like it

with which to compete. The product was patent protected, virtually eliminating the possibility of direct competitive duplication.

All communications to the channel ran through one channel communications manager, who had independently elected to remove from the sales tool kit, the most compelling case study, testimonial, and evidence of the cost-savings opportunity for clients.

Why?

Because he personally did not believe the value claim – despite the customer generated and validated case study and testimonial.

Once that bottleneck was discovered, the individual was coached and re-trained. He corrected the sales documents, adjusted his approach, and communicated the value message to the channel. Revenues quickly began to turn around – increasing by 15% in an industry that experienced an overall decline in growth of 18% that same year.

Moral of the Story: Just as the value quotient needs periodic testing in the *Market Viability Test* gear, the effectiveness of client value messaging and delivery must be periodically audited in the *Channel Alignment* gear.

End of Story

The Sales Process Discipline Gear

The Sales Process Discipline Gear comprises two equally important parts.

Part 1: A standard sequential sales process with several distinct steps. In our case, Navigational Selling™ is a simple four-step process, incorporating:

1. *Qualification*: of both account-level and offering-level opportunities,

2. *Discovery*: of specific customer needs, objectives, circumstances, decision makers and influencers, and the client's decision-making process,

3. *Solution Formulation*: comprising the formulation of both creative, competitively advantaged solutions to the client challenges, and the crafting and delivery of proposals or quotes which the client can approve,

4. *Follow Through to Winning*: to assure that: a) the proposal or quote does not atrophy or stall, b) that it receives client approval or, c) is modified as needed to facilitate the client's decision.

It's a bit like a golf swing-routine: Aim, Setup, Swing, Follow Through. Easy-peasy. At least in theory. In reality, like golf, not so much. But, with practice anyone can improve.

Part 2: The second component of the Sales Process Discipline Gear is the training and preparation of the sales force and the channel to tell the specific offering's value-quotient story. This is an extension of the Channel Alignment gear.

While Part 1 of the Sales Process Discipline Gear will likely be applicable across large swaths of the firm's product/service line, Part 2 will require crafting for each individual product/service offering.

As you can see from our Marketing & Sales Engine model, there are four gears that precede the Sales Process Discipline gear. The cold truth is:

It is unreasonable to expect that any fundamental weakness in any of the preceding gears can be totally compensated for in the Sales Process. Yet so many sales methodologies seem to assume the preceding gears, if they exist at all, are fine.

That is why we begin *this* book with a Marketing & Sales Engine discussion. After introducing it, we will not dwell on it. But first, we must complete the engine explanation.

The Market Intelligence Feedback & Analytics Gear

Visibility and analysis of the target market's economic health, as well as the need to understand primary demand for your offering, competitive alternatives, and competitive differentiation situations, are all essential to make appropriate strategic adjustments.

To maintain a healthy, growing business, it is important to understand: a) the insights and implications of the information produced from your client engagements, both wins and losses, b) economic and competitive information within your primary target markets, and c) the effectiveness of your own business processes. Since the Market Strategy gear includes market strategy development and the evolution of your business model, it is the best place to deposit this raw, real-world data.

Such analytics are crucial to increasing the productivity of your marketing, sales, and new offering investments. Analysis may reveal vertical market momentum trends, common client problems, challenges for which you may or may not have solutions, and insights you may have learned about the most effective ways to engage a decision-making executive. Feeding data from sales and analysis back into your strategy gear for processing, staves off business obsolescence and diminishes competitive threats.

Throughout the 30 years of my practice, the greatest sales, revenue, and profitability breakthroughs experienced by my clients, have been triggered by assuring that the Market Feedback gear was working, and the data the engine was producing were fed into the Market Strategy gear. In several cases, small adjustments to strategy produced orders of magnitude increments of new business.

With that final gear explanation, we have completed one turn of the engine. However, we have one more important ingredient to consider, organizational Culture.

Corporate Culture: The Lubricant of the Marketing & Sales Engine

Every engine needs a lubricant to prevent the gears from grinding, overheating, and seizing up.

The "oil" of the SMB2B Marketing & Sales Engine is the Culture of the firm. A healthy corporate Culture keeps every part of the Marketing & Sales engine running smoothly and provides a clear competitive advantage. An organization's culture keeps a business humming, producing repeated client success, revealing market insights, generating cash, attracting new clients, garnering referrals, and assuring uninterrupted operation.

Your personal and business disciplines, behavioral expectations, values and ethics define your culture. Your culture produces your clients' successes and defines your brand. Therefore, your clients' successes define your success.

Your Culture, demonstrated through your firm's operational disciplines and personnel behaviors, creates your client experience. That client experience drives the market's perception of the Relative Perceived Quality of your offerings, which drives both competitive advantage and profitability - both crucial to business success.

Assessing Marketing & Sales Engine Effectiveness

A Marketing & Sales (M&S) Engine effectiveness diagnostic is shown in Figure 3. This diagnostic assessment is helpful in identifying shortcomings in the key factors required for overall business success. This assessment identifies seven key Marketing & Sales related dimensions (processes, skills, and disciplines) related to your M&S Engine. If SMB2B organizations want to give their sales soldiers the best chance for victory, they must master these dimensions before their competition does.

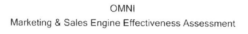

Figure 3: The OMNI™ Marketing & Sales Engine Effectiveness Assessment

If you wish to profile your firm's Marketing & Sales Engine Effectiveness against these performance dimensions, you can request a free Marketing & Sales Engine Assessment from QMP1@qmpassociates.com.

An understanding and crafting of a working and efficient Marketing & Sales engine is essential for long term success of an SMB2B firm. It is essential to increasing the company's value. Creating, maintaining, and preserving that engine, therefore, should be a long-term foundational goal.

*****

Chapter 3 : Assessing Organizational Sales Effectiveness

In this Chapter…

Revealing Your Organizational Starting Point

The Organizational-Level Sales Effectiveness Assessment

Interpreting Assessment Results

Caution: Chasing False Prophets

The Mission of Navigational Selling™

Revealing Your Organizational Starting Point

Most SMB2B firms, new or mature, have sales objectives they want to achieve, and sales challenges they want to overcome. Moreover, each salesperson is faced with their own individual business-related and personal set of objectives and challenges. As a business firm or individual, getting from where you are to where you need to be, is a journey which at its beginning offers alternative paths.

Further pressuring the need to improve, is the realization that time is critical, and resources are limited. Most SMB2B firms are not afforded the luxury of a fake-it-till-you-make-it or multiple try-and-fail and try-again-and-fail cycles. Competitors are not standing still, and clients cannot put their problems, opportunities, and gaps (POGs) on hold, waiting patiently for you to figure it out.

No two business situations are precisely alike. What works for some may not work for others. Different industry characteristics, capabilities, market situations and competitive starting points create a near infinite number of improvement roadmaps.

Given the breadth of circumstances, perspectives, and roles, selecting the right place to start to improve your sales skills and process can be a challenge. What seems to be most urgent is not always most important, and what seems to be missing may only be a symptom rather than a root cause. Addressing the urgent, leaves the important unattended. Investing in fixing a symptom rather than a root cause, will not work for the long term, and in the short term, will waste valuable time and money - leaving your business competitively vulnerable.

To achieve corporate success, every individual in a sales role, a sales-support role, or responsible for assuring the quality of the client experience, needs to be on the same path and be supported by a solid corporate foundation. Each player must understand and use the same vocabulary and operate with the same understanding of appropriate next steps. Every sales and support role must be aligned along the same target market messaging, sales process, client experience expectations, and behavioral disciplines playbook. All players must execute their roles well, as culturally lubricated cogs in an overarching Marketing & Sales Engine.

To rapidly improve, the EIC must first acknowledge their most critical organizational deficiencies. Moreover, in order to launch the best rapid-impact improvement initiatives, they must assess and understand the root causes of the challenges those initiatives are intended to overcome.

In both business and medical situations, the first step in improvement must always be a diagnostic step.

To identify the best place to begin, at the end of this chapter you will be invited to take a ten-dimension Organizational-Level Sales Process & Skills Effectiveness Assessment. Within the ten performance dimensions are 30 individual contributing factors, measuring corporate level capabilities.

The Organizational-Level Sales Process & Skills Effectiveness Assessment is designed to identify the effectiveness of the sales function as a whole. By simply rating the accuracy of each of the 30 statements, on a scale of 1 to 5, as it compares to your current business situation, the assessment generates a gap analysis curve, like that shown in Figure 4 below.

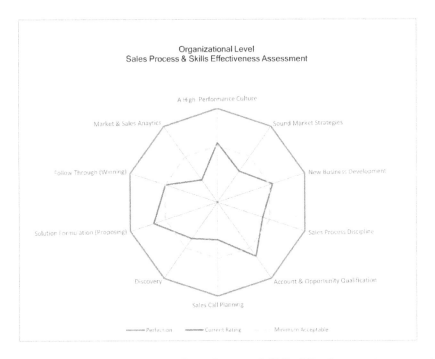

Figure 4: Organizational Level Sales Process & Skills Effectiveness Assessment

This assessment provides a snapshot of the firm's current state in those ten dimensions essential to sales success. It profiles organizational capabilities, sales processes, behavioral disciplines, and other crucial success-enabling factors. It reveals the highest leverage starting points for an improvement journey.

Five of the performance dimensions are essentially the same as the Marketing & Sales Engine effectiveness assessment of Figure 3, namely Performance-Driven Culture, Market Strategy, New Business Development, Sales Process Discipline, and Market & Sales Analytics. However, to make the assessment more specific to Sales, we supplemented it with the basic four process steps of Navigational Selling™: Qualification, Discovery, Solution Formulation (Proposing), Follow Through (Winning). Finally, we added a Sales Call Planning dimension to recognize the importance of time management to a salesperson's productivity.

The overlap of dimensions between the M&S Engine and Organizational-Level Sales Effectiveness Assessment should not surprise anyone. The requirements for a high-performance M&S Engine and a high-performance Sales Process are deeply codependent.

Do not be discouraged if your Organizational-Level Sales Process & Skills Assessment reveals weaknesses. Few SMB2B firms score well in their first run through. Consider each performance weakness as an opportunity to leap ahead, using the ideas and concepts revealed in this book.

The good news is that the bigger the gaps, the bigger the rewards for closing them. You simply need to know what it is you need to improve, in what order, develop a roadmap, and steel the will and discipline to improve.

At the end of this Chapter, you will be invited to take an Organizational-Level Sales Process & Skills Effectiveness Assessment.

Caution: Addressing Performance Shortfalls Are Most Effective if Done in the Proper Order

Here are four fundamental considerations for assessing and planning remedial efforts:

1. *Not all performance gaps are equally important*. Certain dimensional gaps are more important than others and should receive attention and investment first.

   For example, if the Market Strategy dimension scores low, it will adversely impact all the successive gears. A gap there must always be repaired quickly. But a sound Market Strategy, in turn, depends on a sound process for collecting and analyzing data. Therefore, the Market & Sales Analytics gear requires immediate attention.

2. The *Market & Sales Analytics gear must be fixed first* before the Market Strategy gear can be repaired. Otherwise, you have no data, or bad data, with which to develop a sound strategy. That won't work.

3. *Cultural deficiencies influence every gear* in the engine; if it is rated low, it must receive a higher urgency.

4. Deficiencies in other gears or dimensions should be addressed only after *deficiencies in the Cultural, Market Strategy and Analytics gears are improved*.

You may sigh and say, "But we don't have time and investment for all that foundational effort!"

To which I say, if you don't commit to fixing those dimensions, at some point, you will be doomed like Sisyphus. He was the mythological Greek King of Ephyra, who because of his stubbornness and arrogance, was punished by the gods for eternity to roll an immense boulder up a hill, only to have it roll down every time it neared the top.

The Cultural, Market Strategy and Data dimensions are foundational. All your marketing and sales initiatives, now and in the future, depend on those parts working well. And good news - they might not take as long as you think to reinforce. But once they are strengthened, they support every subsequent decision. The quality of the client experience you deliver, compared to your competitors', depends on it.

After such improvements have been achieved, the long-term challenge is to maintain high performance. High performance in those dimensions must be sustained through the ups and downs in the economy, as well as through the management and personnel changes that will inevitably occur over the years.

The Organizational Level Sales Effectiveness Assessment

Looking at Figure 4, the solid line along the outer perimeter of the chart, indicates perfection. The dashed line indicates a barely minimal level of acceptable performance in any dimension, and the irregular solid line reflects your personal subjective assessment of the current situation within your firm.

In years of compiling such assessments for SMB2B firms, and crafting programs to fill the gaps, the example shown in Figure 4 is close to what one might expect from the self-rating of a firm with up to six people involved in the sales process. These groups would likely comprise, inside and outside sales, marketing, executives, and customer service personnel.

We will delve into the specific graphical results in the example later in this chapter. For the moment, however, we should first discuss each dimension, and why each is important for achieving sales success. Understanding the "what-and-why" of each of the ten dimensions is critical.

Starting at the top of the chart:

Dimension 1: A High-Performance Culture

A *Performance-Driven Business Culture*, in any business entity, assures that promises are kept, organizational outcome and process measurements are used to track performance, and sales-support-related processes and systems are in place and functioning at optimum levels.

To achieve improved business outcomes, overall sales effectiveness requires more than just individual salesperson improvements. Sales support activities such as delivery, quality, order entry, inventory management (if a manufacturing or distribution business), scheduling (if a service business), and accounts payable & receivable, all need to exhibit strong performance so that they do not derail a deal that the salesperson has worked so hard to win.

All business functions and processes must have the salesperson's back. And the salesperson must sell what can be delivered within the capabilities of the organization. Collaboration is essential to deliver what clients want and need. High sales performance requires the support of a high-performing organization. Together, they must collaboratively deliver an excellent client experience.

Moreover, it is not adequate to simply measure outcomes: such as bookings, revenues, and deliveries. Each of those goals are *dependent variables* – meaning their achievement is totally dependent on some other process or behavior within the business. Those "other" processes must be executed with precision in order for sales goals to be achieved.

The achievement of outcome goals (dependent variables), sales or otherwise, is totally dependent on quality performance of certain antecedent behaviors within the company (independent variables).

For example, measuring the number of discovery meetings involving a client Decision Maker or EIC, is meaningless if the calls are of poor quality. Poor quality discovery meetings are characterized by poor planning, inadequate preparation, insufficient information gathering, poorly documented client needs and decision criteria, little information gathered regarding decision makers and decision-process, and critical information undiscovered – all requiring repeat visits to gather.

The quality of the activities and antecedent behaviors is much more important than simply the perfunctory performance of those activities.

Navigational Selling™ is all about the quality of sales behaviors - rather than just their perfunctory execution and measurement. A high performance, behavior-focused culture is the best soil for growing success.

Dimension 2: Market Strategy

The previously related story of the Battle of Stalingrad illustrated that a well-considered strategy is much more effective than a brute force frontal assault against an established enemy position. A sound market strategy delivers more wins with less effort. A sound market strategy leverages the strengths of your offerings, and targets markets that will receive the highest relevant value from them. Rather than attempting to sell to "everyone" and encountering resistance because of a less than perfect match of offering capabilities to client needs, the focused approach wins more with less effort and enables higher selling prices.

In practical terms, that means understanding the value quotient of your offering, selecting the most lucrative target market for it, articulating its competitive positioning in the context of that market's needs, and assuring the channel understands how to communicate that position.

A Market Strategy, therefore, is a combination of: a) an economically healthy target market with a common problem and a sufficient number of under-satisfied clients whose needs you can meet, b) an offering that meets those needs and in doing so delivers highly-relevant customer-perceived value, c) a distinct and differentiated competitive advantage which helps you stand out from others trying to service the same market, and d) a channel-to-market that communicates and provides complementary or supplemental value to the client (installation, training, information, or service, as examples).

Since clients in different market segments have different needs, it is likely that what they perceive as value varies as well. Thus, we want to assure that our value proposition is focused on the segment(s) of the market that will perceive and receive the highest value quotient from it.

Not every client receives the same magnitude and type of value from your product or service. It makes sense that those who perceive the greatest value are more likely to buy it, pay more for it, be happier with it, tell others like themselves about it and return when they need more. Always begin there.

The more the perceived value you deliver, the deeper and stronger the client-to-salesperson bond of trust.

Moreover, value is a quotient. Value is equal to benefits divided by costs. And both benefits and costs are multi-dimensional, comprising not only economic factors, but also, the emotional, physical, social, and political dimensions of value as well. A salesperson must be keenly aware of what their client needs and values in all value dimensions, and if they can deliver it comfortably and ethically, do so.

The first hint there is a strategic gap, either in market focus or value-quotient, is a prospective client not immediately recognizing and appreciating its value.

Dimension 3: New Business Development

New Business Development (NBD) is the brackish water between strategy and sales. It encompasses a lot, incorporating both corporate initiated activities such as tactical marketing communications and sales promotions, as well as individual salesperson-initiated activities, such as prospecting, networking, formulating alliances, and building productive referral networks.

In addition to the normally expected tactical marketing activities (advertising, websites, email promotions, trade shows, etc.), New Business Development includes a salesperson's individual efforts to find sources of multiple pre-qualified leads on their own, through:

- identifying and mapping *target market client Communication Networks*, peer-to-peer, formal and informal,

- building a cadre of *Referral Sources* within those networks,

- developing a *LinkedIn presence* and using it for potential client identification,

- participation, through *Talks and Networking*, in Industry Associations and their events,

- participation in peer groups and professional societies to *build a Referral Network*,

- developing complementary, mutually confidential, and *referral-producing Alliances*,

- evaluating *Additional Channels* for distribution of their offerings, and

- market focus and *Target Account Research*.

Each of the activities within New Business Development should have as a primary objective the discovery of *streams of opportunities*, as well as landing individual new clients.

Dimension 4: Sales Process Discipline

Dimension 4 measures the degree to which you believe that your firm's sales team is practicing a formal, disciplined, and effective sales process. Another word for sales discipline is sales rigor – or rather attention to detail and thoroughness of process step execution.

There are many sub-dimensions of sales process discipline.

At the highest level, there are the four basic sales process steps: *Qualification*, *Discovery*, *Solution Formulation* and *Follow Through*. Yet within those basic four steps there are many finer points and behaviors that also require discipline and rigor to execute well. Such rigor and discipline assure that each sub-step is completed effectively, efficiently, and contributes to a successful completed sale.

Sub-steps include pre-qualification, time management, sales call planning and preparation, sales call execution using agendas and objectives, detailed discovery, documentation through discussion summaries, effective questioning/listening skills, discovery of the buyer decision-making process and authorities, reading people, revealing personal and business motivations, and crafting inclusive solutions - to mention a few.

Dimension 5: Account & Opportunity Qualification

Dimension 5 measures the degree to which both your ideal target client criteria, as well as your opportunity qualification methods, are effective and result in a high win rate.

It is generally recognized by both sales managers and salespeople, that time is a salesperson's most valuable asset. Smart allocation of available time is essential for success. While there is no precise, generally accepted time-allocation mix, there is general agreement that the best way to improve effectiveness is to learn to qualify real opportunities quickly and accurately, so that wasting time on dead ends is minimal.

There are three types of qualification activity:

1. *Account Pre-Qualification:* Is a new account worth pursuing? What is the likelihood it will receive value from your offerings, while generating a repetitive stream of meaningful revenue and profits in return?

2. *Opportunity Qualification:* Are there needs within the account for specific offerings that can be won?

3. *Referral Source & Alliance Relationship Qualification:* This task of qualification is aimed at identifying sources of multiple account or offering opportunities, through a trusted mutual-referral arrangement.

Research has shown that typically 30 to 50% of a salesperson's opportunity pipeline will eventually be lost to "No Decision". This means the customer did not actually buy anything to solve their problem, most commonly because, in their minds, they never had a critical enough problem to act on.

Poor client targeting, weak qualification and lax discovery techniques conspire to waste a huge amount of a salesperson's time.

Dimension 6: Sales Call Planning

I will say it again. The most valuable asset a salesperson has is their time. While it can reasonably be argued that Sales Call Planning should be included under the Discovery performance dimension, I have chosen to establish a separate sales performance dimension for Sales Call Planning, to focus attention on how critical it is to a salesperson's productivity.

Sales Call Planning comprises three fundamental activities:

1. *Pre-qualification* before requesting or accepting a meeting,
2. The use of *Agendas, Objectives and Participation* requests, and
3. Pre-meeting *Preparation and Homework*, by both the client and the salesperson.

Good sales call planning minimizes the time allocated to client visits that do not have a specific purpose or premise related to a client POG. That POG may have been identified through account research, target account pre-qualification efforts, a referral, or phone discussion.

As mentioned previously, upwards of 50% of a salesperson's pipeline is lost to "no decision" – an indication the client did not have a compelling need. Visits to clients that do not have a compelling need just to see what is going on wastes valuable time – yours and your clients.

Dimension 7: Discovery

Discovery is the core of good sales. It must be 100% client focused. It provides the opportunity for the salesperson to build unquestionable trust, by objectively and unselfishly assisting the client in identifying their POGs, their root-causes, and the best approach for addressing them.

One of the most common challenges an SMB2B company faces through the Discovery step, is the disproportionate emphasis many salespeople place on working the client's technical challenge, to the detriment of understanding the decision process, the competitive situation, the decision-makers' motives, the client emotions associated with the need, and the bigger picture.

This limited perspective arises from the often-erroneous assumption on the part of the salesperson, that the client wants only two things: 1) a technical solution that meets their needs, and 2) the best price possible. While I won't argue that those are not important considerations, many more factors influence the ultimate decision.

What other decision-influencing factors might exist?

Here are a few:

- the competitive alternatives available to the decision makers, (including doing nothing, or DIY),

- important subliminal considerations of perceived value beyond just the economic – including emotional, political, social, and physical considerations,

- the management styles and personality types of the decision makers,

- the client decision-making process, decision influencers in an outside of the client firm, and the complete set of decision criteria, and

- the timing and long-term implications of the decision

At first glance, these additional considerations may not be clear. They will be clear after you read Chapter 7, Discovery and Chapter 8, Reading People.

But to reassure you that this is not an empty boast, here is an unsolicited testimonial quote from an SMB2B business co-owner of a Midwest metal-stamping company, where industrial tooling is an extremely competitive market.

"(I) Wanted to let you know that we just won a HUGE program that, alone, will increase our annual revenue by 20%. I wanted to thank you for all of your help and guidance. We incorporated numerous techniques from the previous proposals that we worked on with you. This was an extremely competitive situation, with 10 bidders and ultimately, "we knocked their socks off". Not sure we would have won this program had we submitted this proposal using the same approach (a simple, one-page quote sheet) we used prior to our engagement!" Exec VP, Co-Owner

---

High quality Discovery is the magic potion to add to the cauldron when you stir up a proposal.

Dimension 8: Solution Formulation (Proposing)

Dimension 8 measures the degree to which your client proposals are comprehensive and compelling. Many SMB2B product firms provide their prospects only a basic two-part offer: a price list or price quote, and a delivery date.

Such an approach leaves a lot of unanswered questions, misses opportunities for differentiation, and provides the prospect only those two criteria (price and delivery) from which to make a comparative decision. There are many additional considerations other than just price and promise date which can influence a decision.

In the world of the 21st century, no matter the level of authority or title of the client's ultimate decision maker, few important corporate decisions are made by a single individual, devoid of input from and discussion with others on the client's team. Proposals will likely be read by more than just the ultimate decision maker, and comments elicited. Each of those readers will look for their selfish needs in the proposal or quote you deliver.

Because of this growing reality, proposed solutions must incorporate the "High-school class photo" technique.

If you look at your high school class photo, whom do you look for first?

Yourself! Unless, of course, in the search for the younger thinner you, you first encounter your high school sweetheart, which typically delays you for only a brief nostalgic moment. Just sayin'.

Back to the point.

To garner their support and approval, client decision makers and decision influencers must easily see themselves, their interests, their needs, and perspectives, explicitly reflected in your proposals.

This is the main reason a thorough Discovery step is essential.

In sales, the well-worn, **ABC** mantra, "**A**lways **B**e **C**losing", may have been effective 50 years or more ago, but since the research done by the Huthwaite Group on the effectiveness of closing techniques, the fallacy of that acronym has been exposed. The conclusion from that research is that customers that have been "closed" with techniques and tricks are less likely to rebuy, less likely to be satisfied, and less likely to recommend you and your offerings to others.

Given that conclusion, but liking the acronym, I'd like you to consider an alternative interpretation of that mnemonic. Think of the **ABC** as "**A**lways **B**e **C**ollaborating".

Buyers appreciate collaboration, assistance, and guidance more than high pressure sales tricks and patently self-interested closing techniques. The Navigator is a collaborator.

Dimension 8 reveals the degree to which your sales process and skill set, is more aligned with collaborative vs. self-interested, trust-eroding, high-pressure closing behaviors.

Dimension 9: Follow Through (Winning)

This outcome (dependent) assessment dimension is included as a measure of the strength or weakness of any of several behavioral areas. It reflects the degree to which solid, compelling proposals have been delivered based on:

- highly qualified opportunities,

- thorough discovery,

- high client-perceived benefits that will be delivered by the proposed solution, compared to its costs,

- strong competitive positioning,

- meaningful competitive differentiation,

- an understanding of the buyer decision-making process, buyer personalities and non-economic needs,

- compelling needs to address an important or urgent client POG, and

- a strong advocate relationship.

It is possible that a sales team might feel confident because they win a lot of deals. But research has shown that closing based on sketchy, tricky, or seller-centric behaviors will not pay in the long term. That is why this performance dimension looks at salesperson behaviors, rather than simply outcomes in the form of wins.

Dimension 10: Market & Sales Analytics

As expressed earlier, the identification of market, customer, and value-quotient trends, generated from the implementation of a basic analytics gear, has been the source of the greatest breakthroughs in revenue and profit I have experienced in my nearly 30 years of consulting. There is no higher return on the investment of time and effort than in collecting, communicating, and analyzing what is really going on: a) in your target markets, b) within your client's business, *their* markets and organization, c) with the competitive situation, and d) in how the perception of your value quotient might be shifting in the minds of your ideal clients.

I am continually amazed at how common it is that the analytics gear is missing in SMB2B firms. I assume it's because most marketing & sales organizations don't think they have the time and have not experienced the benefit of such a small investment of effort, reflection, and money. Furthermore, many SMB2B firms that *do* embrace analytics during an engagement, let it atrophy after the first breakthrough.

Storytime: I Told You So

> Less than 90 days after beginning an engagement with a client whose new-product sales had stalled, their team ran an analysis of the value received from their product by their installed base. They discovered, hidden within that customer data, a huge under-served market with enormous growth potential.

> At the time of the analysis, they had only a single client in that under-served market, but through that client's feedback discovered that the client was receiving much higher economic impact from the product than any other client, in any of their other markets. Moreover, their analysis revealed that there were over 20,000 similar clients like that sole example, across the country, all experiencing the same challenges and having the same needs - with no good solution alternatives available.

> Refocusing marketing and sales efforts on that new market created a true breakthrough, resulting in more than *one thousand new installations* within a couple of years.

> On completing the engagement, and after the momentum rapidly picked up, I strongly cautioned and advised that they needed to invest a small amount of effort on an ongoing basis to the analytics gear.

> They did not.

> A few years later when their new market hit a wall and experienced a segment specific economic downturn in demand, their business cratered - and they called me back to help them find their next breakthrough.

> My first question was whether they had been continuing their analytical work, so I could look at it and start there.

> The answer was no. Undiplomatically, I said, in my best Dutch Uncle voice, "*I told you so!*"

> They rehired me and we ran analytics and found a second market to shore up the lagging first market.

> Why would they want to pay me twice? Why would they not have prepared for an inevitable market turn-down? Why would they not have embraced the wisdom and payback available through a small continuing effort in analytics? Why would they reject a proven approach that discovered breakthroughs?

> I do not have the answers.

> Go figure.

Moral of the Story: When repairing a broken process, institutionalize, nurture, protect, and use the new process.

End of story

Interpreting Assessment Results

The output of the assessment in Figure 4 is relatively easy to read.

The heavy line along the outer edge of the chart signifies perfection. The light shaded dashed line indicates a barely acceptable level of capability within the scope of skills and experience required in that dimension. The irregular solid black line is the actual self-rated current situation.

The profile shown in the graph in Figure 4, illustrates a typical situational profile of an unenlightened SMB2B. Any time the irregular black line approaches or dips below the dashed line, there is a self-recognized need for skills, process, and/or capabilities improvement.

Focusing on the irregular black shape in Figure 4, notice the dips and scores in the following dimensions: Market & Sales Analytics (1.4), Sales Call Planning (2.0), Market Strategy (2.3), Sales Process Discipline (2.4) and Discovery (2.6). Even if this SMB2B is limping along and satisfied with their performance, such scores leave them vulnerable to competitive moves.

The implications of an SMB2B's vulnerability to competitive moves and economic hiccups can be assessed by asking the following questions:

1. How much do we believe these gaps might have cost us over the last several years?

2. What would the near and long-term implications be if any of our toughest competitors scored significantly higher in each dimension that we are deficient in?

3. What would the implications and consequences be if a competitor discovered and exploited those weaknesses?

4. If a suitor wanted to buy a business like our SMB2B, and had other similar businesses to consider as well, what would be the impact on the economic value of our business, if during the suitor's due diligence process, these deficiencies were revealed? Based on those revelations, in the eyes of the suitor, would the business be worth more or less?

If, as a result of the assessment these questions frighten you, perhaps that's good and it will encourage an immediate effort to improve your SMB2B sales process capabilities. That is its purpose and I hope this book helps.

Don't be discouraged. No SMB2B business scores high in all categories at the outset. The good news is that all the dimensions can be improved upon with strong focus and commitment. Again, we will explore each of these dimensions in much greater detail in the coming chapters.

A short, non-graphic version of the Organizational-Level Effectiveness Assessment is included in Appendix A. A full graphical assessment is free for readers. To access it, simply request a link to the Navigational Selling™ Sales Effectiveness Assessment from QMP1@qmpassociates.com. We will respond with the link and password that allows you to take the assessment. Please note, passwords are only valid for 24 hours after you receive your link.

Your assessment will help you plot your journey to success and provide you a benchmark against which to assess your progress.

Caution: Chasing False Prophets - Process Effectiveness vs. Process Automation

Notwithstanding the arrival on the scene in the last 30 years of the internet, websites, e-commerce, marketing automation, SaaS CRM software, social media, cloud-based Apps, Zoom™, blogging, webinars, podcasts, audio books, et al - the foundational science and principles of Marketing & Sales as integrated into the Marketing & Sales Engine, parts of which all of these new tools would aspire to automate, remain unchanged.

Those foundational principles include:

- long term success requires a sound, yet flexible and evolving Market Strategy,

- products or service offerings should not be launched before they are market-and-client value-tested,

- customer value-received plus the client' perception of the relative Quality of your offering compared to competitors, define your competitive advantage and brand - and ultimate success,

- field data must be continuously collected, analyzed, and processed to keep a market strategy fresh and an offering's value-quotient relevant,

- client value messaging must flow quickly and accurately through a channel-to-market from offering design, through marketing, through sales, to the client, and

- focus assures rapid market penetration.

With no intent to diminish the value of the marketing & sales innovations listed at the beginning of this subsection, at their core those innovations are simply automation. Based on my many early years in manufacturing, I can provide first-hand testimony that automating a manufacturing process of fundamentally unsound effectiveness, will very quickly create a bunch of junk and waste – and do it much faster than what would have been produced manually.

The same is true for automating unsound marketing and sales processes.

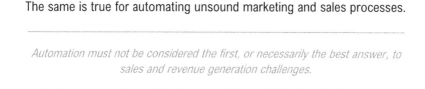

Automation must not be considered the first, or necessarily the best answer, to sales and revenue generation challenges.

If the fundamental market strategy, value proposition, market focus, qualification criteria or sales process that is being automated are flawed, great outcomes cannot be produced and should not be expected through automation - no matter how efficient the automation process is.

It is the difference between efficiency and effectiveness. One must achieve effectiveness first, before driving to automation efficiency.

A highly automated sales process cannot produce good results if the market strategy on which it is based is flawed. Do not gamble on marketing automation investments, sales process training or a comprehensive branding initiative, devoid of having a sound, proven market strategy in place first. Those gambles will not individually or in combination, save the day.

The Mission of Navigational Selling™

The mission of Navigational Selling™ is two-fold:

1. to communicate the proven, foundational principles of marketing and sales science and illustrate how they directly influence sales success, and

2. to reveal how an individual or SMB2B business can become more effective in selling - no matter your current target market, competitive situation, skill level, and culture of discipline.

Both parts of the mission are yours for the reaping - if you empower the concepts of Navigational Selling™ with your personal commitment.

*****

Chapter 4: Five Considerations that Influence SMB2B Success

In this Chapter …

Five Considerations that Influence SMB2B Success

Consideration 1: The Limited Impact of Tactical Marketing

Consideration 2: The Leverage from New Business Development

Consideration 3: The Often-Overlooked Client Decision-Making Process

Consideration 4: The SMB2B Salesperson's Adherence to Sales Process Disciplines

Consideration 5: The Client Experience and RPQL

Five Considerations that Influence SMB2B Success

If you are an EIC, it is important to understand that there are five interwoven considerations that will influence, to one degree or another, SMB2B sales success.

They are:

1. *Tactical Marketing:* The approach and investments the company will use to attract potential clients to engage with a salesperson. This includes the company's website, advertising, email promotions, blogs, social media efforts, trade shows, branding programs, and digital marketing. The relative merits of each of these investments and their likely returns will be discussed in coming pages.

2. *New Business Development:* The approaches and methods the individual salesperson will employ, supplemental to the firm's tactical marketing efforts, to attract potential clients to engage.

3. The *Client's Decision-Making Process:* This is the most ignored and yet most important of the considerations.

4. Your company's *Standard Sales Process:* This comprises the steps, techniques, tools, and skills the salesperson uses once the prospective client is engaged.

5. The *Client Experience and RPQL:* This is the value and consistency the client experiences in the delivery of market-leading, high customer-perceived value and RPQL (Relative Perceived Quality Leadership) in each client engagement, from their first, to each subsequent involvement.

To achieve optimum return on investment and sales effectiveness, all considerations must dovetail. Close alignment of those considerations assures there is consistency of behaviors, objectives, and messaging, thus eliminating any wasteful overlap of effort and investment.

Alignment begins by assuring that each contributing factor is formulated from answers to the following questions:

- Which group(s) of clients will receive the highest value quotient from your offerings, aka your target market? This group should be your primary market focus.

- What critical and important problems, opportunities, and gaps (POGs), are clients in those target markets facing?

- Which of your product/service offerings will meet those client challenges?

- What meaningful impacts, (economic, emotional, physical, social, and political), will the resolution of those POGs deliver to clients?

- Of the target markets you have identified, which will receive the highest value from your offering's resolution of their POGs?

- What price premiums can be charged in exchange for that market-leading delivered value?

- What proofs (case studies, testimonials, references, examples) exist of that value having been delivered in the past to other clients in that market or situation? These examples will comprise your proof of relevance.

- Within the selected target markets, how will your offerings and firm become the best known, most effective, and trusted "solution of choice"?

- How will you position and differentiate your business and its offerings from competitors?

- How will you engage the market to communicate those offerings and the value they deliver to the target client base?

- As a salesperson, beyond the efforts of your tactical marketing programs, how will you attract qualified client prospects into your sales pipeline?

- How will you navigate these client prospects through the sales pipeline to a signed deal?

- What approach(es) will you use to discover and engage new clients on a continuing basis?

- Based on what clients appreciate, what do you need to do to assure the highest client-perceived value delivery in each client engagement?

Many SMB2B's do not thoroughly think through these questions ahead of launching an offering, leaving the salesperson to figure out the answers and approaches on their own. Additionally, many salespeople and managers do not recognize that the five considerations must be designed into an integrated and aligned system.

As either an executive or a salesperson, it is critical to think through these considerations and questions, anticipate their implications, align investment initiatives, and prepare for a range of possible selling scenarios. Such integrated process design will accelerate both individual and corporate success.

Consideration 1: The Limited Impact of Tactical Marketing

Using a fishing metaphor, tactical marketing activities can be described as "Bait-to-Bite". Such activities attract clients to the front-end of the company's sales pipeline, where they can be taken under a salesperson's wing, engaged in a collaborative dialogue about the client's needs, qualified, and assisted in finding and deploying a good solution to their POG.

You might ask, "Why are we discussing tactical marketing in a book about sales?"

Because an SMB2B salesperson must know what to reasonably expect from their firm's marketing investment.

In most SMB2B cases, only a small fraction of new, promising, pre-qualified opportunities arriving at the front end of a salesperson's pipeline, will actually be the direct result of tactical marketing activities and investments. Based on my work with hundreds of SMB2B clients, tactical marketing expenditures, while they may consume a large portion of the non-personnel related marketing and sales budget, produce low-level results as a source of new, highly pre-qualified leads for the salesperson. This is particularly true in highly competitive markets like banking, Information technology, professional services, and consulting.

Consideration 2: The Leverage of New Business Development

New Business Development (NBD) activities are commonly within the realm of what a salesperson does to discover and cultivate sources of multiple pre-qualified leads. NBD efforts are supplemental to a firm's tactical marketing efforts.

NBD comprises developing Primary Referral Sources (well-connected people that the salesperson wishes to be introduced to), Alliance Partners (business entities that provide complementary services to clients and businesses the salesperson wishes to engage with), and Networking (virtually, in-person and through social media channels).

Some might classify this type of activity within the realm of tactical marketing, but it is rare for a tactical marketing team to take on these tasks. I believe that is mostly because: a) it is simply too difficult and time consuming to expect a marketing department to build an individual salesperson's network (particularly if there are multiple salespeople in the SMB2B), and b) these kinds of relationships are developed very personally, based on the high degree of trust that is developed between the salesperson and the NBD referral source.

New Business Development is discussed extensively in Appendix D, and the relationship between the various marketing and sales roles is illustrated in Figure 39 in that section.

The Unfavorable Math of Cold Calling

Cold calling is a real challenge for most people. Nonetheless, many companies require it, and a high proportion of inexperienced salespeople still believe in it.

Companies that embrace a cold calling method, commonly consider sales a numbers game. They establish cold calling goals that target a minimum number of cold calls per day, per week or per month. The expectation is that *perhaps* 10% of those calls will lead to an appointment and 2% will turn into a won business opportunity. Think of the painful scenes from the movie "Glengarry Glenn Ross".

A few years ago, in a closed-door meeting with 25 senior salespeople from different firms, we shared the secrets of our New Business Development success. The revelations astonished me.

I believed that most successful salespeople would identify some mix of the same approach I used – namely speaking, writing, and nurturing well-connected primary referral source relationships. In actuality, the answers were all over the map. Referrals, however, were the most common and most productive approach.

Only one individual cited cold calling as the primary trigger for her new business development success. The room was stunned to silence. Could that possibly be true?

It was!

Then simultaneously, after momentary confusion and considering the idea, the light of recognition began to appear on our faces. We all understood why. This salesperson was a consultant – a specialist in, guess what…. training companies on the skill set of cold calling. I will say, unless a salesperson is consulting on cold calling techniques or has completely exhausted every other approach, they should try another, more productive path.

Let's just review the math of cold calling.

Assume the salesperson has a target to cold call 200 prospects in a week. The goal is to arrange five meetings with individuals who are ultimate decision makers for purchasing the salesperson's offerings.

Of those 200, the salesperson gets voice mail at a rate of 25% - which means they will probably need to call the individuals back. That means 50 additional calls, that will probably achieve the same success rate. So, the number of required phone calls keeps increasing, though at a diminishing rate.

Now, let's assume that after leaving numerous voice messages, reaching wrong numbers, and finding a way around gatekeepers that have graduated from "Protect-the-Boss-from-Cold-Calls-at-All-Cost" University, the salesperson finally reaches an economic decision maker. Of those calls that achieve success in connecting with an EIC or other decision-making authority, let's assume the salesperson can set-up and confirm two appointments in ten.

How many hours do you think a salesperson would need to invest in all that effort?

Let's say 40 hours to work through 200 leads, including call-backs, repeat calls and phone tag. The possible outcomes: a) don't call again, b) not interested, c) call me back in a few months, d) a voice mail, e) a protective admin that promises to leave a message or, f) the ultimate reward, an acceptance to book a face-to-face appointment with a decision maker that has a real need in the salesperson's sweet spot.

If the salesperson is good at cold calling and it's working for them, that's great.

For the rest of us, we need a more productive use of our time. Consider a pre-qualified lead generated from a warm referral, peer, alliance partner, or a talk focused on a specific audience of decision-makers.

What to expect from Considerations 1 and 2

Tactical marketing efforts are intended to generate leads for the salesperson. In reality, SMB2B tactical marketing activities, on their own, rarely generate enough pre-qualified leads to achieve sales targets.

Therefore, the salesperson must make up the difference. They must generate their own new-opportunity sales leads from: returning clients, networking, referrals, alliance relationships, cold-calling, local event participation and personal market research. Such leads are typically much better qualified at the outset.

Figures 5 and 6 illustrate the most common lead generation approaches, and their contribution to filling the front end of a salesperson's pipeline. (Source: QMP Research)

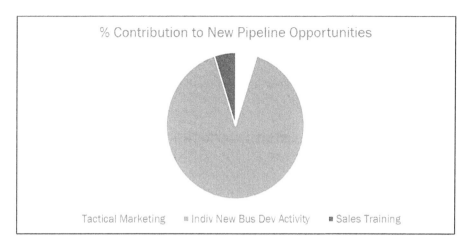

Figure 5: % Contribution to a Salesperson's New Opportunity Pipeline

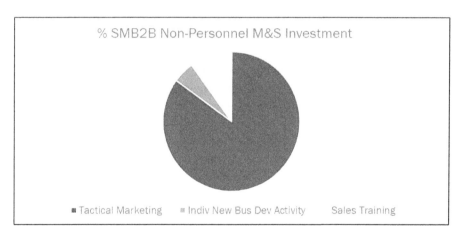

Figure 6: % SMB2B Non-Personnel-Related Marketing & Sales Investment

The conclusions from these charts:

1. The salesperson's individual and independent New Business Development efforts, in many cases, will become the largest single contributor to their own pipeline activities. So, they must learn to become both effective and efficient at it.

2. Tactical marketing costs are a large percentage of non-personnel related marketing and sales expense. Yet they return only a small portion of the leads a salesperson processes through to success.

An extensive discussion of New Business Development activities and approaches are covered in Appendix D.

Consideration 3: The Often-Overlooked Client Decision-Making Process

Internal decision-making processes can vary widely from client-to-client.

In their book "The Challenger Customer", the authors (Brent Adamson, Matthew Dixon, Pat Spenner, and Nick Toman) state *(parentheses mine)*,

> *"Much of the problem (in achieving consistently successful sales performance) lies less in a supplier organization's inability to sell effectively, and far more in a customer organization's inability to buy effectively. And a large part of that challenge lies squarely in customers' struggle to achieve common agreement across the wide range of stakeholders now typically involved in virtually any solutions purchase."*

Many B2B client organizations have inefficient and inconsistent decision-making processes, or worse, no formal decision-making and buying process at all. Moreover, approval and authorization levels of people with identical titles will vary from client to client. For example, if the typical ultimate approval authority for what is being sold is the Chief Operating Officer (COO) in one firm, it may be the CEO at another client firm. The EIC ultimate decision-maker can range up and down the client's published organization chart.

Another variable is the number of people contributing to the final decision. This collaborative decision-making team may comprise one to seven individuals. The Challenger Customer research pegs this number at 5.4, not including outside advisors.

Individual considerations and motivations of each of those decision-makers and influencers will certainly not be the same from client-to-client.

Finally, not all decision makers will be experienced or qualified in conducting the kinds of evaluations and making the important decisions required concerning what the salesperson is offering.

Some clients may have never had to find and evaluate a solution or make a decision regarding their current POG. In such a case, they are inexperienced buyers, uninformed solution evaluators, and therefore may become reluctant, cautious, and painstakingly slow decision makers.

What if the client does not even recognize their own decision-making process?

It is possible, and not uncommon, that some clients have never purchased the salesperson's particular offering in the past, and therefore have not formalized a process for making informed decisions about such offerings. This is particularly the case, if for example, what the salesperson is selling is a true innovation. Furthermore, even if the client has purchased a similar offering in the past to address a recurrent POG that hasn't occurred for some time, personnel changes and the current people on board may have not participated in that last decision.

In such cases, the client may need assistance in how to go about making the best decision. If a salesperson finds themself in this situation, they might consider communicating the following to the client.

"With no disrespect intended, it appears you and your team may not have developed a process or be familiar with how best to evaluate available solutions to your current challenge. If you are open to it, perhaps I might offer an approach, or refer someone that I know, that has effectively navigated this decision journey in the past."

The decision-making process in Figure 7 below, sketched on a whiteboard or napkin can be received by clients as revealing to them the secrets of the universe. It's simple and logical. In my career, inexperienced clients have appreciated such a suggestion. It gets them off ground zero and moving faster toward POG resolution. At minimum it provides them a logical approach to share with other members of their team or their EIC.

SMB2B salespeople must be prepared to assist with a recommendation of precisely how the client might evaluate alternatives. In this situation, the salesperson must Navigate for the client – collaboratively offering to assist by plotting the client's decision-making course and carefully piloting the client's team through decision shoals that require steering finesse.

A Typical Client Decision-Making Model

Attempting to drag a client into the salesperson's *sales process*, if it is different than the internal *decision-making* process they would prefer to follow, leads to friction. Not necessarily the kind of friction that creates conflict, but rather the kind of friction that complicates communications, slows things down, and in the worst case, results in lost sales.

In all cases, the client's decision-making process will trump the salesperson's sales process.

Navigational Selling™ recognizes that success requires helping the client navigate their own decision-making culture.

The decision-making approach may vary from client to client and offering to offering. Common types are:

- *Consensus*, in which the ultimate decision-maker strives to *achieve agreement* from all stakeholders,

- *Consultative*, in which the ultimate decision-maker elicits input and recommendations from all stakeholders depending on their expertise, reserving the final decision and authorization for themselves, or

- *Collaborative*, wherein the team develops *objective evaluation criteria* and scoring according to their specialties, shares the tasks associated with proper *data gathering*, and contributes their evaluations to the score sheet - *the results of the score sheet points to the best decision*.

No matter the approach, the salesperson should assist the ultimate EIC decision-maker in navigating internal stakeholders through their decision process.

Figure 7 illustrates a common decision-making process that a prospective client might use in deciding whether to purchase a salesperson's offering.

Figure 7: A Common Client Decision-Making Process

Beginning at the far left, here are brief explanations.

Step1: *POG Awareness*, wherein the prospective client becomes aware of a specific performance problem, opportunity, or gap in their business.

Step 2: *Solution Limits & Risks*, wherein the client team begins to recognize the constraints, limits, and risks they need to consider when deciding how best to solve the problem, exploit the opportunity or close the gap.

Step 3: *Evaluate Alternatives*, wherein the client's team evaluates alternative approaches given the constraints, limits, and risks identified in the previous step.

Step 4: *Value Analysis*, wherein the client team assesses the potential value and benefits of resolving the problem or availing themselves of the opportunity, compared to the anticipated costs.

Step 5: *Approvals*, wherein the client project leader requests formal approval or agreement from the EIC ultimate decision maker or whomever is higher up in the client firm's chain of command. It could be their Board of Directors, owners, partners, CEO, CFO, bank, lawyers, etc. Sometimes other approvals are not necessary, as in the case of a sole CEO/Owner decision maker.

Step 6: *Deployment*, wherein the client team, with support from the seller, implements the offering.

Step 7: *Progress Monitoring*, wherein the client team measures, monitors, and reports on how effective the solution has been. If progress is not being made, they still have a problem – and the process repeats until it eventually results in POG resolution.

A salesperson may find some variations in the decision-making process from client to client, but the main flow, steps and purpose will be largely the same.

Think of it.

If you buy a new car, a new set of wireless ear buds, or the services of a personal trainer, you will likely follow the same steps. Businesses making capital investments follow the same logic – formally or informally.

Remember, the NavSell salesperson's purpose in selling, is to help the client Navigate the best decision for optimum results. A salesperson should think of their sales responsibility as finding ways to help the client's decision makers and influencers work through their own decision process most efficiently.

To build trust, the salesperson must continually assist the client to do what is best for themselves.

Decision-Making Facilitation Tools: Helping the Client Navigate Their Own Process

To assist clients, there are several decision-making enablers we can attach to this decision-making process model. See Figure 8.

Tools can help the flow of the customer's decision-making process. More specifically, we mean tools that are designed to assist the client in moving smoothly from one step to the next.

An experienced salesperson is typically able to anticipate and proactively provide the kinds of facilitating information that will help the client's decision-makers achieve their objectives. They are likely familiar with what helps in certain circumstances and have discovered, over time, what most clients need to make such a decision.

A well-crafted sales tool kit injects information in parallel with the client's decision-making process. Such tools may include: a needs assessment which reveals latent gaps and opportunities, economic benefits analysis tools, case studies that prove the performance impact of the salesperson's offerings in similar circumstances, client testimonials which illustrate past clients' delight with the results, and/or the competitive comparisons of the salesperson's approach – including the very real and common alternatives of "Do-it-Yourself" and "Do-Nothing".

Each tool should be designed to act like a little oil injector, greasing the flow of the client's decision-making process from one step to the next.

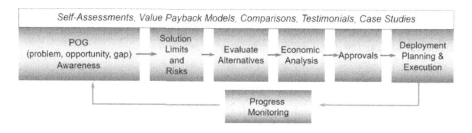

Figure 8: Adding Sales and Decision-Enabling Tools to the Client Decision-Making Process

Latent Need Triggering Techniques

One can consider the client decision-making process like a piston. See Figure 9 below.

All pistons need some sort of explosive force to move them forward to drive the engine. That explosion is illustrated by the starburst in the figure below, and the piston movement illustrated by the thick arrow moving toward the right.

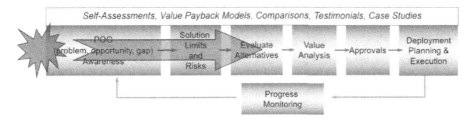

Figure 9: Initiating an Explosion to Drive the Client Decision-Making Process

There are multiple ways to trigger the buying-process motivational explosion.

Sometimes the explosion is self-triggered by the client. The trigger might be a sudden downturn in business, an operating crisis, unexpected loss of a huge customer or an important employee, an opportunity to invest in new equipment, or the need to quickly shore up business performance factors in anticipation of selling the business. The list of internal motivational triggers is endless.

There may be no current motivational trigger fuse already lit. That does not mean that an explosion cannot be triggered through diagnosis.

Probably the best way to illustrate this is with a medical analogy.

Imagine going to the doctor for an annual checkup with no specific symptoms and discovering your blood pressure is dangerously high. That piece of unexpected diagnostic data triggers the need for doing something soon: increasing exercise, adjustments to diet, medication, lower alcohol intake – or all the above.

In the process of selling, diagnostic assessments designed around the salesperson's specialty can be effective in revealing unexpected, latent problems, opportunities, or gaps (POGs). Such assessments can create trigger motivational explosions that drive the client's decision-making process.

The Client POG Self-Assessment

A client self-assessment is an effective way to trigger a potential client's decision-making process. Such an assessment is designed to reveal latent or hidden needs. It also has the potential to reveal secondary issues, perhaps related to the already current POG the client wishes to address.

Clients, even if they call the salesperson in to discuss a specific challenge, do not always know the best solution, or the root cause of their problem. They may be convinced that they need something that addresses symptoms, not root causes. A symptom-only solution is rarely in the client's best long-term interest.

It is a bit like a patient coming to the doctor with an excruciating pain in their lower back and asking for chiropractic service, when in fact the problem is a non-passable kidney stone, not a muscle cramp. An ethical doctor would not take the patient's request as wise, schedule a chiropractic visit or provide powerful pain killers without diagnostic testing. Rather, they would run a battery of tests, diagnose the root cause of the problem based on the results, consult with the patient, then recommend an appropriate course of treatment.

The point is: Treatment without diagnosis is malpractice.

Doctors must first do no harm. This means they need to treat the root cause of disease, not just the symptoms.

Salespeople should also live by that guideline.

An SMB2B firm's sales process must incorporate assessment tools that can be used by the client to reveal their needs. If these needs are serious enough, the pre-treatment consult should then trigger a client's decision-making process to resolve whatever issue has been revealed in the assessment.

We will discuss the POG Self-Assessment approach in Chapter 7, Discovery.

Consideration 4: The SMB2B Salesperson's Adherence to a Disciplined Sales Process

There are two parts to the salesperson's sales process: individual New Business Development activities intended to supplement tactical marketing lead generation and the actual Selling Process through which the salesperson and the client-prospect collaboratively formulate a plan for resolving the client's POG.

Because Tactical Marketing rarely provides an ample supply of qualified opportunities, a salesperson's New Business Development efforts will need to bear the brunt of attracting new prospective clients. It must be effective, time-efficient, and multiplicative.

Part A: Individual Salesperson New Business Development Activities

In preparation for initiating New Business Development activities the salesperson must be clear with regard to their client-relevant, value-quotient messaging, and the client decision-maker and decision-influencer targets for those messages. Each type of decision-maker or decision-influencer will likely respond to slightly different messages – those messages that resonate most closely with their primary concerns and functional perspectives.

Figure 10 illustrates how that might be captured for a salesperson selling Marketing & Sales related products or services.

Within a client's organization there are typically two levels that are instrumental in a collaborative decision-making approach to what to purchase to resolve a Marketing & Sales related POG - the *Decision Makers* and the *Decision Influencers*. Each has their own set of perspectives. The benefits and messaging communicated to each needs to be tailored to their position and role in the firm, as well as any revealed motivators of their performance and compensation.

For each of the Decision Makers and Decision Influencers, a role-specific message is postulated in the graphic.

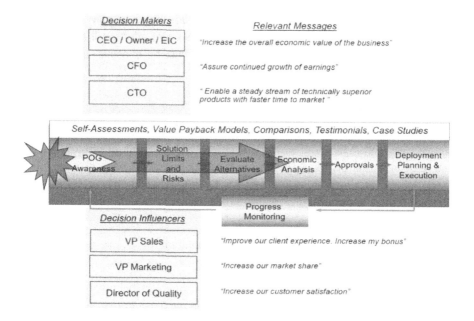

Figure 10: Relevant Support-Building Messages within a Client Decision-Making Team Process

In the example above, note that the motivation of the CEO, Owner, or EIC is ultimately "the overall economic value of the business", while that of the VP of Sales will likely have "increase my bonus" as a key consideration.

The different perspectives mean that the salesperson must frame their Value Quotient benefits messages accordingly. Benefits messages must be crafted to resonate with the primary motivations of each of the key influencers and decision makers. Crafting these messages needs to take on equal importance to building a sales-enabling tool kit. The salesperson needs to know how, when, at what stage, and to whom within the client's organization to deliver each message.

New Business Development: Generating Sources of Leads

Before a salesperson can deliver a tailored message, they must discover and target the client prospect companies, and the decision makers and decision influencers within those companies who need to hear those messages. Continuing to build on our model, the left vertical column in Figure 11 below identifies mechanisms for discovering target client firms and key people within them.

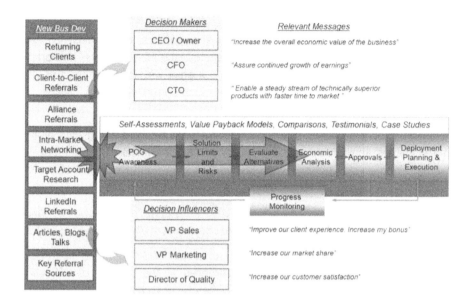

Figure 11: Adding New Business Development Sources of New Opportunity

Let's take a brief look at each of those New Business Development blocks in the column at the left of the graphic.

Returning Clients: The easiest people to sell to are those with whom the salesperson has already established trust and delivered value. It is critical therefore, to keep in regular contact with them. I am continually amazed at how some salespeople become complacent and let those clients languish for long periods of time without checking in.

Client-to-Client Referrals: Referrals are a transfer of trust. If the salesperson has established a high degree of trust with a client, then asking that client for a referral to their peers in other companies that might be beset with the same or similar POGs, should be a relatively easy thing to do.

Alliance Referrals: No EIC I have ever met makes decisions to buy only the salesperson's offerings. Identifying the other kinds of decisions and purchases they make, points the salesperson to the types of businesses with whom they should develop trusted alliances.

For example: My consulting practice offers Marketing & Sales Organizational transformations. Periodically this generates a need for recruiting salespeople, marketers, and marketing or sales executives. So, I have developed trusted relationships and bi-lateral referral alliances with two Executive Recruiting Firms.

Intra-Market Networking: Every industry I know of has associations, journals, blogs, opinion leaders, experts, conferences, events, and local chapters. Networking within a target market's intra-market network is a great way to stay abreast of who the opinion leaders are, the relevant common issues currently faced by clients, and the overall health of the industry.

Target Account Research: There is an enormous amount of information on-line about industries, their POGs, specific companies, and individuals. Between industry databases, industry associations, websites, articles, blogs, and LinkedIn profiles, just about anyone, in any company, at any level, can be found.

Is the salesperson not getting enough leads from corporate tactical marketing? This is no excuse for poor sales performance. They must start digging and asking for referrals.

LinkedIn Referrals: I am continually surprised at the number of B2B sales professionals that are still not fully literate in the use of LinkedIn. It is like having a thousand people in a Rolodex with whom the salesperson can play the *"Who do you know?"* game.

Articles, Blogs and Talks: To succeed, a salesperson must be an expert in what they sell. Experts sell more, receive more respect and referrals from their clients, and build more memorable brands. Assuming that shining a light on the salesperson's expertise is of value, they might consider becoming a speaker at an industry event.

Speaking opportunities must never become blatant promotional pitches, but rather an opportunity to share insightful perspectives about industry POGs and how to approach them.

Such talks establish the salesperson as a "go-to" resource, provide opportunities to reinforce their personal brand, and occasions to speak and answer questions concerning industry POGs, to a captive audience of industry executives, uninterrupted for up to an hour. Speaking about a common meaningful industry challenge, to audiences with the right people in attendance, will likely produce at least one invitation to "come by and chat" with someone experiencing some issue related to that POG.

Primary Referral Sources (PRS): This category captures all those professionals in a salesperson's network with whom they have developed credibility and trust. Salespeople must periodically remind that network that they will accept referrals to potential clients that are experiencing challenges related to their offerings.

Salespeople must also inform their network of new offerings they have to sell and how they might recognize a prospect that could benefit from them.

As you might imagine, a PRS relationship must be bilateral.

Part B: The Navigational Selling™ Process

The process of selling includes qualifying, listening, discovering, understanding, formulating, and winning high-client-value proposals.

It takes a bit of patience and coaching to convince non-sales professionals that there are productive ways to sell – approaches that avoid the derisions and consequences associated with the negative connotations of sales: hyping, talking too much, pestering, closing tricks, badgering, and manipulation.

The way to become Navigational and client-helpful in a personal sales approach is simply by not exhibiting or practicing any of those negative behaviors. Success does not require it. In fact, it is just the opposite.

Think of this scenario from another common aspect of people's lives, a visit to the doctor.

When you visit your doctor with some ailment, what do they do?

They ask questions, run some tests to get an accurate diagnosis of the ailment and then recommend a course of treatment. They do not immediately open the pharmaceutical formulary and walk you through a list of all the possible medications they have available or describe in detail all the possible surgical procedures they are familiar with.

Nor do they ask you which combination of treatments, medications, and procedures you think is best. They do not attempt to convince you to take the most expensive drug or submit to the most expensive surgical procedure, or the one that is "on special this week for a limited time only."

Why don't they do that?

Because that would be malpractice and it would be laughable if the potential consequences for all involved were not so significant.

Prescription without diagnosis is malpractice. The salesperson should consider good sales behaviors like a visit to a good doctor. The salesperson is like the doctor, the expert, the specialist. The client is the patient, the person with the malady - the POG. The salesperson must question, assess, and diagnose before recommending a course of action based on their expertise.

The more methodical the doctor, the more questions they ask and the more thorough the exam and testing process. Their thorough diagnostic process builds trust with you. The more accurate the diagnosis, the more effective the treatment plan.

The priority in any good sales process is to accurately diagnose the root cause of the client's malady and prescribe some effective course of action. Both doctoring and selling in that way builds trust.

The salesperson must *help the client navigate a reliable path to resolution of their challenges*. Helping the client requires a thorough assessment of their challenge and its root cause, analysis, diagnosis, recommendations, and advice through the treatment regimen.

Helping is the most important sales behavior. Helping builds trust. Trust produces wins.

At the foundation of trust-building with a client is their perception of the salesperson as the + – an expert sincerely and honestly focused on helping them solve *their* problem and meeting *their* challenge in a way that is in *their best interest*. In other words, that the salesperson is attempting to help them achieve *what they need*, by recommending and providing what is, based on the salesperson's expertise, necessary for them to heal.

Consider the "sweeper" in the Winter Olympics sport of curling.

The "thrower" of the stone initiates the play with the specific intent of sliding the stone over the ice into the center of the target or some other strategic location, depending on the number of stones already on, or near, the target (called the "house").

The sweeper's job is to prepare the path ahead of the stone to direct the moving stone to where the thrower desires it to stop. If a salesperson's behavior emulates the Doctor, or the Sweeper, a solid foundation of trust with the customer is built. Both Sweeper and Doctor are operating with the best interest of the client in mind – trying to beneficently lead them to where they need to be – in an improved condition.

So, listen, assess, diagnose, recommend, reassure, and encourage. Through it all, the salesperson should sincerely work to ***help*** their clients achieve the client's objectives first. In other words, when selling, help Navigate the client's decision journey.

Consideration 5: The Client Experience and RPQL

The relative competitive position of an SMB2B's offerings, no matter how much faster, feature laden or fabulous looking they are, can be adversely impacted by one bad client experience anywhere along the process.

Extensive research has revealed that within a target market, offerings which achieve a Relative Perceived Quality Leadership (RPQL) position relative to their competitors, will ultimately garner higher market share, generate higher profits, and command higher prices.

Don't be fooled by the word Quality. In this context, it does not mean more reliable, fancier, or longer lasting - though those factors certainly contribute. Quality in this context means providing superior value in the eyes of the clients in that market – and in that context the definition of quality is specific to the customers or clients within that segment, and encompasses the complete, long-term *Client Experience*.

Quality is defined by the client's perception of the complete client experience.

The client experience does not begin with a sales call and end with a closed deal. Rather, it encompasses all in-person and virtual interactions the client has with the SMB2B firm and its representatives. It includes every experience, exposure, communication and use of its offerings. It spans from their first awareness of the SMB2B's offerings, to their review of the website, any demo they may need to see, pre-sale meetings, emails, proposals, delivery, installation, startup, training, packaging, un-boxing, help line and chat box - to any post-delivery follow-up. It must all build trust by being as close to flawless as possible.

So, in some way, the SMB2B's sales process, is really the sum of all an SMB2B's business processes. They should all be designed and operated with one purpose in mind – to enhance the client's experience. RPQL encompasses the whole corporation - every department and every individual that connects with the client in some form or another, at any point of the client-SMB2B business relationship. Each interaction the client has with an SMB2B business and its offerings, before and for a long time after the sale, contributes or detracts from RPQL.

*****

Part 2: The Navigational Selling™ Process

Part 2 provides a detailed description of the Navigational Selling™ methodology. It will be most relevant and helpful to salespeople, sales managers, those sales draftees whose function is not primarily sales, and EICs and Entrepreneurs whose professional backgrounds are not in sales.

Navigational Selling™ is a basic 4-step process comprising Qualification, Discovery, Solution Formulation and Follow-Through (aka Winning). Reading People is a sub-category of Discovery and is allocated a chapter of its own because of its importance.

Chapter 5: The Pillars of Navigational Selling™

Chapter 6: Qualification

Chapter 7: Discovery

Chapter 8: Reading People

Chapter 9: Solution Formulation

Chapter 10: The Proposal

Chapter 11: Follow-Through & Winning

Chapter 5: The Pillars of Navigational Selling™

In this Chapter ...

The Pillars of Navigational Selling

A Navigator Mindset

Trust - Your North Star

The Client's POG

Collaborative Problem Solving

The Primacy of the Client Value Quotient

The Pillars of Navigational Selling™

Sales success, both at individual and organizational levels, must be built not only on the individual skills of the salesperson, but also the organization's foundational principles – the pillars that will support a successful, sustainable, client-oriented sales culture for the long term.

There are a handful of pillars that support Navigational Selling™. They underpin its values, process steps, and recommended personal selling behaviors.

Those pillars are:

1. a Navigator Mindset,

2. *Trust:* your North star,

3. the *Client POG* (Problem, Opportunity, or Gap),

4. *Collaborative Problem Solving:* helping more than hyping, and

5. the primacy of the Client Value Quotient.

Pillar 1: A Navigator Mindset

Great tools are not sufficient to assure success as a salesperson.

I am confident that any PGA or LPGA tour golf professional would win a match against me, using either their personal set of golf clubs or mine – the tools we would bring to a match. While good tools provide the potential to help performance, the salesperson must know when and how to use them and have developed a high degree of skill.

Long term sales success requires a personal commitment to continually learn, improve, and build your skills. More so, it requires a personal "mindset" which puts the client and their objectives first. To succeed as a salesperson, the ultimate personal, emotional state we wish to achieve is the "Navigator Mindset."

The Navigator Mindset is characterized by a primary focus on achieving the client's goals through a win-win solution, a priority to listen over talk, a motivational imperative to help - not hype, and a drive to build trust over "closing at all costs."

If you lose a deal, but built *Trust* with the client decisionmakers and influencers, you have won something of value. It is the one thing that is completely within your control. The Navigator Mindset is the lighthouse that guides you to that win.

The Journey to a Navigator Mindset

The journey to achieving the Navigator Mindset requires different paths for different people, depending on where they currently are in terms of emotional maturity and their place on the spectrum of sales skills and experience.

Journeyman salespeople, those assigned to fulltime sales roles, typical exhibit a normal range of skills, personality, and experience. But an SMB2B's sales presence in the market is broader than just its assigned experienced sales team. A sales presence encompasses the whole range of individuals that may get involved in a sale, from the ambitious yet unseasoned Journeyman salesperson, to the senior relationship farmer, to the support specialist Draftee, to the gung-ho, "Close-at-all-Costs" driver. Each impacts your clients' perception of your firm and your brand.

Each must come to understand and embrace the Navigator Mindset.

To the Journeyman Salesperson

Your long-term success depends on how well you improve your sales skills, hone your process disciplines, build your reputation, grow your referral base, and develop your expertise. Navigational Selling™ addresses those needs.

Foundational to all, however, is the need to keep the Navigator Mindset in the forefront of all you do.

To the Gung-Ho, "Close-at-all-Costs" Salesperson

By virtue of simply picking up this book, you are at a crossroads.

Road 1: You may choose to continue on your current path, because you've been successful with it so far and have the belief that, "*If it isn't broken, don't try to fix it.*"

Road 2: You may elect to learn and evolve over a period of time to the Navigational Selling™ process and mindset.

If you are not open to Road 2, close this book. It isn't for you. I wish you well on your journey to your version of sales success. May you not hurt anyone along the way.

To the Draftee: The EIC and Inside Specialists Occasionally Asked to Assist in Selling

EICs with no sales experience and specialist-draftees shanghaied into the sales effort must also embrace the Navigator Mindset within an SMB2B. They represent the SMB2B firm and must understand and exhibit the kinds of sales behaviors that reinforce the SMB2B's brand image. In such pressure situations, the draftee may experience insecurity and anxiety when asked to participate.

There are two common challenges that face the individual who, through one circumstance or another, is suddenly faced with a need to become a successful salesperson. Those challenges are: 1) crystalizing their understanding of what it means to sell (the mindset), and 2) the knowledge of how to sell (the mechanics).

During my talks, I periodically ask non-sales professionals to rate their immediate reaction when they hear the word "salesperson". Using a scale of -5 (Unfavorable) to +5 (Favorable), with 0 in the middle, meaning neither Favorable nor Unfavorable, the responses typically range from a high of + 1 to deep negative territory.

The words they use to describe salespeople are not very complimentary: pushy, irritating, in your face, relentless, arrogant, talks too much, manipulative, sneaky, self-centered, un-trustworthy and more.

Why is this?

It's because too many people have experienced those kinds of behaviors when personally dealing with a salesperson. So, it is no surprise that when an individual finds themself in a circumstance that they need to, in effect, become a salesperson, they feel a visceral aversion to such a thought. They can't imagine personally behaving as they envision a salesperson behaves, in their worst personification of the word.

They fear being branded with negative connotations. They do not want their names used in the same breath as any of those negative descriptors. They do not want to cloud their expertise or stain their reputation with the offensive behaviors they think are expected of a salesperson. In thinking so, they delay their success.

So, they shut down. Freeze.

To those readers in this category, understanding, embracing, and practicing the concepts and pillars of Navigational Selling™ by living the Navigator Mindset, will help overcome such fears and ease your journey.

Pillar 2: Trust - Your North Star

One hears a lot about the importance of Relationships in sales. For some, it is the ultimate treasure. The implication is that "*good relationships result in sales*". I once knew a car salesperson who lived by the mantra, "*Make a friend. Sell a car.*" So, perhaps the implication deserves some consideration.

Let us stipulate, then, that good relationships help – to a degree. However, I think that stipulation requires clarification.

Consider this. Assume you own an SMB2B business employing 70 people. Imagine further that you have a sibling with whom you have a great relationship. He is a salesperson and does not work in your business. You fish together, are godparents to each other's children, and even vacation together at the family cabin on the lake.

If that sibling tried to sell you something that you perceived would damage your business, or jeopardize the wellbeing of you and your employees, would you buy it?

Probably not - even if the sibling threatened to tell your mother of the refusal.

I actually survey my training classes with this precise question and the answer is always the same. No matter how good the relationship, every person would reject buying anything with a fundamentally bad value quotient, even if it were their sibling offering it.

I think salespeople overlook that what they really need to develop is Trust - earned Trust. Good selling is not solely about the relationship. Trust is the magic ingredient. Trust is the foundation of the relationship.

If your sibling were trustworthy, he would not have even offered to sell you something that obviously was a potential problem for your business. Could that breach of trust damage the relationship? Perhaps a bit. Vacations together at the family cabin might become strained.

Trust can be compartmentalized. You may trust someone about some things in one area of your life, but not trust them in other areas. You may trust your spouse on some things, your accountant on other things, and neither of them on the best place to get your car repaired.

Can one have trust without having a personal relationship?

I think so.

How many people have a great personal relationship with their pharmacist? Your life depends on trusting that person to provide precisely what you need in the proper dosage to sustain your life.

In certain types of compartmentalized decision-making, Trust can, and often does, trump relationship.

Moreover, trust is the underpinning of a good long-term relationship. People buy from people they trust. Salespeople must work on building trust first. The relationship will follow – and be stronger.

Even if a prospect ultimately does not buy your solution, you win when you go your separate ways and know you have established a high degree of Trust. The foundation of that Trust is the competence, expertise, collaboration, assistance, and empathy you offered during your discussions.

Who do *you* trust?

In survey after survey, people express that they trust nurses, doctors, scientists, firefighters, pharmacists, and teachers more than they trust other professions. Car salespeople are commonly rated at, or near the bottom of the list.

The range of favorability between the highly rated and low rated professions, is embedded in beliefs in the minds of the public, that the top-rated trusted professions are:

- assumed to have as their primary professional ethic, objective, and purpose, to *help their clients* (as is the case for doctors, pharmacists, teachers, and even dentists),

- guided by noble and *ethical standards* of behavior,

- *trained and certified* to deliver the services they provide,

- influenced by *diagnostics, facts, and data* more than opinion, and

- demonstrating a higher degree of *interest in their client's well-being* than their own during an engagement.

Many sales programs and books have been written about the power of self-motivation in creating successful salespeople. One of the sales books on my bookshelf suggests that if you are motivated by a big new home or a fancy car, you should tape a picture of that object of desire on your refrigerator door or bathroom mirror to remind you of your ultimate goal each day and to motivate you to sell, sell, sell!

That approach works for some. But it implies a disproportionate self-interest factor in the salesperson's efforts to assist a client in solving *their* problem. That self-interest obsession can bleed through in client discussions, emerging as a high-pressure close - a colossal turn-off to clients. Imagine visiting a surgeon in their office. On the wall is a framed picture of an exceedingly large yacht, sporting the hand-written caption "My Dream". At the end of your visit, the doctor recommends elective surgery – that they would be pleased to perform personally.

The title of this book, Navigational Selling™, is intended to encourage the reader to reconsider and reject an over-weighted self-interest approach to achieving success. Instead, it suggests that, in sales, trust-building is the single most important behavior you can practice. The best way to accomplish this is to demonstrate a near complete concern for the well-being of your client, the achievement of *their* goals, the resolution of *their* problems, and a sublimation of your own Self-Interest.

The Trust Formula

Let's look at the trust formula below. The formula is totally dependent on the prospective client's perception of the strength of each factor.

Trust = (Referral + Insight + Proof + Familiarity + Dependability) – (5 x Self-Interest)

Figure 12: The Client Trust Formula

A client may filter, shut down or block your attempts to help if they do not trust you first. Let's review the factors that make up the Trust Formula.

Referral Credibility

A client EIC, facing a challenge they cannot resolve on their own, will ask a close colleague if they know someone that might be able to help. They typically will ask a peer EIC, a lawyer, board member, banker, consultant, or accountant. But they will only request, and accept, referrals from people they know and highly trust.

> *Referrals are a transfer of trust from the seller, through the referrer, to a prospective client.*

A client prospect is more likely to engage in a dialogue with you when your referrer is known and trusted by the client prospect. It is therefore critically important to select your primary referral sources, centers of influence (COI), and alliance partners carefully, based on their high credibility, competence, and trustworthiness – not just the size of their contact database.

Insight

Thought Leadership (speaking and writing about your specialty) builds credibility. It is extremely effective in opening the channels of communication at the beginning of a client/salesperson dialogue. For example, research into the high-service profession of consulting reveals that thought leadership and referrals are the two most important factors in a client's willingness to begin a dialogue.

However, Thought Leadership is only effective as a lead generator if it provides true insight and demonstrates how those insights produced meaningful results for clients similar to the listener or reader. The more insight and meaningful results, the higher the likelihood the client prospect believes that the salesperson can offer something of value, something that the client may have not considered.

Proof

Proof is delivered in the form of verifiable case studies, references, and testimonials from clients highlighting past successes from their engagement with you. Testimonials must demonstrate that people of rank and stature similar to your client's - people that the prospective client will readily identify with - are willing to provide their contact information and statements that verify the value you delivered in their world.

Familiarity

Familiarity is the plausible, logical, and verifiable connection that you communicate to your prospective client, of your deep understanding of their situation, role, industry, and business challenges. The higher the demonstrated Familiarity, the higher the credibility and trust.

Dependability

Dependability is your proof that you will deliver what you say you will in a timely manner, and do it with empathy, understanding, reassurance, and an intense focus on the client's POG. Dependability must be demonstrated, not just after a contract is signed, but also throughout the selling process.

Self-Interest

Self-Interest is the final factor impacting trust. Even a little bit of Self-Interest, if perceived by the client, has a huge disproportionate negative impact on their willingness to engage with a salesperson.

Empathy and reassurance reinforce trust. Expressing and demonstrating both are vital in client communications - from your very first meeting, to every time you communicate going forward. Some years ago, I read a study published in Harvard Business Review, that revealed that Empathy and Ego are the most significant personality traits that predicted a salesperson's success.

Sincere expressions of empathy reduce the client's perception of Self-Interest, thereby increasing Trust and reducing a client's anxiety concerning the challenges they might be facing.

Ego, in this case, means strong self-esteem, such that the loss of a sale or the rejection of an offer, is not taken personally by the salesperson and can be graciously accepted. Strong self-esteem reduces the anxiety a salesperson may feel when engaged with a client. Reduced anxiety diminishes the panic or urge to push too hard, or overly promote vs. collaborating to find the best solution.

A strong Ego, in the sense of strong self-esteem, also means that a salesperson can put the client first, without feeling that it somehow diminishes their own goals and importance. In this sense, strong Ego permits an intense focus on the other person in the relationship – in this case the client.

Both traits, the ability and desire to express Empathy, and the other-centered dimension of Ego, can be strengthened and toned over time.

A highly valued, trust-based client experience enables a successful engagement. It also positions the salesperson favorably for a follow-on engagement with that same client, and as a referral to one of that client's peers in another company or organization.

I have never met a client who had only one challenge and no friends, peers, or colleagues.

An example Trust Calculation:

Here is a somewhat extreme example Trust calculation, made for the purpose of demonstrating the damaging power of high self-interest. In this example, we rate each factor on a scale of 1 to 10, with 10 being highest.

Perfect scores (10's) in the first 5 factors will give you a subtotal of 50 points within the first set of parentheses. A perfect score!

But if you are promoting instead of collaborating, talking instead of listening, pushing instead of guiding, the client's perception is that your Self-Interest is also high, let's say a 10.

Five times 10, equals a Self-Interest factor of 50. The sum of the positive trust-building factors, (+50) is completely wiped out by the Self-Interest factor (-50). Trust therefore becomes a big fat 0.

$$Trust = (10 + 10 + 10 + 10 + 10) \text{ minus } (5 \times 10) = 0 \text{ Trust}$$

The Self-Interest factor when multiplied by 5, can have a huge negative impact. That is why caution is recommended and client-centered collaboration is emphasized.

On the other hand, Self-Interest can also be a negative number.

If you demonstrate and take action that is overwhelmingly in the prospective client's best interest, it is theoretically possible to have a Self-Interest factor that is a negative number. A negative self-interest score means you have completely sacrificed your self-interest on the altar of the client's interests.

A negative number multiplied by a negative number, yields a positive number. So, a negative Self-Interest rating actually adds to a total Trust score. Even if it is as small as a -1, if everything else is rated a 10, this small increment of negative Self-Interest increases your total Trust score from 50 to 55. That's a 10% improvement!

I am not suggesting you do that. Realistically you would be an easy mark for a client that is a Taker or Opportunist – personality types we will discuss later in the section dealing with Reading People.

Suffice it to say, from the beginning of your dialogue and communication, to the delivery of your service, and for years afterward, the second pillar of Navigational Selling™ is to consistently build Trust, continually reinforcing those variables in the Trust Formula.

Pillar 3: The Client's POG

Peter Drucker, the lauded author, consultant, and professor (1909 - 2005) is purported to have said, "If you would offer me a million dollars-worth of market research, or a day in the kitchen with a housewife, I'll take the day in the kitchen."

Now, before you get all riled up about Peter Drucker's use of the word housewife (and my decision to use that quote) please consider it was 1949 to 1959 when Drucker was in his prime. It was the post WWII baby boom in the U.S. and the dramatic growth of the suburbs. It was the era of stay-at-home moms, one-car households, and one bread-winner – typically the Dad. Housewives spent much of the day at home managing the household - cleaning and preparing meals until the children rolled in after school for cookies and milk, and Dad arrived in time for dinner. It was a time before Uber Eats, microwave ovens, stay-at-home Dads who loved to cook, two or three-car families, and a preponderance of working moms.

The point Professor Drucker was making, which still holds true today, is that:

Only by detailed observation, first-hand experience, dialogue, and empathy for a client's situation, can one discover the conscious, subconscious, explicit and implicit challenges that clients are facing in a target market.

We call these challenges a customer's POG - their Problems, Opportunities or Gaps.

The earlier the salesperson is able to discover, understand, and internalize the nature of the client's POG, the better support they can provide to navigate the client to the best solution.

Step 1 must always be diagnosing and discovering the client's POG, their root causes, and implications. We will discuss POGs, and the use of client self-assessments to reveal hidden POGs, in Chapter 7, Discovery.

Pillar 4: Collaborative Problem Solving

If a prospective client had the skills, talent, experience, solution, or inventory to address the sales challenges in their own organization, they would not need to discuss anything with a salesperson. By virtue of a client asking a referral source for assistance in finding a resource to fill their need, the need is likely important. Your task, should you accept it, is to discover and help.

We discussed the meaning of Navigational Selling™ earlier, and the role the Navigator plays in helping the captain safely reach the ship's destination. That is primarily a role of helping.

In summary, the fourth pillar is a call to unselfishly help your client through all stages of their decision process: diagnosis, understanding, evaluation, planning, selection, and deployment.

Pillar 5: The Primacy of the Client Value Quotient

Communicating the value of your offering requires a clear understanding of the concept and fundamentals of Value, from the client's perspective.

A simple example of the concept of value is in the well-worn mime that people do not want to buy drill bits. What they want is what a drill bit produces, namely "holes". The drill bit is the enabler of producing the hole – the individual's real goal. Without the hole they cannot accomplish their goal.

Clients do not want what the salesperson is offering. They want what the offering produces – meaningful value in a form relevant to them, that they can quickly experience. And they want it at a cost that is not prohibitive.

The First Law of Value: The Value Quotient

At the foundation of all successful businesses lies a single, supportive principle, the Law of Value, which states:

All economic value accruing to the salesperson and their company, begins with a client's perception that they will receive greater economic, emotional, physical, political and/or social benefit from an offering, than the economic, emotional, physical, political, and social costs associated with acquiring, deploying, and using it.

That law is at the core of the concept of a high-quality *Client Experience*.

This means that to achieve meaningful perceived value in the eyes of the client, the benefits need to be greater than costs. The Value Quotient needs to result in a value greater than 1.

Value Quotient = Benefits / Costs

A winning Value Quotient must be > 1

Contrary to commonly held ideas within the B2B world, meaningful benefits are not exclusively economic. Moreover, client-received benefits exist at both the conscious and subconscious levels and can be grouped into five categories.

Economic Benefits = B_{ec}

Emotional Benefits = B_{em}

Physical Benefits = B_{ph}

Political Benefits = B_{po}

Social Benefits = B_{so}

Recognizing the multiple dimensions of both benefits and costs, the resulting Value Quotient equation is shown in Figure 13.

$$Value = \frac{Bec + Bem + Bph + Bpo + Bso}{Cec + Cem + Cph + Cpo + Cso}$$

Figure 13: The Client Value Quotient

Each component of client-perceived benefits in the numerator of the Value Quotient has a corresponding factor associated with client-perceived costs in the denominator.

Value Quotient Implications

Client-perceived value is not all about economics, in either the numerator or the denominator, no matter what anyone tells you. If perceived value were only about economic benefits and costs, people would only buy one model of car – the cheapest.

In the U.S. there are over 250 different car models offered, including 43 new models introduced in 2020. This statistic demonstrates that many value factors exist and are at play in a large percentage of consumer purchases – that it is _not_ solely economic.

Ask yourself, "In considering my last automobile purchase, did I buy the absolutely cheapest car I could have?"

I predict your answer is no. You likely purchased the car that best suited your lifestyle, personality, and needs – with cost as the second consideration after deciding on the most appropriate model.

Storytime (Fictional): "This Will Not be Perceived Well at Home", or "Peace vs. Vanity".

> A successful, 48-year-old businessman yearned to purchase the brand-new red Corvette he saw prominently displayed outside a dealership that he passed every day on his way to and from work.
>
> _Economics_ was not a problem. He had more than enough discretionary cash to easily make the purchase. He harbored a strong _emotional_ desire for the car and imagined the _physical_ adrenaline rush from the speed and pick-up the car could attain. He dreamed of the _social_ acknowledgement and pleasure he would derive from running that beauty up to the Country Club and having his golf buddies drool over it (not literally).
>
> Yet, he did not buy the car. In his perception the _political_ consequences likely to reveal themselves when he drove in the driveway and surprised his spouse, whose appreciation of those other benefits is nowhere near the same given they have a young family, would be a cost too big to bear.
>
> In this specific case the _political_ cost consideration greatly outweighed the four benefits factors of _economic_, _physical_, _emotional_, and _social_.
>
> _Moral of the Story:_ When discovering a client's needs and wants, do not fail to consider the emotional, physical, social, and political considerations that will influence their decision-making process, as well as the economic.

End of Story.

This auto example is appropriate for the consumer automobile market. But does it retain its validity in B2B markets?

The answer is yes. Absolutely!

I have worked, as an engineer, operations manager, marketer, strategist, and consultant in many industries: medical equipment, industrial controls, plastics, healthcare, law, accounting, raw materials, metal fabrication, solar power, wholesale distribution, protective packaging, software, information technology, audio-visual systems, banking, opto-electronics, and manufacturing. These are just a few. In none of these markets did I, or any of my clients, make business decisions solely based on economics.

In B2B, a decision to evaluate and purchase an offering, can involve any combination of the value-quotient factors. The decision can be driven by emotion (fear), physical factors (loss of sleep and worry), or political (courage to fight for the right solution vs. the boss's opinion).

As illustrated in the red Corvette story above, a client's decision-making process does not just evaluate like-factor vs. like-factor ratios, such as economic benefits vs. economic costs. There is much more involved.

In general, while a strong economic benefits factor may be easily identifiable as the first hurdle in selling an offering, and the lead-in attractor to a business executive, decisions to engage will inevitably incorporate the other client-relevant considerations as well.

As you design your offerings and discover your clients' needs, consider how you will articulate the mix of benefits that will accrue to decision-making executives, and how those benefits will significantly outweigh the costs associated with achieving them.

Value-Quotient-Based Sales Tools: Case Studies, Testimonials, and References

Each offering in your suite should have at least one documented, verifiable, validated case study that illustrates the meaningful value you have delivered to a real-world client. Testimonials from successful client EICs provide real-world validation when they attribute that success directly to their engagement with you, your offering, and your firm. Case studies can illustrate the combination of benefits and costs (economic, emotional, political, social, and physical) experienced by the client without revealing client-confidential information.

Takeaways

In the heat of the moment, when a salesperson is face-to-face with a client, discussing an opportunity, it is difficult to maintain the presence of mind required to remember all the right steps, questions, phraseology, tidbits, and advice that this or any other sales methodology book might suggest. In the military, this challenge is addressed by supplementing the detailed orders to a unit, with something known as "The Intent of the Commander".

Here is an explanation from Wikipedia.

The commander's intent succinctly describes what constitutes success for an operation. The role of the Commander's Intent is to empower subordinates in the operational unit and guide their initiative and improvisation as they adapt the plan to the changed reality of the battlefield. Commander's Intent empowers initiative, improvisation, and adaptation by providing guidance of what a successful conclusion looks like.

The five pillars described in this chapter should be considered like the Commander's Intent. All client engagements should be handled with an operational purpose to demonstrate to the client the salesperson's commitment to the five pillars of Navigational Selling™.

They are, again:

- behaving with a *Navigator Mindset*,

- continually building client trust through attention to the *Trust Formula*,

- discovery of, empathy with, and resolution of the *Client's POG*,

- *Collaboration*, demonstrated through a sincere desire to help, not hype, and

- understanding and delivery consistent with the *Client's Value Quotient*.

*****

Chapter 6: Qualification

In this Chapter …

Account Pre-Qualification

Account Re-Qualification

Opportunity Qualification

Qualification Factor 1: Compelling Need

Qualification Factor 2: Match of Capabilities to Needs

Qualification Factor 3: Value Quotient

Qualification Factor 4: Competitive Advantage

Qualification Factor 5: Advocate

Qualification Factor 6: Leverage

Rating Your Opportunity Qualification Factors

How to Rate Opportunity Qualification Factors Consistently

Opportunity Qualification Exercise

There are three types of qualification associated with an effective sales process:

1. Current Account Re-Qualification,
2. Target Account Pre-Qualification, and
3. Opportunity Qualification.

Current Account Re-Qualification

Current Account Re-Qualification is a personal revisit with a client to share mutual situational information, discover new opportunities or share relevant information that might help them. A salesperson needs to stay abreast of their current clients' situations. Economic circumstances change, new challenges appear, and industry and personnel changes can occur after any successful sale.

Account Management is the activity of servicing a current customer and keeping abreast of what is happening within their business. Current Account Re-Qualification is part of Account Management.

I mentioned previously that it continually surprises me to discover salespeople within my client base who have not kept up with their current accounts. They seem to feel that as long as the client is happy, as evidenced by the fact that they haven't received any panic calls or complaints, account requalification efforts are unnecessary. As long as the order momentum is steady, and their commissions are being paid, they need not allocate the time to revisit. They believe the time is better spent in finding new fields to plow.

It is too easy to become complacent with clients with whom you have already closed business. The high performing salesperson must not let the recurring commission and revenue streams of the last sale flow in unattended. They must pay continuous attention to changing client circumstances.

Complacency is the field in which competitive weeds flourish.

Complacency erodes your existing client business relationships, trust, familiarity, and credibility – all essential to maintaining Trust. More often than not, such conscious disregard eventually meets with surprises with negative potential consequences, such as:

- organizational structures and responsibilities change within the client's organization, demanding that trust and credibility be re-established with the new players,

- competitors make inroads,

- new opportunities arise and the salesperson is uninformed or contacted late in the client's evaluation and decision process,

- technology and industry economics shift,

- new people, (unfamiliar with you, your offerings, and your company), are promoted, hired, and brought on-board,

- new policies, processes or standards are put in place,

- an acquisition of the client's business is pending, with the expectation of a consolidation of suppliers, or the sourcing of what the salesperson delivers is being shifted to the suppliers used by the acquiring firm,

- usage of what they are buying unexpectedly declines, and because the salesperson doesn't understand why, the salesperson's forecasting becomes wildly unreliable, and/or

- based on unreliable forecasts, the salesperson's firm is burdened with too much, or too little, inventory.

All these factors impact your current and future business.

Whether the news is good or bad, the sooner you know it the better.

In the extreme, the client organization may eventually evolve to where it is no longer a desirable client to do business with – for ethical, economic, procedural, or other reasons. So, SMB2B EICs and sales managers must insist on periodic current account requalification reports from the salespeople assigned to those clients.

The opportunity to reconnect is crucial.

Reconnecting also provides an opportunity to elicit feedback on the long-term impact of the last solution you delivered and determine if there are any new POGs you might help with. A Re-Qualification effort might present an opportunity for a re-take of the previous assessment you used to trigger the client's recognition of their first need.

An assessment re-take would offer a quick look at whether their situation has improved or degraded. An improved situation offers an opportunity to request a referral or testimonial, and a degradation provides an opportunity to offer something new to address the degradation.

Not all Re-Qualification initiatives, however, need to be diagnostic.

Keeping clients in mind when you find something of general interest of which they should be informed, is also helpful in letting them know you are always looking out for their best interest. Periodically staying in touch with past clients by sending them relevant, meaningful, and valuable content, reinforces the trust relationship and your credibility as an expert resource. And the formulation and use of plausible premises or requalification visits are just as valid and helpful in Account Re-Qualification as in Account Pre-Qualification.

Please remember that sending relevant, valuable tidbits of information has the most impact if personalized. Email blasts will not elicit near the amount of attention, appreciation, or reflection as a personalized message. Those blasts are specifically what junk-email folders were designed to capture.

Caution: A Note to Managers about Maintaining a Balance between Current Account and New Account Efforts

An over-zealous effort on new client growth, reinforced by commission plans which reward new client wins at premium commission rates vis-à-vis current client growth, can create a conflict with Account Re-qualification efforts. It is much easier to sell something additional (a new product, service, or application) to an existing client, than to a totally new client. Yet, if market share growth is to be achieved, new client growth is essential.

This situation creates an inherent dilemma, which is often reconciled by the assignment of separate titles and accountabilities within the sales force. In such a structure, Account Managers manage existing client base customer relationships, while New Business Development Managers become responsible for new client account growth. The sales commission structure must be designed to track achievement of specific goals associated with each assignment.

Target Account Pre-Qualification

Target Account Pre-Qualification encompasses the efforts applied to investigating and researching a target account's challenges, their executive decision makers as they relate to your offerings, and your path to personal introductions to those people. In some sales processes, this is called developing a list of "suspect" accounts.

Target Account Pre-Qualification activities are aimed at prospective clients with whom you have no past or current business. You may have identified these as targets through some basic territory and industry research. Or they may have been referred to you by an alliance partner or primary referral source. Target accounts within this category may include clients within a market sector you have not serviced before, larger clients that you have discovered are facing serious challenges you believe you can assist with, or potential clients you have noticed as you have travelled around your sales territory.

In such cases, preparatory research will comprise discovering important account and people information, as well as determining any relevant issues and challenges currently facing their business and industry.

Hints about those issues can usually be found by: a) a simple Google search of "What are the major challenges facing the (blank) industry in the coming year?", b) calling and asking the same question of the membership chairperson of the industry association to which the account will likely belong, c) visiting the target client's website and looking at "*Our Team*" and "*Latest News*" tabs, or d) asking someone you might know who is already doing business with the account.

Discovering such basic information before a first sales call, even if it is a cold call, provides a head-start.

Building a basic understanding of the prospect's potential challenges, within the context of their industry, helps you become immediately relevant, by enabling meaningful dialogue with any contacts you may make. Such research supports the *Familiarity* factor in the Trust Formula discussed in Chapter 5. Familiarity helps build rapport.

Pre-Qualification effort also helps in the formulation of a *premise*, aka a reason for any introduction or referral request you hope to make.

A premise is a credible, logical, and valid benefit a key decision maker or decision influencer within a target account might receive from speaking with you. Premises must always be formulated from the primary perspective of their relevance and benefit to the specific client with whom you will be speaking.

Despite the amazing capabilities and power of today's technology to increase productivity, people remain remarkably busy. They do not have time to waste with someone calling "*just to say hello and introduce themselves*". Armed with your research, and before speaking with a prospective decision maker, you should prepare a valid premise that is relevant to the client's challenges.

Effective premises might include:

- offering an industry update about an approach to a common industry challenge,

- news or insights about an industry innovation,

- sharing relevant business or management insights, or

- providing a technology update (particularly effective with technology types).

When asking for a personal introduction or referral from one of your referral sources, it is always better to pair that introduction request with a premise that will be relevant to the person you are asking to be introduced to.

Of course, this all assumes that the client has not called you first to discuss a specific issue that is causing them pain. In that case, the premise is defined by the request.

Targeting the Premise

A premise must be targeted and tailored to a specific decision-maker or decision-influencer within the target account. Thanks to the advent of LinkedIn, and its common use in the B2B community, discovering who those people might be, is not anywhere near as difficult as it was in the past.

To discover to whom the premise will be meaningful and the best person to contact, begin by asking yourself the following questions:

- Does this organization exemplify the type of potential client that might experience the challenges that we have the offerings, expertise, and experience to address?

- Who, by name and title, would likely be involved in an initiative to meet those challenges and participate in the decision to buy a solution? This information can often be determined by a search of LinkedIn, Google, the company's website, or other data bases like Reference USA (RefUSA). The RefUSA database, as of this writing, is remotely accessible online at no cost through many public libraries. The database is robust and lists extensive data by company, zip code, industry, geographic region, etc.

- What current news can you discover about the target client from their website, news releases, or through a Google News search?

- What background information can you find about key individuals that are likely be decision makers at the firm?

- Are any of these key people connected to people I know? Who in my personal network can provide an introduction and debrief about the company?

- Who are the key people (EIC decision makers and decision influencers) within the target client's organization? Who in your network (personal, LinkedIn) can help you with a referral to those key people?

An Example:

Let's say you are a salesperson for a company that sells custom formulations of plastic resins.

In researching the manufacturing industry in your area, looking for target accounts that might use such resins, you discover that Amalgamated Manufacturing Enterprises (AME) has just completed construction of a 100,000-square-foot facility, 15 miles from your office. Further research reveals this facility will house their Aerospace Division, including research, design, and fabrication of parts for the next generation of commercial, heavy duty delivery drones.

Your firm produces lightweight, durable plastic resins suitable for aircraft parts, so you figure that the latest advances in that capability may be a premise for a discussion with AME.

Next, you go to LinkedIn to discover the names of people who might be within that on-line database and have built a profile which identifies them as; a) an AME management employee, b) in the aerospace research or product development department, and c) of sufficient title to likely hold sway in decision-making about which resins to use.

LinkedIn also has the capability to identify all those people you are connected to that also have connections to any other individual you are targeting. If you have a strong LinkedIn presence, chances are someone in your network will have a connection to the targeted individual. If you have previously built a trusted relationship with the referrer, and they have a more than superficial relationship with the introduction target, and you have developed a sound relevant premise, that mutual connection will more readily agree to provide an introduction.

Now you have the information you need: a contact, a referrer, and a relevant premise.

End of example

Opportunity Qualification

Opportunity Qualification refers to *specific* needs within a new or existing account, for the sale of a specific offering. Not all *Opportunities* that arise in discussions with a pre-qualified account will be attractive or appropriate.

For example: Referring to our previously identified Amalgamated Manufacturing Enterprises (AME) target account.

Assume some parts designed for a short-range, limited payload drone for use in cities, have been produced by AME, using the lightweight, durable plastic resins your firm supplied. Those parts have proven extremely reliable in maintaining their dimensional integrity within a specific limited temperature range.

AME has informed you that they are designing a new, longer-range, heavier payload, high-speed, higher-altitude drone for use in sub-Saharan Africa. This new drone, funded by the World Health Organization (WHO), will deliver important medical equipment and pharmaceuticals to remote villages.

That new, higher performance drone requires a plastic resin similar to what you previously designed and supplied for their short-range drone. However, the new part will be much larger and must maintain its dimensional stability over a much higher temperature range and through a significantly more demanding high-speed vibration profile. This will require a slightly modified resin formulation.

The first plastic part application was highly qualified and within your organization's capability to deliver. This newest higher-performance part may not be.

Even within highly qualified target accounts, some specific applications and opportunities will be a good match – while others may not. It is important to evaluate and qualify each opportunity independently, even if they originate within the same account.

Navigational Selling™ recommends qualifying all opportunities by the following six criteria:

- *Compelling Need* - the degree of urgency and importance the client feels to address their POG,

- *Match* - of your offerings and firm's capabilities to meet that specific client need,

- *Value Quotient* - from the perspective of the client,

- *Competitive Advantage* - also from the perspective of the client,

- *Advocate* - based on their position and power within the client organization, and

- *Leverage* – the long-term positive implications a win will have on your organization.

Detailed explanations of these criteria follow. Each can be rated on a scale of low-to-high – we use 1 through 5.

As you read through their definitions, remember:

In Opportunity Qualification, in rating the first five Qualification Factors, the only perspective that is valid in determining a factor's score is that of the prospective client decision maker.

Qualification Factor 1: Compelling Need

The Compelling Need factor rates the degree to which a challenge or problem faced by a client is critical, needing to be addressed immediately or there will be significant consequence for not doing so. Regulatory compliance, safety considerations or the need to meet bank covenants are just a few examples of needs that fall into a high Compelling Needs category.

To put the importance of this factor in perspective, research has shown that upwards of 50% of the "qualified" opportunities in a typical salesperson's pipeline are lost to "No Decision". A truly Compelling Need cannot be lost to "No Decision". Consequences of a "No Decision" to resolve an acute Compelling Need would be grave for the client or other stakeholders.

A client with a high Compelling Need must find a solution or there will be some significant ramification or negative consequence to their business. Moreover, the degree of Compelling Need cannot be judged exclusively through the perspective of the salesperson. As convinced as a salesperson may be that a client needs a solution, no purchase will be made until the client decides they need to act on their POG.

Salespeople often discover what they believe to be a customer's compelling need - one that their offering can resolve. Motivated by this discovery, the salesperson goes all out to convince the customer of the need and is flabbergasted by the client's persistent reluctance to do something about it.

The salesperson may obsess about it. The opportunity remains highly visible and painful in the salesperson's pipeline – like a stone in their shoe that they stubbornly refuse to remove in hopes that it will dislodge itself.

> *If the client's ultimate decision maker does not see the Compelling Need the same way as the salesperson, nothing will happen – no matter how hard the salesperson tries or how long they wait.*

In such a circumstance, there are many possible reasons for the client's recalcitrance. Perhaps the client does not understand the implications of leaving the need unaddressed. Perhaps there is a personal psychological barrier to fixing the problem, borne of fear, embarrassment, lack of understanding, or their degree of perceived risk.

We will address different aspects of this situation in the Value Quotient qualification factor also in Chapter 7, Discovery, and Chapter 8, Reading People.

For the moment, let us just stipulate that without the client's self-awareness of the implications of their own compelling need, nothing will move. For the salesperson, note how much time you are spending banging your head against a brick wall!

The Opportunity Hidden Beneath a Client's Compelling Need

Storytime: One Client's Compelling Need Hid a Vein of Gold!

About 10 years ago, I was asked to assist a client in overcoming a sales roadblock. Market adoption of their flagship, a highly innovative product and software offering, had been excruciatingly slow. My client believed the product had enormous potential and economic benefit to clients. They simply could not understand why their prospective clients did not see the brilliance of their solution and immediately jump on board.

Their marketing and sales team was constantly bickering amongst themselves about which market would be best to focus on.

Nothing they attempted seemed to be working. While most customers they spoke with could easily identify with the problem the system solved, and to a certain degree all were experiencing the same challenge, too few had the need to the extent they would immediately embrace the solution.

While it was true that just about any company could benefit from use of the software, the core of my client's problem was their failure to identify any single, specific market segment in which its value quotient was uniquely and disproportionately beneficial to the client.

To focus and trigger faster growth, the question they needed to answer was: *"Of all the clients and markets we have sold to thus far, which are experiencing the highest pain, have no good current solution, are in a market that contains a large number of businesses experiencing the same challenge, and would receive the highest economic return from relieving that pain?"*

Through historical sales analytics and some client value-quotient validation, the data revealed a single highly satisfied client that represented a market with an under-satisfied client potential exceeding 25,000 business entities in the United States.

Nearly all those business entities were faced with a common set of compelling needs that were driving high internal costs. No easy-to-deploy solution had been found. Moreover, the clients within that segment met frequently to share best practices. A single high-visibility win planted within that collaborative solution-sharing environment promised to generate many opportunities within a short period of time.

After a shift of market strategy and sales focus, sales took off. Resources were redirected toward that single segment, and the benefits message tailored to the context of the clients in that segment.

Having done well by my client, as I left the engagement, I advised them to dedicate a small amount of ongoing effort to continually analyze sales and discover their next high client-value-received market. I knew that their new golden goose would not produce eggs forever. Continual diligence was essential in anticipation of a time when the first market demand waned, most likely due to the inevitability of periodic shifts in the economy.

Completely distracted and blinded by their new-found success, they did *not* follow my recommendation. Until that is, as I had warned, due to an economic downturn in the primary market, the golden goose shut down. They called me back to help them find a backup market - but not until the negative impact was being acutely felt.

After some analytical catch-up, a second market was found. While not as strong in its compelling need as the first, it supplemented the company's revenues sufficiently to hold until the economic conditions within the primary market recovered.

Moral of the Story: Highly satisfied clients within your current customer base may be representative of larger populations of clients with similar compelling needs. It is highly productive to constantly analyze client motivations, client satisfaction and investigate how large a population of other potential clients they represent.

End of story

Qualification Factor 2: Match of Capabilities

Qualification Factor 2 rates the degree to which your service offering precisely meets the challenges presented by the prospect's Compelling Need.

It is insufficient to believe, in your own mind and heart, that your offering is a good match to their problem. As in Factor 1: Compelling Need, the client's perspective is the only perspective that counts. To precipitate a purchase, the client must believe, unequivocally, that the Match is spot on.

For salespeople of technical products, this factor has an obvious rut which the wheels of your sales effort can very easily be pulled into, i.e., the technical performance specification. Often, other considerations may also be equally, or more, relevant, such as:

- an ability to ramp up capacity if the client's demand takes off,

- the availability of technical design and testing support services,

- the ability to demonstrate certified Quality standards,

- parts inventory buffer storage,

- just-in-time delivery coordination,

- assurance of an ongoing cost reduction plan, or

- installation or integration services.

The best technology does not always win.

A *Match of Capabilities to Needs* means more than just a match of technical requirements.

Qualification Factor 3: Value Quotient

The client Value Quotient was discussed in detail, in Chapter 4. It is pillar 5 in the Pillars of Navigational Selling™.

The client Value Quotient Qualification Factor rates the long-term value a client will realize as a result of acquiring and using your solution to address their POG, as compared to the costs borne by the client of implementing that solution.

The Client Value Quotient is both a subconscious and conscious calculation in the mind of the client. It comprises both, the five perceived benefits (economic, emotional, physical, political, and social) divided by the five perceived costs (economic, emotional, physical, political, and social). See Figure 14.

$$Value = \frac{Bec + Bem + Bph + Bpo + Bso}{Cec + Cem + Cph + Cpo + Cso}$$

Figure 14: The Client Value Quotient (redux)

Value Quotient is depicted in this representation as a mathematical formula (Bec = economic benefits, Bem = emotional benefits, Cem = economic costs, etc.).

Except for the economic component, the other contributing factors within the formula cannot be objectively quantified. The result of the formula is completely subjective and only valid from the perspective and perception of the client. Therefore, the complete Value Quotient can only be judged and felt by the client.

Let us consider that Amalgamated (AME) has a problem with a component in their standard drone. The part keeps cracking. The Chief of Engineering was the person who designed the part and selected the material – but the material was not your resin. It was sourced from one of your competitors.

What would the implications of that situation be on the perceived value quotient of your solution?

Could there be an emotional (embarrassment) component that needs to be considered? How about the political and social appearance of the admission of a failure of design skills by the Chief of Engineering?

For this circumstance, touting only the technical capabilities of your resin might not fulfill the value the client needs. The salesperson may need to find a way to position the solution so as to make the Chief of Engineering a hero, instead of a goat.

It is crucial to remember, in every discussion with a client decision maker and influencer: a) Value Quotient is the result of both subjective and objective client perceptions, b) Value Quotient is only valid from the perspective of the client, c) Economics is only one part of the equation, and d) the salesperson must be effective in assisting the client in recognizing other dimensions of value beyond just the economic.

In my experience, clients will *Trust* you more if you patiently and discretely help them recognize all the parts and implications of the Value Quotient.

Trust (Pillar 2: Chapter 5) is an emotion – a feeling. Many decisions are made, not because of price, but because of a feeling of trust between the client and the salesperson.

Nurture Trust and you have a solid beginning.

Sustain Trust and you have a long-term relationship.

Break Trust and you lose everything.

Qualification Factor 4: Competitive Advantage

Qualification Factor 4 rates the degree to which the client believes you have a competitive advantage over other alternatives. Do not forget that "Do it Yourself" and "Do Nothing" may be legitimate forms of competitive solutions in the eyes of a client – whether they are wise alternatives or not.

And, as mentioned previously in the Qualification Factor explanation of Match, technical specifications advantage should not be the only advantage promoted. What good would a 50% superior performance in a key engineering specification be if the product had poor long-term reliability or could not be delivered in time or in sufficient quantity to meet the client's needs?

Storytime: You're Not Listening! Gas Mileage is NOT my Primary Concern.

I was test driving cars a few years ago and found one I thought could be a contender for my next purchase. The salesperson came along for the test drive.

Sitting in the back seat, he inflicted upon me an incessant barrage of capabilities and features – not even taking a breath long enough so I might ask a question or two. And he never asked me one. The one feature he kept repeating was the car's great gas mileage.

Growing extremely impatient and frustrated, I pulled over and asked him to stop talking for a minute, almost having to shout to be heard over his incessant chatter.

I explained that my consulting business required little long-distance driving. Additionally, I was single and had two cars - an old SUV for fishing and Oregon adventures, and another older luxury car for business that was in remarkably good condition. My search was for a possible business car replacement. Gas mileage was *not* an important consideration.

I politely asked him to cut back on the selling barrage pounding on my ears from the back seat and let me listen to the car as I drove. The level of road noise *was* important to me since I spoke with clients on our way to lunch meetings, and I needed to hear them clearly when they spoke. They did not typically sit in the back seat and shout in my ear.

We started up again. So did his chatter and promotional push about great gas mileage.

I drove back to the dealership. I did not buy the car. I cannot even remember what model the car was - or why I had even wanted to test drive it.

What I do remember, all too vividly, was the pushy, unskilled, unhelpful salesperson and the dealership where he worked.

Moral of the Story: Question and listen carefully to the client. Then decide which tack to take.

End of Story

Not everyone will need or equally appreciate all the performance, benefits, and capabilities of your offering. So, your offerings need to be targeted at markets and clients to whom its benefits and value can be relevant - and the benefits story you communicate must be tailored to the individual client's specific expressed needs. You find that out by questioning and listening – not talking.

Qualification Factor 5: Advocate

Advocate refers to a key person within the client organization that has high regard and respect for your approach and offering. This person endorses you and your approach even when you are not there. They keep you informed as to the progress of the decision and maintain their steady support for you during the selection process.

Advocates without influence or some form of power within the target client's organization are relatively ineffectual. Just because they avail themselves for lunch or join your golf foursome, does not make them a true Advocate.

Storytime: The Failure of a Lifetime and an Unforgettable Lesson Learned

Before I left my corporate role to consult, I was a strategic marketing manager, called on occasionally to support the sales team in the field – a Draftee.

A major, multi-million-dollar project was about to be awarded and I travelled across the country to help the regional sales manager convince the client we were the best solution. The salesperson introduced me to his internal Advocate, who was more than pleased to have lunch with us that day.

On returning from lunch, the Advocate politely excused himself while he made a quick phone call in response to a message that had been left on his desk while we were out.

After just a few seconds of muted conversation, I saw the Advocate's face drop.

Visibly shaken, he looked at us sheepishly and said something like, "*I'm really sorry, but I was just informed that the contract was awarded – and you guys didn't win.*"

Now it was our turn to be shaken.

We left quickly - stopping for coffee to try to figure out what had just happened. Quite frankly on top of our disappointment, we were concerned about the home office reaction and career consequences of such a major, high visibility opportunity slipping through our fingers.

In our autopsy of the loss, it quickly became apparent that what we had interpreted as a strong Advocate was way too low in the client hierarchy of decision-making power and influence to truly help. With news of the final decision, it was obvious he had not been in the inner circle of decision makers and influencers.

But he was friendly, and always responded to the salesperson's calls – and such receptive behavior had lulled the salesperson into a false sense of confidence.

Moral of the Story: Not everyone in the client's organization that likes you, is available to talk and have lunch, has the influence, power, and decision-making authority to really help.

End of Story

Good Advocates fight for your solution when you are not there, have a sound logical basis for their advocacy, and have the courage and political clout (if not the power) to influence decisions in your favor. If you do not have a true, highly placed, influential Advocate within an opportunity, find and create one.

Qualification Factor 6: Leverage

Leverage is the only Opportunity Qualification Factor that is valid from both the seller's and buyer's perspectives.

From the *seller's perspective*, Leverage estimates the degree to which a win of this opportunity provides any or all of the following benefits to you and your business:

- for more business,

- to enter a new industry,

- to build a strong and *impressive case study*,

- to gain a strong *testimonial*,

- to tout an industry leading organization as a client, and

- for strong in-market referrals.

From the *buyer's standpoint*, Leverage can be evaluated by the client's recognition that adopting your solution might provide an opportunity to:

- *fan out the benefits* of your offering to other projects, departments, or divisions within their company,

- *enhance the quality perception of their products* in the marketplace, (remember the Intel-Inside branding that earlier models of laptops and PCs had),

- *enhance their own personal, professional expertise*, or

- provide *internal recognition* of their ability to innovate.

Rating Your Opportunity Qualification Criteria

All Opportunity Qualification criteria can be rated on a scale of 1 to 5, with 5 being the highest score. The question then arises as to how a sales manager or salesperson can be assured as to a common understanding, consistency, validity, and value of any of the factors.

The first question to ask the rater is: "Is this factor rating a validated perception in the mind of the client – or is it just based on your own perspective?"

Followed by: "How have you validated that client perception? Have you actually asked the client? Your Advocate?"

Such questions, assuming honest responses, quickly reveal the validity of any specific Opportunity Qualification.

Some important things to note:

First, the total score, the sum of all the criteria ratings, means nothing. Theoretically, a score of 25 out of a possible 30 points could lead you to believe you have a highly qualified opportunity – a sure deal. In reality, if any of the first 5 criteria is a rated a 1 or zero, you will still have a great total score, but the likelihood of a win ensuing is virtually eliminated.

Second, the first five scores are only valid from one perspective, the client's.

Last, an objective assessment of the ratings from the customer's perspective should direct your next action.

Here is an example. Let us say an opportunity in your pipeline has a true, customer perspective of:

Compelling Need = 4

Match = 4

Value Quotient = 3

Competitive Position = 2

Advocate = 2

Leverage = 4

Your Advocate, the previous client Executive-in-Charge (EIC), retired unexpectedly for health reasons and you have not yet built a relationship with the new manager in charge. That has had the effect of eroding your customer-perceived competitive strength because the new person in charge is not familiar with your value proposition and competitive strengths.

You realize that your position is in jeopardy.

Given this situation, your next steps are clear.

Step 1: Meet, build trust, and befriend the new EIC.

Step 2: Ask for an opportunity to review your proposal and/or firm's differentiated capabilities with the new manager.

For good measure and to assure yourself, ask if the compelling need is still perceived as high. A new person may not share the same perspective as their predecessor.

In this regard, it is important to establish communications and relationships with as many people within the client company that are associated with the client's challenge – up, down and across the organization. In the situation where your primary point of contact or Advocate leaves or changes roles, it is likely they will be replaced, at least for the short term, by someone already in house. So, treating the team that supports the ultimate decision maker with respect, and acknowledging their opinions and needs, can go a long way.

How to Rate Qualification Factors Consistently: The Color-Matching Swatch Technique

Questions may arise as to how a sales manager or salesperson can assure a common understanding, consistency, validity, and value of any salesperson-rated factors. How can a sales manager feel confident that everyone on the team is using the same criteria, process, and guidelines for rating each factor?

Storytime: The Power of the Color Swatch

> Over an extended Christmas holiday one year when I was in college, my Uncle Al offered me a job working in a lady's shoe store he managed. This was long before Zappos.
>
> Since it was the Holiday Season it was busy, as many women were preparing their outfits for Holiday and New Year's celebration parties - along with a smattering of Weddings.
>
> Uncle Al had a small workbench in the back of the shoe store, on which he could color dye white pumps. For those unfamiliar, a white pump is not a Nike basketball sneaker - rather it is a high-heeled women's dress shoe. Those suitable for dyeing had a fabric outer surface that would absorb dye.
>
> To match a client's dress and or handbag, customers would typically arrive with a small fabric swatch, which clarified the precise color needing to be matched. Uncle Al would immediately take the swatch, run to the workbench in back, and mix up a precise color match.
>
> *Moral of the Story:* When you need to quantify a qualitative characteristic that does not have an objective measuring device, you must use descriptive swatches against which to match your ratings.

End of Story

To assure consistency of qualification ratings, from one customer, sales pipeline opportunity or salesperson, to the next, there must be a standard set of criteria and circumstances against which to compare each factor. Navigational Selling™ suggests a *swatch technique* that enables the salesperson to consistently consider a match of circumstances when rating a factor.

In Appendix B, you will find a complete table guide for each of the six Qualification Factors. By comparing your specific opportunity situation to each of the criteria statements, you can then rate the Qualification Factor appropriately and consistently from one opportunity to the other. As an example, the rating swatch-matching table for Compelling Need is shown below in Figure 15.

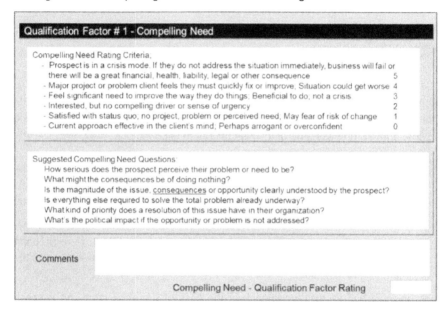

Figure 15: Opportunity Qualification Factor Rating - Compelling Need

Opportunity Qualification Exercise; Try it out!

If you wish to understand opportunity qualification in practice, it might be helpful to work through the following exercise, using real account opportunities that exist in your current sales pipeline.

In the table below, Figure 16, select a specific opportunity from your sales pipeline and, as objectively and honestly as you can, using the swatch-matching techniques and guidelines in Appendix B, rate each of the six qualification criteria from both your perspective and the client's perspective.

For example, it is common that an SMB2B salesperson will identify a circumstance within a prospective client's business that could be improved by one of the salesperson's offerings. This observation may lead a salesperson to rate the Compelling Need qualification factor high. From the perspective of the salesperson, the observed situation is creating a need that screams for improvement.

Through a quick mental calculation, the salesperson may even be able to estimate a significant economic benefit from such a solution. They would therefore rate the Compelling Need factor as high – let's say a 4 or 5, as well as award a high rating to the Value Quotient factor.

In practice, the prospective client may: a) not notice the same need, b) agree with the need but have other priorities, c) not wish to disrupt the current organizational effectiveness with any perceived risky change in how things are done, d) not have the cash to invest, or e) have some other extenuating consideration which prevents moving forward with the salesperson's solution.

If there is a reason within the client's mind (ignorance and lack of awareness included) that they cannot move forward on addressing such a need, no matter how obvious it is to the salesperson, this opportunity cannot honestly be rated over a 3.

Any discrepancy in ratings should compel an action on the part of the salesperson to address and move the ratings into alignment. For a sale to happen both the salesperson and the client must be on the same page and see things congruently.

Using the table immediately below, select any opportunity from your pipeline to test how well it is qualified.

Opportunity Name:	Your Rating	Client View	Action to close gap
Compelling Need (example)	4	2	Client does not understand economic implications of the challenge; Run the numbers and review with client EIC
Compelling Need			
Match			
Value Quotient			
Competitive Position			
Advocate			
Leverage			

Figure 16: Opportunity Qualification Exercise

Your sales action plan must address discrepancies between your rating and what the client thinks.

If an opportunity within a salesperson's pipeline is not moving toward closure, and the client's Compelling Need rating remains low and unchanged, it is most likely because the implications of the Compelling Need have not been made clear by the salesperson and embraced by the client. If the client's need *has* been resolved by a DIY or competitive approach, the problem was with some other qualification factor – probably Competitive Position.

If a salesperson is ever at a loss for what to do, a good step is to review the qualification ratings of major opportunities within their pipeline and create an action plan from the exercise.

Qualification Notes to SMB2B EICs

1. In judging qualification scores for different opportunities in an account, there will be significant differences in compelling need, value quotient, advocate, and leverage. Decision-makers and decision influencers may well be different from opportunity to opportunity. Therefore, each opportunity must be considered, and qualified, independently – on its own merits.

2. Qualifying a new target account through Account Pre-Qualification activities does not automatically qualify all opportunities arising from your relationship with that account. Certain opportunities may not meet acceptable opportunity qualification criteria scores for warranting an effort to move it through your sales pipeline. You can easily recognize poorly qualified opportunities by the amount of dust on them. They have likely been dormant for an extended period.

*****

Chapter 7:   Discovery

In this Chapter …

What is Discovery?

Planning the Discovery Meeting

Discovery Meeting Agenda

Conducting the Discovery Meeting

Super-Charging Discovery: The Client POG Self-Assessment

PITA vs. Thoroughness

The Discussion Summary

What is Discovery?

<u>*Discovery*</u> is the process of engaging in detailed dialogue with a client or prospect, about a specific challenge they are facing. Thorough Discovery may occur in a single 90-minute Discovery Meeting, take several months, or even last years.

The difference in timing is typically related to how long it takes the client's ultimate decision maker to recognize the gravity of a problem and its implications. At the longer end of the spectrum, are situations characteristic of a serious client problem or challenge that the client has not yet recognized.

In one case, I was invited by a Director of Operations to guide and advise in the formulation of a market strategy. The competitive situation, persistent weak revenue growth, and a lack of strategic expertise at the firm, all screamed for help. Despite the obvious need, the business owner was not moved to action.

Some years later, after the Operations Manager had left the company out of frustration, I received a call from the owner to come and help with the problem we had discussed several years earlier.

With a client you have not previously done business with, Discovery should begin immediately following Pre-Qualification. The role and specifics of Pre-Qualification is discussed at the beginning of Chapter 6.

With a current or existing client, Discovery is typically triggered when a specific need is revealed during your periodic Re-Qualification efforts.

In either situation, the objectives of Discovery are to:

- ferret out the details of any specific challenge or problem the client is facing, that you can assist with,

- understand the dynamics of how they will decide what to do about it, and

- collaboratively agree with the client or prospect, about how best to proceed.

In the previous chapter, we discussed six opportunity qualification factors. Achieving a common understanding of these six factors with the prospect, will reveal whether there is an opportunity to help. Your path to sales success is substantially advanced if the client is already self-motivated to action and driven by their recognition of a challenge or opportunity with significant negative or positive implications, respectively.

However, in addition to the six qualification factors, there remain important pieces of information that a salesperson should discover about a specific opportunity. These additional tidbits of information will affect how you approach an opportunity to increase your probability of a win. They include:

- the management styles, personalities, perspectives, values, and roles each person will play in any decision,

- the client's decision-making process,

- the client's perception of the Value Quotient, and

- the form, format, and content of your offering proposal.

Discovery is your opportunity to find out as much relevant information as possible - information that will enable you to recommend the most appropriate and competitively advantaged solution. Deep Discovery enables you to tailor your value message to those issues and sensitivities most relevant to the key decision makers and decision influencers within the client organization. Further, it will allow you the opportunity to align your selling process with the client's decision-making process and formulate a competitively advantage proposal.

Discovery typically occurs face to face. However, I have been able to conduct a Discovery meeting and win business with clients thousands of miles away via phone and video conference. Independent of which mode of Discovery you elect, careful preparation and planning provides enormous benefit.

Planning the Discovery Meeting

A Discovery Meeting is Just Another Phrase for a Sales Call. Isn't it?

No. There is a difference between a Sales Call and a Discovery Meeting.

A Sales Call may have a variety of objectives: to pick up a signed contract or sales order, personally drop off samples or prototypes, address a quality problem, introduce a new member of your support team, meet a new member of the client's team, view a user problem first-hand, or work out a revised delivery schedule – to mention a just a few of the dozens of reasons a salesperson may need or want to call on a customer. At some clients, this has included periodically dropping off donuts as a gesture of goodwill.

In contrast, a Discovery Meeting, differs from a Sales Call in its specificity and focus on a specific new client POG – which you anticipate may turn into a sales opportunity.

A Discovery Meeting differs from a Sales Call in its specificity. A Discovery Meeting is designed to reveal the specifics surrounding a new client issue or POG they need to address. A true Discovery Meeting is rarely associated with any previous sale or administrative issue.

To some salespeople, every customer discussion, by phone, face to face or video, is considered by them a Sales Call, whose only objective is to reveal an opportunity to quote or propose something – anything. They seem to believe that their measure of success is to have a lot of quotes in their pipeline and lots of customer "touches". It looks good to the boss. They play the numbers game – believing that the more quotes, the more wins. The more wins the more sales. The more sales the higher their commission.

Devoid of any pre-qualification effort, such an approach will waste a lot of your and your client's time, and time is a salesperson's most valuable asset. This "visit for any reason" approach can diminish your credibility, erode brand respect, and take valuable attention away from other, better-qualified opportunities.

Discovery Meetings are reserved for when you have a high confidence that there is a specific and significant client problem or challenge to address. This confidence must be supported by a valid reason, such as: the client calls you and invites you to discuss some specific issue, you are "tipped off" by an alliance partner that during some of their own work with a client they discovered a need you are qualified to address, or you are referred by a previous client of yours who believes you can help their colleague.

Storytime: Can I Send You a Quote?

When I was an electronics circuit design engineer, I remember a going-away party for Sam, an electronics tech who was leaving our Design & Development Lab for a job as an independent electronic component manufacturers' rep, aka a salesperson.

He seemed unmotivated and bored as a lab technician and was excited about this opportunity to break away. We were delighted for him.

Several months after his departure, I received a call from him. As I remember the dialogue, it went something like this:

Sam: *"Hey Jerry. It's Sam!"*

Me: *"Hey Sam. Good to hear from you. How's the new job?"*

Sam: *"Great! (without stopping to take a breath...) Hey Jerry, I've been selling a lot of components. I've got resistors of all sorts - diodes, thyristors, capacitors, integrated circuits – just about every component type you would ever need. What would you like me to quote?"*

Me (stunned at his approach): *"Uh, Sam. You know how things work around here."*

"First, if things are working fine in our current designs, we have no need to go through all the rigmarole to test and changeover what we've already designed in."

"Even if you can save us a little money, I am already on to the next project and don't have the need or priority to execute any component changes. There is simply no time to redesign, retest, change our documentation, rid ourselves of the current inventory of parts, get purchasing involved, handhold the manufacturing team to reassure them the new part is OK, change the assembly drawings, train the assemblers, and all the other stuff. You know that's a lot of effort."

"But, if you insist ol' buddy, you can send me a quote if you feel the need to. But I don't have a need to replace anything at the moment and it simply won't get any attention. And my new designs are already in the final testing phase."

"The timing is wrong. The need doesn't exist. The time and expense costs compared to the benefits doesn't make sense."

Sam: *"OK. Take care."*

Click.

Moral of the Story: A legitimate and productive sales call Discovers first.

End of Story

I imagined Sam, sitting at his desk somewhere frantically punching out phone numbers then using his inane, nonsensical, and completely inappropriate script. He was probably being measured by how many calls he made and how many quotes he delivered.

Great guy!

Bad approach.

What was wrong with Sam's approach? Where do I start?

First, he was familiar with the narrow time window projects have in which to select components. Unless there was a problem with something already in production, he would need to have hit the timing perfectly. Sam's first question should have been to ask about what new designs I was working on, what the project timing was and/or what component needs there might be.

Secondly, preparing and delivering an unsolicited quote under those circumstances of no need and no problem, was an absurd waste of time for *his* team.

Third, a bucket full of quotes delivered and intended to service "no need and no problem" situations would not be worth the economic value of the plastic in the bucket.

Fourth, even if he were under pressure to look productive by stuffing the sales pipeline, it would eventually catch up with him.

Fifth, he was wasting his time - the most valuable personal asset a salesperson has to invest.

Discovery Meeting Planning and Prep

There is nothing more time efficient and productive than a well-planned and prepared Discovery Meeting. Preparations for a Discovery Meeting should include:

- a visit to the company's website,

- a LinkedIn search to find the key individuals likely to be involved in any buying decision, and

- a quick Google search of the key issues and challenges currently facing the client's industry.

This small effort increases the probability of discovering a premise and increases the relevance of any discussion you may have with the client.

Selling takes time. But selling time is not always within the control of the salesperson. Frequently, the time it takes to qualify, discover, and win an engagement, is solely in the hands of the client. Assuring client-relevance improves the effective use of time, both yours and your client's. It is an important way to manage your sales efforts.

Consider this scenario – it's a little test for you.

Imagine, for a moment, that you are a financial analytics software salesperson. The corporation you work for is FinCo. At 4:30 p.m. on a Tuesday afternoon you are reviewing your sales pipeline and contemplating how thin it is.

The phone rings.

The person on the other end introduces herself as Jan Grant, the CEO of Grant-Holly Industries. She asks for a few moments of your time and shares her concern about two of the five Grant-Holly divisions that are struggling to achieve their target profitability goals. The internal reports she has received raise more questions than answers. She does not trust what she is reading in these reports.

She recently heard from a colleague about FinCo's financial analytics software for high-tech firms and its consulting support. She also heard your talk *"Smart Profitability Management for the 21st Century"* at the Association of Corporate Recovery monthly meeting. She tells you she is impressed with how you think.

She wonders if you have time for a meeting next week.

What do you do?

a.   Immediately say yes and open your calendar to set a date?

b.   Engage her in a relationship building conversation?

c. Act coy and say, "Hmmm let me see, I'm pretty busy at the moment."

d. Decline to meet.

Based on the number of times I've posed this situation to attendees of my sales training sessions, nine out of ten people responded that they would open their calendar, set the appointment, thank the sales gods for the gift of a call-in, and think they had done a good job in quickly booking the appointment.

But is that really the best thing to do?

Instead, consider this approach. Turn the phone call into an opportunity for both Pre-Qualification and Pre-Discovery sales call planning.

Here is the dialogue.

You: *"Thanks for the call Jan. Glad you had a chance to hear my talk."*

Jan: *"Yes, I never thought of things that way before".*

You: *"I'd be happy to come by and talk with you about your challenges. To help me prepare appropriately, it would be helpful if you could share a bit more about the details of the challenges you are facing. Can you take 10 minutes to do that now?"*

This premise and question are gold. And since you are asking the question to enable improved discussion preparation, which is in her best interest, she will likely be willing to take the time to explain the challenge in a bit more detail. As a result, you will be able to prepare the right material, case studies, testimonials, and problem-solving materials to lead the discussion where it needs to go when you visit.

Jan: *"Yes. I have a few minutes."*

You: *"What do you believe might be the root cause of those problems? Are they the same for both divisions? How long have you been facing this challenge? What have you tried already to resolve it?"*

As the conversation continues, you should be able to discover enough about the situation to prepare well.

You might consider asking a few more great questions. The first is about participation in the coming discussion.

You: *"Are there any other people in your organization that might be able to join us for the discussion? It helps to hear multiple perspectives, particularly from those who have first-hand, front-line experience with the issues, or those who might be greatly affected by anything you decide to change."*

And yet, another question. This one has to do with their preparation for the meeting - homework for the discussion.

You: *"Is there any data that you or someone in your organization might prepare for the discussion? I would be happy to sign a non-disclosure agreement. Having data available brings some urgency to the situation and allows everyone in the room to see it at the same time. That way the team is aligned on the issues."*

Another question:

You: *"What would be your ideal outcome of the discussion?"*

And one final question, a preliminary assessment request.

You: *"Based on what you've shared with me so far, I can prepare. We have a general assessment designed for those types of challenges. The assessment is free and takes about 10 minutes to complete. We ask folks to take this and return it before we meet. It helps us develop a common understanding of your situation and its root causes, at a deeper level. Is that something you might be able to do?"*

At this point you have begun to prepare well for your sales meeting with Jan and her team. Now you can set the date and time.

But the conversation is not quite over.

In your best Columbo voice, you say…

You: *"One more thing. Would you mind if I sent over a suggested Agenda and Objective for the meeting? It is helpful in keeping the discussion on track and informs all attendees of what to expect from our discussion."*

Again, this suggestion is clearly in the client's best interest.

In my experience:

- No one has ever refused to further discuss their challenge over the phone before they set the meeting date and time.

- Rarely has anyone declined the offer of a suggested meeting Objective and Agenda.

- Very few have declined the opportunity to invite others. If they have, it was an early warning sign of a closed communication culture.

- Very few have declined to take the assessment.

- Few have required an NDA.

- Not many have relevant, sufficient, and accurate root-cause data to bring regarding the problem or challenge - which is a major contributor to why the problem exists in the first place.

Good collaborative planning for a Discovery Meeting, in dialogue with a client EIC, will accomplish three critical things: 1) build credibility and trust, 2) accelerate the time it takes to identify the best approach to address the client's POG, and 3) help them.

The Discovery Meeting Agenda

Establishing a mutually agreed upon objective for a detailed face-to-face Discovery meeting, and assuring such objective is clearly in the best interest of the client, accelerates their decision-making process.

Here is an example of a mutually agreed upon objective established between fictitious Grant-Holly (the client prospect) and FinCo (the financial analytics software company).

Meeting Objective: To understand the details and implications of Grant-Holly's financial performance challenges and assess the appropriateness of FinCo's current analytics and financial software to meeting those challenges.

Attendance: Assuring that all the right people are in the room and participating in the discussion is a great time saver. Ideally participants in the discussion should be those involved in the decision-making process, those in a position to recommend the solution or those who might be impacted by the solution.

In this case it would be helpful to suggest to Jan Grant that she invite her CFO, Division Managers, and IT systems people into the discussion.

By my count, this would mean a meeting of five participants, all with a stake in the outcome.

Client Pre-work: Preparation for the meeting should include the financial analysis and report information that is needed to understand the problem. Having samples of the reports for review, coupled with participants' sharing their specific concerns, would provide greater clarity and save time.

Pre-Discovery Client POG Self-Assessment: We will discuss this a bit later in this chapter. Briefly, a client POG self-assessment, taken and returned to you from the client EIC prior to a Discovery Meeting provides you relevant information to prepare well for your discussion.

Agenda: Suggesting an agenda, your email might say …

"Thank you for agreeing to meet next week to discuss Grant-Holly's financial analytics and reporting challenges. To make best use of our time and assure maximum progress, I'd like to offer a specific meeting objective and agenda for your consideration."

Agendas demonstrate that during any face-to-face discussion you are mutually working toward the same, pre-stated objective.

An effective five-part, 60 to 90-minute Discovery Meeting Agenda with nominal times for each part, follows:

•	Personal Introductions & Backgrounds	5 to 10 min
•	Grant-Holly Challenges (incl. self-assessment review)	30 to 40 min
•	FinCo's Approach	10 to 15 min
•	Applicability	10 to 15 min
•	Next Steps	5 to 10 min

Here is what should occur during each part of the Agenda.

Part 1: Introductions and Background Sharing

Success for both parties depends on building a trusted relationship between the salesperson, the ultimate economic decision maker, and the decision influencers. Dedicating a few minutes to get to know one another and briefly share professional and personal backgrounds, provides an opportunity to get comfortable with one another.

Finding something in common helps as a conversation warmer, but do not overdo it. Your primary purpose is to help solve a business problem. In Navigational Selling™ the Introductions portion of a Discovery Meeting allots 5 to 10 minutes max – best done in a "go-around-the-room" format.

Not long ago, I discovered in this portion of a Discovery Meeting, that the CEO-level EIC loved salmon and steelhead fishing as much as I do. Another client EIC CEO is a musician - a rock drummer. I am a schooled musician and composer. We always have something interesting to chat about for a few minutes when we meet. But we get down to business very quickly.

Part 2: Client Challenges

The first things you will notice about the suggested time allocations of the Navigational Selling™ Agenda are: a) the amount of time dedicated to questioning and listening to the client's challenges is a minimum of 2X the amount of time you will be talking about your offerings and what you do, and b) the client challenge part of the discussion arrives quickly.

As antsy as a salesperson may get waiting to give their pitch, that pitch cannot be the first item on the agenda.

Storytime: Getting the Agenda Backwards - or - Talking Before Listening

A client of mine travelled to a foreign country to promote his diagnostic product to the head of a major hospital. For certain critical health issues, this product significantly reduced the amount of time a patient had to spend in an intensive care unit (ICU). This reduction of ICU time saved both insurance companies and hospitals a lot of money and made the hospital a more attractive place for doctors and HMOs to admit their patients.

After quickly launching into his sales pitch, then sitting down, the Director of the Hospital said to my client:

"Mr. Schmidt (fictitious name), that's a pretty amazing product you have there. I do believe it delivers all the benefits you say. However, my government pays me for the number of days I keep people in the ICU – not how fast I transfer them out."

If Mr. Schmidt had questioned and listened first, he may have discovered that he needed to promote a different benefit about his system. Rather than touting the rapidity with which his product could enable patients to be released from the ICU, he might have touted the accuracy and reliability of its diagnostic capabilities.

Moral of the Story: Listen first. Talk second. Then listen again.

End of story

Not all clients receive the same types and levels of benefits from your service or product. Questioning and listening first reveals which of your offering's capabilities will most likely resonate with the client prospect, indicating which benefits will be most important to highlight when you speak.

I encourage the QLCLW approach: Question. Listen. Clarify. Listen. Write it down.

It is also within the Client Challenges part of the Agenda that the results of any pre-meeting self-assessment are discussed.

Part 3: Your Approaches

If you have done a good job in your preliminary phone screening and been able to extract a preliminary self-assessment from the client before the Discovery meeting, you should be well prepared for the issues the discussion revealed.

Part 3 is your opportunity to describe the approach, the benefits delivered to the client, relevant case studies and testimonials, deliverables, and overall outcomes produced – all within the context of the types of challenges the client is facing.

Part 4: Applicability

Once you have worked through the listening and capabilities review, it is time to face the music by asking a series of direct questions.

"What value do you believe your firm will realize by resolving these issues and challenges?"

"To what degree do you feel that the approach we offer might be able to close the gaps and challenges that were revealed in the preliminary self-assessment and this discussion?"

"If you believe our approach is directly applicable to your challenge, how do you feel about the urgency of moving forward?"

These questions should reveal what further effort is required to help the client decide. Remember we are *not* trying to trick or *push* the client into signing a proposal. We are trying to build trust and belief in a collaborative effort to fix what ails them. We assume that if the problem is serious enough, the client will want to act sooner rather than later.

Part 5: Next Steps

This is just what it says, the collaborative identification of the actions that any of the people in the room might need to take to move ahead with resolving the problem together. At the conclusion of the Discovery Meeting, these actions, and who owns them, must be clear.

Conducting the Discovery Meeting

Questioning and Listening

If you are not spending more than 65% of a sales call questioning, listening, and writing things down, learn to adopt that discipline.

Just a few more points about questioning:

- Keep the questions relevant to the challenge the client has expressed in Part 2 of the agenda.

- Use open ended questions. Open ended questions begin with the words, What, How and Why. Those types of questions cannot be answered with a yes or no. Closed ended questions begin with, Did you? Do you? or Have you?

The point is to ask questions in such a way as to elicit as much additional information as possible.

I play this game with my granddaughter. I never ask, "*How was school today?*" Phrasing the question in that manner will usually elicit a one-word response like, "*Good*". Information gathered = none.

Instead, I ask, "What kinds of new things did you discuss in school this week?".

I typically receive a response such as, "Did you know, Grandpa, that (fill in the blank)."

This approach triggers a much more rewarding dialogue.

Open ended questions begin with:

- How?

- What?

- When?

- Why?

I am not suggesting you treat your client prospect like a child. I am suggesting you ask questions in such a way as to gather as much relevant information as possible, so you can better help your client address their POG. Always question, question, question, and listen intently and actively.

And, for goodness' sake, write things down!

Why is writing things down so important?

You, your team, their team, your management decision makers, and their management decision makers will all need to be on the same page if a challenge is to be tackled. What you write down and share with all involved, will align everyone's efforts and optimize the solution offered and benefits realized by the client.

Super-Charging Discovery: The Client POG Self-Assessment

Adhering to a disciplined discovery meeting is a sound approach to reveal the details and circumstances surrounding a client's POG. But what if a prospect is not even sure they have a POG? Or overconfident that they do not have a POG?

What if they just feel a general malaise, expressed in a resigned, "things could be better" shrug of the shoulders? What if they are expressively displeased with the current performance of their business, but are unsure of any specific cause, or combination of causes, at the root of the deficiency? Or they might be smugly overconfident, complacent, or ignorant of the telltale signs or hidden problems, which if left unaddressed, are quietly building to a crisis.

The best and most powerful motivational moment for encouraging a client to address one of their challenges occurs when a client comes to the *self-realization*, sometimes slowly and sometimes like a bombshell, that they absolutely must do something about a Problem, Opportunity, or Gap. Until that happens, most of what you say and offer, while it may make sense, will not motivate action.

A client POG self-assessment is an effective way to trigger or accelerate a client's self-realization, crystalize their purpose, and energize their decision-making process. A client self-assessment can reveal latent or hidden POGs or bring into clearer focus any problem areas related to an already existing POG.

The reason self-assessments are so effective is that they reveal critical needs and opportunities based on the client's own perception and admission of organizational weakness or need.

Clients, even if they call you in to discuss a specific challenge, do not always know what their core problem is. They may be convinced that they need something that addresses symptoms, not root causes. A solution that only addresses a symptom is not always in the client's best interest.

It is a bit like a patient coming to the doctor with an excruciating pain in their lower back, asking for chiropractic therapy, when in fact the problem is a non-passable kidney stone, not a muscle spasm. An ethical doctor would not simply take the patient's request as wise and schedule a chiropractic visit or even provide powerful pain killers - until they had run a battery of tests, diagnosed the root cause of the pain, then recommended an appropriate course of treatment.

The point is that treatment without diagnosis can lead to malpractice. Doctors must first do no harm. This means they need to treat the root cause of disease, not just the symptoms.

The Sales role is similar. The best salespeople must do no harm. What the client wants may or may not be what the client really needs.

> *The Salesperson should do no harm. Providing simply what a client wants may be the fastest route to closing a sale, but if it is not what the client truly needs, it is highly likely that the outcomes desired will not be achieved or long-lasting.*

One of the most effective ways to identify the root cause of a problem and make best recommendation is through a diagnostic assessment.

The general form of a useful diagnostic assessment is shown below in Figure 17. This type of graph is called a spider or radar graph. Figure 17 is an example self-assessment that could be used to assess selling operational effectiveness software, financial consulting services or any other operations-related offering to a Mental Healthcare Practice.

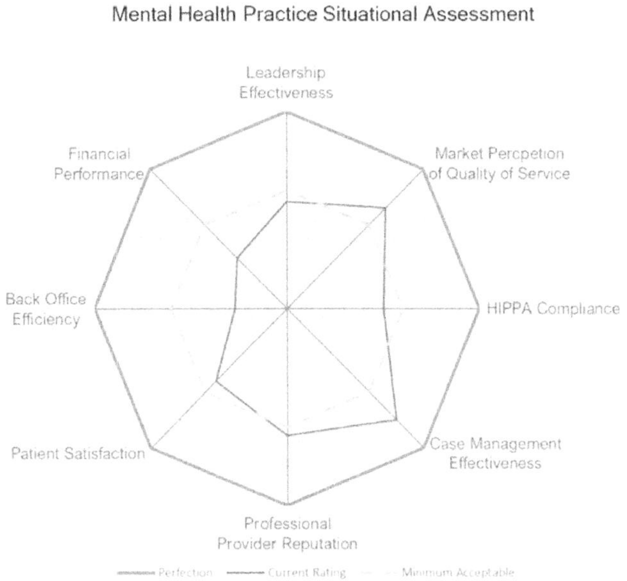

Mental Health Practice Situational Assessment

Figure 17: Mental Healthcare Practice Situation Self-Assessment

This example has eight dimensions against which a manager, owner or key employee of a Mental Healthcare Practice can self-evaluate their organization's performance.

Reading a POG self-assessment

Referring back to Figure 17, the thicker solid line along the outside edge of the graph signifies perfection. The dashed line, about halfway between the outer perimeter and the graph's center, is the border of minimally acceptable performance. The irregular polygon represents the client's self-score - their perception of their performance along each dimension.

Any score that falls below the dashed line signifies unacceptable performance and a gap that could be addressed.

In this example, you can clearly see that there four performance gaps, the most significant is Back Office Efficiency – which may be closely related to, and a root cause of the other performance gap in Financial Performance. In addition, Patient Satisfaction is below acceptable levels as well, which may mean that patients are dropping their care programs earlier than recommended and not returning. That would certainly have a detrimental impact on the Financial Performance of the practice, as well.

Such an assessment serves as an effective approach to triggering the kind of EIC self-awareness that drives a client's urgency to address the multiple interrelated issues. It does not however assure the client will buy something from you. They may elect to fix things themselves, opt for a competitive approach, or flying in the face of their own self-judged poor scores, decide to do nothing.

The number of dimensions in an assessment is unimportant, as long as the assessment covers the major characteristics of good performance. I have created and used assessments with as few as five and as many as ten dimensions. Typically, seven or eight dimensions are adequate.

Two cautions about selecting the performance dimensions of your assessments:

1. The dimensions that you choose should identify gaps that can be addressed by your expertise and offerings, or those of your alliance partners.

2. As much as possible, try to associate the dimensions with both root causes and common symptoms.

Improving the performance of root cause dimensions is more likely to create lasting results, which in the long run are much more valuable to clients and much more in their (and your) best interest. Including symptoms dimensions helps those taking the assessment more easily identify with what they observe in their daily business activities.

The Four Magic Implications Questions

The results of the completed assessment provide a pretty clear visual representation of perceived gaps, but the salesperson needs to assure that the *implications* of those gaps are explicit and clear to the EIC Decision-Maker.

Four questions bring home the implications of any gaps that may have been revealed.

Question 1. How much do you think those gaps have cost (economically) in the last three to five years, in terms of lost or foregone revenue, profit, or clients?

This question drives home the economic impact of doing nothing. As they silently ponder the answer, you can typically see deep self-reflection on the face of the client EIC, followed by disappointment. You do not need to get a specific answer. A quick shake of their head tells you all you need to know.

<u>Question 2</u>. What would your competitive situation be if your toughest competitors had significantly higher performance in those dimensions where you have gaps?

That concerned look on their face usually gets deeper as they ponder this additional perspective and begin to imagine the consequences and implications of unattended gaps.

<u>Question 3</u>. What would your competitive situation be if your competitors discovered these gaps and found ways to exploit them to win business?

Deeper concern.

<u>Question 4</u>. What do you think the impact might be if, at some future date, a suitor was considering buying your business and these gaps were discovered during the due diligence process? Would visibility of these gaps increase the perceived value of the business in the eyes of the prospective buyer - or reduce it?

This final question usually hits the CEO/Owner hardest.

The four questions serve to drive home the negative implications and consequences of leaving self-revealed gaps unaddressed. If the client remains reluctant to engage in a remedial program to close the gaps, one can always offer a more inclusive assessment which collects input from the firm's key managers to capture their perspectives - through both assessments and interviews.

Such a follow-on assessment continues to move the ball forward and provides a firmer, data-driven foundation for a remedial program proposal. It also allows you, as the salesperson, the opportunity to provide an objective perspective of the true depth and implications of the gaps.

The impact of Question 4 is deeply meaningful to EIC/Owners. They have likely worked and sacrificed a large part of their adult life to create something of value, and when they ultimately sell the business, or hand it to their progeny, they want four things:

1. a fair price that recognizes their hard work and what they have created,

2. to leave a legacy,

3. to assure some continuity, recognition, and job security for employees who have helped them achieve what they have, and

4. something meaningful to do with their life afterwards.

Storytime: The Perception of "Good" that was "Bad"

I recently conducted a POG assessment with a manufacturing firm that identified their Culture as the most important and strongest component of their organization's success. Both the owner and his management team gave consistently high ratings to the Culture dimension of their assessment scores. It garnered the highest individual rating of any dimension in the assessment.

However, my personal objective assessment revealed that the reason it was rated so high, was its easy-going, low pressure, employee-centered atmosphere - to a fault. So much so, that setting goals, getting things done, a sense of urgency, and individual accountability were almost non-existent.

That is a nice comfortable place to work I guess, but not a very productive one.

Moral of the Story: Subjective self-assessments need to be validated by objective, expert perspectives to be considered meaningful and diagnostically accurate.

End of Story

Another Quick Storytime: Different Perspectives - or - Does everyone in this room work for the same company?

In another case, a more extensive assessment of eight partners in a business revealed a significant difference in perspective between the CEO and the seven other partners. The CEO provided consistently and substantially higher performance ratings than all other respondents - in all dimensions. That discrepancy of perception took some time to sort out, but I'm pleased to say, the business became successful.

Moral of the Story: Differences in individual assessment ratings by important executives within the client organization can reveal barriers to acknowledgement of performance gaps and their implications.

End of Story

Assessments help identify shortcomings, both subjectively and objectively, and focus the client's attention on performance gaps and their serious implications.

Building Your Own Client POG Self-Assessment Tool

POG self-assessments, tailored to your specific market, offerings, value propositions, and differentiated capabilities are relatively easy to craft.

Here are the steps:

Step 1: Identify up to nine dimensions of performance that are indicative of problems, opportunities, and gaps that clients in your target market commonly experience, and that your offerings have proven to successfully address. You can have up to nine dimensions, but seven or eight dimensions are adequate.

Step 2: For each performance dimension, identify three descriptive situational statements that can be rated on a scale from 1 to 5.

Referring back to Figure 17, the example of a POG self-assessment for a Mental Health Practice, let us take the dimension of Back Office Efficiency as a case in point. The three sub-dimension statements might be:

> S1. *Timeliness* - Our back office is always effective in assuring that our provider billing is timely, without the persistent need for overtime. Rating ___

> S2. *Accuracy* - The accuracy of our diagnostic groupings (the classification of patient condition, treatment provided, and charges) is more than 97% accurate, and rarely delays reimbursement approval and payment for services. Rating ___

> S3. *Post-Visit Communications* - Our post-visit and post-treatment communications with patients are timely and, based on post-visit interviews with patients, highly appreciated by them and their families. Rating ___

Each of these can be rated on a scale of 1 to 5, with 5 being the highest degree of agreement with the statement, and 1 being the lowest degree of agreement. A simple average of the three statement client ratings yields the composite score for that dimension.

Dividing the dimension into a minimum of three rating statements, permits a more specific circumstantial rationale for those rating the dimension. Additionally, a set of three statements per dimension allows for a deeper-than-surface-level understanding and behavioral diagnostic of a POG result.

Step 3: The last step is to plot the averaged results on a radar, or spider graph. The graph is easily created within Excel.

It is important to identify performance dimensions that are useful in revealing specific and relevant gaps that you could address within the markets and target client organizations you wish to serve. Do not include dimensions or sub-dimensions your offerings, or those of your alliance partners, cannot address.

In formulating your own assessment, assure that a minimum of half of the dimensions are related to root causes. Because clients are more likely to understand and relate to symptom dimensions, you must include both root cause and symptom dimensions.

At the end of this exercise, you should have a multi-dimensional assessment tool suitable for use with client prospects. The assessments have proven to be a valuable "visual" tool in helping clients recognize performance gaps and their depth. The assessment coupled with implications questions motivate clients to action.

When designing an assessment, don't make it so exhaustive that it cannot be completed within five or ten minutes. If an EIC has not taken a pre-Discovery meeting assessment, they must be able to work through one quickly during the meeting.

Where, When, and How to Use a Client POG Self-Assessment.

POG self-assessments are useful in several circumstances:

1. *As a pre-work assignment for the client prior to a pre-qualified Discovery Meeting*

   In planning a prospective client Discovery Meeting, having POG self-assessment results ahead of time contributes greatly to the accuracy and relevance of your preparations.

2. *During a Discovery Meeting, if the only participant is the EIC and, at most, one other executive*

   Early on I used only a composite score, no graph results with the POG assessments. On one occasion, an EIC/Owner and his Operations Executive arrived at my office to discuss their challenges. I gave them each a self-assessment to fill out. A perfect score was 85 points.

   One of the executives scored the situation at 10 points total - the other at 8 points. Up to that time, the lowest scores I had ever witnessed in the history of my business. Though I did not mention that record-breaking result, I am certain they saw me struggling to hide the surprise on my face.

   I asked the four implications questions, and they struck home. They quickly enlisted my consulting services.

3. *During a Talk or Webinar*

   Several years ago, I delivered a focused 20-minute talk to a peer group of fourteen SMB2B CEO's regarding the difference between tactical marketing and strategic marketing. I handed out a condensed version of a client Marketing & Sales self-assessment and gave the group just five minutes to complete it. Once the time was up, I asked the four implications questions.

I did not ask to see their scores. We did not have time for in-depth discussion. The look on their faces told me all I needed to know.

Four of those participants became clients within three months.

4. *As a Pre-Qualification Tool*

Occasionally when I receive a phone or website inquiry, I ask the caller if they would be willing to take a POG self-assessment. About half do. About half of those who do agree, follow through and complete an assessment. I assume the other half, for one reason or another, disqualify themselves. That's OK with me. If a client is not given to honest self-reflection, they will not likely be given to follow-through during execution.

5. *As a Post-Engagement Assessment*

This use determines if the situation has improved after the sale and implementation of your product or service.

You may identify more opportunities for using a client POG self-assessment. They are easy enough to create that I now have a collection of more than a dozen I use in my own business for different offerings. And I have helped clients craft dozens more for their own use – across a wide range of markets and industries.

Irritant vs. Thorough: The Balancing Act

You may be considering that such an over-emphasis on thorough Discovery would eventually run the risk of the client perceiving you as an irritant. That can happen, so the telltale signs of such irritation should be monitored closely.

There are several ways to minimize the likelihood of such a client reaction.

Be patient

There are two threats to patience: 1) you and your bosses' collective sense of urgency about the importance of winning new business quickly, and 2) the client's urgency to resolve their POG, as first identified in the Compelling Need factor of the six opportunity qualification criteria.

The degree to which you are calm, methodical, thorough, explanatory, and reassuring throughout your discovery activities, will help the client understand your intent and the benefits of working with you. If the salesperson senses acute need brought about by an intense and urgent compelling need, you might consider even saying something reassuring like …

"I sense that this situation is really causing you some anxiety and deep concern. I'm pretty confident we can arrive at a solution to your challenges. But to assure that we build that solution precisely to your needs, I hope you understand that I might need to gather quite a bit of information. So, I beg your patience as we have this discussion. I will be asking a lot of questions to assure you get a proposal that delivers precisely what you want, what you need, and the kind of value that will flow through your internal approval process quickly. I appreciate your understanding."

This suggestion would help with a decision influencer. With an ultimate decision maker, you might consider a slightly reworded version.

"I sense that this situation is really causing some anxiety and deep concern. I'm confident we can arrive at a solution to your challenges. But to assure that we build that solution precisely to your needs, I hope you understand that I need to be thorough and gather quite a bit of information. So, I ask for your patience as we have this discussion. I will be asking questions to assure you receive a proposal that quickly delivers precisely what you want and need and delivers real value. I appreciate your understanding."

Note the minor changes to the wording. We eliminated the approval clause, since we are speaking with the ultimate decision maker, and emphasized quickly delivering value. EICs and Owners typically have a higher sense of urgency than those lower in the organization.

Use the right phraseology:

In anything you ask or say, think about how to phrase questions, statements, and recommendations from the perspective of the client first.

Instead of asking, *"Do you have this budgeted?"* or *"What is your budget?"*, begin by asking a client about the value of implementing a solution to their problem or challenge – or gain an estimate of the value that might be generated by availing themselves of the opportunity they think will open up by implementing your solution.

Continually Build Trust:

As you continue to dig through the mine of Discovery, remember that your primary objective is to elicit information that will help you both achieve the client's goals. This means that you must ask questions and discover information in such a way that clearly shows you are working in their best interest.

I once was trusted by a client EIC to such a degree that he signed a multi-page, very lucrative, six-figure contract by immediately jumping to the last page and writing his name on the line provided for his approval of the project.

Why would he do that?

It was the second contract we engaged in. He signed quickly because he felt that I had built enough trust and understanding of his business through the first engagement, that he had no problem in knowing that what I was offering was in his, and his firm's, best interest – even though it was for a different service.

In signing in that way, he communicated very clearly, without words, "*I trust you. I have confidence that you will do what is in our best interest. We have built mutual trust.*"

Collaborate:

Make sure that every question you ask clearly supports the idea that you and the client are working together to solve the client's problem. Explain to the client why the question is relevant to achieving that objective. Use the word "we" a lot and continually refer to the value the client will receive from the implementation of what will be proposed.

The Discussion Summary

Let me clarify a semantic issue. To this point in this chapter, I have been talking about a Discovery Meeting. Now I am calling the written summary and record of the *Discovery* Meeting, a *Discussion* Summary.

What gives? What's the difference between Discovery and Discussion?

To the salesperson it is all about *Discovery*. If you think solely about *your* objective, it is to maximize what you can *discover* about the client needs, the decision makers and influencers, the competitive approaches under consideration, how the client's decision-making process works, and how best to position yourself for a win.

However, to the client, it is all about *Discussion*, information exchange and their evaluation of alternatives.

You are *Discovering* everything you need to address their needs, solve a problem, and win a deal. *They* are *Discussing* and evaluating approaches in a quest to find the best solution.

Using the word Discovery, runs the risk of the client feeling as if they are the object of scrutiny – an amoeba under the lens of a salesperson's microscope – observed, tested, poked, and prodded for reaction. In contrast, the word Discussion implies and facilitates a collaborative effort to reveal the best path to an optimum solution to address their POG.

So, while you may track your progress in your own CRM pipeline system as being in the Discovery Stage, when you summarize the _Discovery Meeting_, please call that summary a _Discussion Summary_ in your communications with the client.

The Discovery step we just covered is comprehensive and comprises digging for a lot of client information. That information is essential to assuring you cover all the bases in whatever proposal and approach you may formulate. But, like the adage, "_measure twice, cut once_", it is helpful to confirm what you have heard from the client before constructing your proposal. The tool for that confirmation is the Discussion Summary.

The Discussion Summary is a post Discovery Meeting email, sent to the EIC within 24 hours of your meeting. The Discussion Summary corroborates the client discussion; what you heard and understood, then requests confirmation or correction.

All Discussion Summaries have the same format in the same order:

- _A Thank You:_ Thank the EIC decision maker for their time and the time of any other attendees that may have participated,

- _Empathy:_ Empathize with their business challenges,

- _Request a Review of the Discussion Summary:_ You need to confirm that the pieces of information you captured during the discussion are accurate. You should also request corrections to those points that you may have misunderstood or mistaken,

- _Itemize the Key Points:_ This is the beef that will form the basis of any proposal you formulate.

- _Detail any Follow-On Action Items_,

- _Thank_ the EIC again, and

- _Promise a Follow-Up Call:_ Explain that you will call in a few days to assure they received and had an opportunity to read the message, hear of and correct any misstatements it contained, and answer any other questions they may have.

Here is a Discussion Summary example:

To: Horace Theroux

From: You

Subject: Discussion Summary

Date: March 12, 2021

Thank you for your time yesterday to discuss the marketing & sales challenges facing your organization. Please express my appreciation also to Bill and Tonya for their participation, perspectives, and the data they brought to the discussion. It really helped put the challenge in perspective. I have attached the results of the preliminary self-assessment you took prior to the meeting. That data formed the basis of much of what we discussed.

As promised, I offer this Discussion Summary to assure I understand the situation accurately. If I missed or misunderstood anything, please let me know.

<u>*Key Points:*</u>

- *Theroux Industries is a 30-year-old business, that you have managed since founding it in 1990.*

- *Over the last several years you have been methodically re-building your management team to include people with current technical skills, to replace several retiring managers in key roles. This effort included Engineering, Quality Management and Sales.*

- *Your current VP of Sales was an industry hire from a major competitor two years ago, but as of January had not formalized either a market strategy or a sales process for the firm.*

- *This slow action is the result of him having to handle priorities dealing with the threatened losses of several major accounts - which represent 60% of the firm's current revenues.*

- *These concentrated efforts on defense have made new market and target account efforts impossible to get to.*

- *There are five sales resources on the team: 1 sales manager, 2 outside salespeople, and 2 internal sales/customer service employees.*

It is your current feeling that:

- *You need a boost of strategic marketing and new business development execution resources to identify new target markets and launch penetration initiatives before your competition does.*

- *An effective current account management process needs to be put-in-place.*

- *Improved forecasting is desperately needed. Inventory turns have been stuck at around 3 for years, and despite a huge dollar value of inventory, there are persistent shortages and poor on-time delivery.*

- *There is no CRM, and you are not sure why you would need one.*

- *There is no active tactical marketing program, though a website redesign has been recently completed.*

- *The most urgent and critical goal is to reduce your vulnerability to a high % of your sales (35%) from one customer.*

- *Your interest is in engaging a sales coach that will help current employees achieve higher performance through training, coaching and education.*

- *You believe that you have a sound approach for selecting markets, though your self-assessment score in that regard suggested it could use improvement. (See attachment)*

Next Steps:

- *Send a sample target market selection tool for review – Jerry*

- *Review the self-assessment and prepare follow-up questions – Horace*

- *Read this summary and correct any misunderstandings - Horace*

- *Based on this message and any corrected misunderstandings prepare a proposal to meet the challenges of the firm - Jerry*

That's all I have Horace. Again, If I missed or misunderstood anything please let me know. I will call in a couple of days to assure you received the message and answer any questions you may have.

Thanks again for your and your team's time and frank discussion.

Sincerely,

Jerry Vieira, CMC

You will see that in the subject line of this message, I referred to the message as a "Discussion Summary" rather than a "Discovery Summary". As explained earlier, we want to phrase communications to the client from the perspective of the client, not our own. To the salesperson, it is Discovery. To the client it is a Discussion. The client will react differently to the word "Discovery" (implying *your own* best interest) than to a "Discussion" (implying *their* best interest).

Benefits of a Discussion Summary

Once you have accustomed yourself to the format, a well-crafted Discussion Summary should take about an hour to prepare. To some, that may seem like a lot of work for little return. That perception is far from reality and ignores the client's perception. The reality is, that from the client's perspective, a well-crafted and thorough Discussion Summary:

- demonstrates that you listened carefully,

- demonstrates you care about the client's well-being by validating what you heard, so that what you propose will meet their expressed needs,

- differentiates you from your competitors who do not offer one,

- builds trust,

- documents action item commitments, assuring continued engagement,

- provides a mutually agreed upon communication mechanism, within a short time after the meeting, for a follow-up conversation,

- improves the accuracy and targeting of your proposal,

- demonstrates your professionalism, and

- communicates to your internal team what is going on and what to expect.

For an important new opportunity or client prospect, it is a small investment of time with great returns in trust building, accuracy, and collaboration.

What the Discussion Summary is not!

The Discussion Summary is *not* intended to be a salesy promotion. Do not hijack its purpose.

Using the Discussion Summary to promote is a common trap that novice users of a Discussion Summary can fall into. Promotional statements within a Discussion Summary corrupt its collaborative problem-solving intent and erode the pillars of Navigational Selling™.

Any statement like this, "We look forward to the opportunity to apply our immense talent and intellectual genius to your problems, the way we have done for 15 years for hundreds of clients in your industry across the U.S. and Canada".

Such blatant promotion is a corruption of the intent of the message.

The first rule of *Navigational Selling*™ is:

Help the client navigate to the optimal solution! Don't push or pull at the helm.

The Discussion Summary is *not* intended to be a proposal. Fees should not be included, nor should solutions, deliverables, or outcomes. The purpose of the Discussion Summary is to simply verify the client's concerns and situation.

The Discussion Summary also is not a tool to "trash" other approaches under consideration, even DIY and Do Nothing.

When you write your first Discussion Summary, find someone that will keep the information confidential, and have them proof it with you. Spelling and grammatical errors diminish your Quality brand and image. Together, review your summary to ensure you have not fallen into the salesy promotion trap.

After a few struggles in crafting a good Discussion Summary, you will learn to use a notebook during your Discovery Meetings, listen carefully, take copious notes, and use spell check.

If you did not take notes during your first Discovery Meeting, you surely will at each Discovery Meeting thereafter. It's tough to accurately capture important details of that conversation and draft a good Discussion Summary from memory. You will learn to hone your listening skills, sharpen your note taking, and utilize spell-check to present a good Discussion Summary.

*****

Chapter 8: Reading People

In this Chapter …

I'm Spartacus!

The Three Personality Dimensions of a B2B Business Client

Decision-Maker Management Styles

Decision Maker I-A-A (Influence, Authority & Affinity)

The Approach-to-Business (ATB) of (EIC) Decision Makers

I'm Spartacus!

There are various versions and movies about the semi-legend of Spartacus, the famous Thracian who led a slave revolt against the Roman empire circa 71 BCE.

In the 1960 movie, starring Kirk Douglas in the title role, Crassus's Roman Legions finally caught up with and defeated the army of the famed ex-gladiator and charismatic slave leader, capturing thousands of his army alive in the process. Not certain what Spartacus looked like (they didn't have milk cartons to publicize his photo at the time) many of his loyal followers claimed to be the famous leader of the slave army to protect him – even though it meant an ignoble and painful death by crucifixion. In all, 6,000 are said to have been crucified along the Appian Way.

In many SMB2B firms, few if any major purchase decisions are made exclusively by just one individual, sitting like a supreme commander atop the organization. In many cases, more than one individual will *claim* decision-making power – thus the Spartacus Syndrome. While one ultimate decision maker will most certainly wield sufficient authority to sign and enter into any kind of contractual agreement with the seller, in many firms, decision-making has become a distributed, consensus-building, team process.

In Chapter 4, we identified the five considerations that influence SMB2B Sales Success. Within the consideration of the client's decision process, we discussed the three C-based decision-making approaches: Consensus, Consultative, and Collaborative. The subtle differences of these three approaches are explained in more detail under the subheading, The Often-Overlooked Client Decision Making Process, which is the third of the five considerations in that Chapter.

Many members of a C-based decision-making team will own advisory or partial approval power over certain aspects of a decision. A designated individual may need to approve the technical considerations of the decision, another the financial and yet others the legal, procurement related, or user-related aspects. At times, it will seem that almost everyone has some input.

Many will claim, (perhaps because there is no fear of crucifixion), their own little Spartacus role within their special area of influence. So, it is not uncommon for multiple members of a client management team to claim, what may appear to the salesperson as, ultimate decision-making authority.

Such claims are, too often, taken at face value by the salesperson. Assuming the truth of such a claim is a trap - which may dissuade the salesperson from testing, validating, and understanding exactly how the client decision will be made.

Research revealed in the book "The Challenger Customer", found that the average number of people involved in a B2B decision to buy, is just over five. Other sources claim the number at seven. Whether the number of consensus decision makers is 3, 5, or 7, the salesperson should expect multiple people involved in the decision-making process. This means there will be a wide range of perspectives, motivations, personalities, emotions, and needs. Furthermore, considerations will range in materiality from economic to emotional, social to political and even physical.

A skilled Navigator salesperson must know how to read people and elicit both their expressed and implied decision considerations.

The Three Dimensions of B2B Client Decision-Makers and Influencers

B2B client decision makers and decision influencers can be characterized by at least three dimensions:

1. their *Management Style*, the way they approach their management role within their business,

2. their degree of *Influence* and *Authority* in the decision, and their *Affinity* for your offering (I-A-A), and

3. their individual *Approach-to-Business* (ATB).

Understanding and being aware of these perspectives is helpful in framing and communicating relevant solutions and formulating proposals. Each member of the C-based decision-making team needs to see themselves and their personal needs reflected in your offer, quote, bid or proposal.

The Management Style of the EIC Decision-Maker

Illustrated in Figure 18 below is an extremely effective approach to understanding EIC Management Styles, so you can frame communication and proposals in a way that resonate quickly.

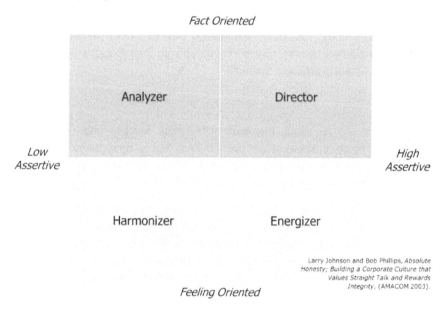

Figure 18: Client Decision-Maker Management Styles

Directors

Directors are the Commanders and Generals of the business world. Directors operate as the unquestioned leader, sole decision maker and ultimate authority of all they purvey. They like order, plans, deadlines, and results. They take their own counsel on decision making and unilaterally decide direction – which all in the organizational hierarchy are expected to follow.

In the Discovery stage of sales, they may decline inviting anyone else in the organization to participate in the initial discovery meeting. In proposals, they will look for schedules, project plans, timelines, checkpoints, milestones, process measurement, team structure, project management responsibilities and specific quantifiable results.

In deciding and executing they will be quick and unilateral, no matter the emotional and organizational carnage inflicted along the path to progress. They are more likely to select an approach that promises to quickly drive to meet all the objectives, rather than one that considers the emotional needs of all the individuals involved. Think General George S. Patton, commander of the US 3rd Army during WWII.

An EIC Director Management Style is not naturally compatible with a C-based decision-making process. But many enlightened Directors have learned to use the Consultative version – listening, considering input from their management team, yet reserving the ultimate decision to themself.

Harmonizers

Harmonizers are all about the team, consensus building and organizational harmony. They thrive on knowing that everyone has had an opportunity to have their say about any initiative under consideration. They typically operate under a Consensus decision-making approach.

In the Discovery stage they are likely to invite as many people as will fit in the room to listen and provide input before a decision is made. Their decision-making style is, at minimum, *Consultative* (they listen carefully to each perspective and ultimately make the decision themselves), or more likely *Consensus* (they give everyone an opportunity to express their concerns, include their needs, and allow a buy-in vote).

The magic words a Harmonizer looks for in a proposal are team, team, and team… in that order.

They will likely select an approach that meets all the team's expressed needs, over the approach that achieves the goal at all costs.

Analyzers

Analyzers like data and detail – and lots of it. They need data to feel comfortable about any decision they make. They need detail to understand the correlation and connection of the data to the process to be followed and the success that could be accomplished. They must connect all the dots.

Before they feel comfortable with a decision, an Analyzer may delay a project start because of their obsessive need to gather and analyze data from every possible angle. The results of any self-assessment are the first pieces of data an Analyzer may inquire about and will surely share them with the other members of the decision team.

If a hard-core analyzer is the EIC and ultimate decision-maker, expect several requests for additional information before a decision is made. If you discover the individual is an Analyzer before the first meeting, come to that first Discovery Meeting prepared with lots of quantified ammunition.

Energizers

Energizers are the blind enthusiasts of the business world.

Similar in style to the Don Quixotes of the ATB scale discussed later in the chapter, they are all drama, unbridled enthusiasm (sometimes unfounded), and ebullience. They harbor visions and a dream of how great things will be. They attempt to create organizational success through infectious enthusiasm alone.

During Discovery, their enthusiasm is obvious, while their follow-through is typically terrible. They just cannot be bothered with the details. In proposals, you must play to the enthusiasm and optimism of the Energizer, but not promise wildly unrealistic results.

If there is going to be any chance of success, the salesperson must identify someone else in the client organization that has some Director traits and assure they are involved in every part of the project. This is best accomplished by collaborating with the Energizer and identifying a detail-oriented project manager. The project manager reports to the Energizer and assumes responsibility for project implementation and management.

Combinations

It is rare to find people who are exclusively one Management Style. In the real world, referring to Figure 18, people typically exhibit two adjacent styles. Yet, there is always a dominant style that rules their decision-making.

Here are a few combinations to expect:

- Director-Analyzers will make decisions quickly and unilaterally but only with backup data.

- Harmonizer-Analyzers or Analyzer-Harmonizers will be more methodical and slower to decide than Director-Analyzers. After all, they must consider as much data as possible, while assuring that everyone is on-board. You must be patient. Very patient.

- The Energizer style combined with a Director component is dangerous. They push hard, then leave the implementation and follow-through effort to others, *demanding* the team produce great results with unclear leadership decision making.

- Energizers mixed with Harmonizer are not dangerous, but never stay with the initiative long enough to see success. This is a pre-condition of languishing initiatives. Great success is unlikely.

- Directors-Harmonizers do not really exist. EICs appearing to emulate this category are most likely acting as Harmonizers as they work a Consultative decision process. Their impatience, however, typically gives them away.

Storytime: An Erroneous Personality Assumption and a Quick Recovery Saves the Day

Late in the day, after delivering a long, one-day sales process and skills workshop concerning how to accelerate the market adoption of an innovation, an attendee approached me.

Here is my recollection of the dialogue.

Attendee: *"I really liked the sales approach you suggested today. It's perfect. I'm the Chief Technology Officer (CTO) at a medical technology company here in town and we just launched a whole new product line – a true healthcare innovation. Our sales team doesn't have a clue about how to sell it. I believe your approach is perfect.*

I'm going to arrange a meeting with our VP of Sales for next week and we're going to show him the light!"

With that, I handed him a business card. He strode out of the room with a determined jaw clench, feeling vindicated. I received a meeting invitation the next day.

No doubt in mind, I tagged the CTO as a Director-Analyzer! A quick decision was assured! I was optimistic.

The CTO, VP of Sales and I participated in the Discovery meeting. The CTO introduced me to the VP of Sales, and following that brief introduction and handshake, the CTO said, "*Jerry, show him what we reviewed last week.*"

Obedient to the desires and style of my Director-Analyzer-Advocate, I began my pitch.

I wish I had taken a photo of the body language and posture of the VP of Sales. He slouched back in his chair leaning to one side, arms folded across his chest, lips clenched tightly together. I knew immediately I was in trouble. I had not lost him – he was never with me. He was not buying into my brilliant approach at all. Nothing seemed to be resonating.

I realized in an instant I had made two errors:

First, this VP of Sales individual was *not* a Director-Analyzer style. I had erroneously assumed that the CTO style was indicative of the general management style and culture of the whole firm. Wrong!

Second, I had failed to let him talk first, after the initial personal introductions. I had violated the Agenda rule. It was obvious I was missing something and had to recover.

After about five minutes I stopped talking, halted the slide show, and took a seat. I realized that this VP of Sales was probably something different than an Analyzer or Director, and I would need a different approach.

I suspected (correctly) that he was a Harmonizer. How and why did I know he had some Harmonizer leanings?

It was an educated guess. My thinking went like this.

The VP of Sales was basically a salesperson. Salespeople typically have more highly developed people skills than engineers, like the CTO.

The next words out of my mouth were, "*I can see this is not resonating with you. I apologize for so quickly jumping into the details. Are there others in the organization that might benefit from seeing this process that the CTO would like you to consider?*"

The VP of Sales reaction was immediate. He unfolded his arms, leaned forward in his chair, put his elbows on the table, looked me in the eyes, and said, *"As a matter of fact, there are. We have a Director of National Sales, a Director of International Sales, a Large Accounts Manager, and a Manager of Internal Sales. They will all be impacted by whatever sales approach we adopt."*

My guess was correct!

Then I asked, *"What benefit do you think there might be in inviting them into this discussion?"*

He responded immediately, *"We're lucky. It's rare, but none of them are travelling today. Let me call and get them to join us."*

They did.

The rest of the meeting was a roundtable discussion, with lots of questions and answers, and little to no slide presentation.

The ultimate results?

- a lucrative engagement to train 50 people over two days in Salt Lake City,

- a follow-on engagement to help the CTO formulate a market strategy for their innovation,

- a corporate buyout that achieved a near 150% business purchase premium based on that strategy,

- a follow-on engagement when the VP of Sales was transferred to Chicago to take over as General Manager of another division,

- two case studies,

- two testimonials,

- a substantial amount of income for me, (they eventually grew to be the 8th largest client in my company's history),

- the birth of several long-term personal friendships, and

- a great story about reading the personality styles of decision makers and adjusting appropriately.

I have used this example for years in blogs, talks, training programs, sales discussions with client prospects, and in two books.

Moral of the Story: Reading the Management Style of the client EIC should influence your approach.

End of story

Decision Maker Influence, Authority, and Affinity (I-A-A)

Contributing decision-makers and decision influencers are not completely understood by Management Style and Personality. There is one additional characteristic that must be discerned to understand decision-making influence, power, and contribution of key people in the client's organization. That characteristic is the person's *Influence*, *Authority*, and *Affinity*, shortened to an individual's I-A-A.

Influence

The degree to which any individual within, or outside of the client's organization (such as a technical specialist, an executive's trusted advisor, a consultant, or a family member) can influence the decision.

I once consulted with a client SMB2B EIC CEO for several years before learning she had a sister who was a partner-owner and behind-the-scenes department manager within the organization. Though the sister had legitimate and equal authority to influence and make decisions, she declined, was never involved, and left all major decisions totally to her EIC CEO sister.

Authority

The degree to which any individual involved in the decision-making process has the Authority, at any time, to make a unilateral decision - whether or not they use that power.

Affinity

The degree to which anyone involved in the evaluation and decision has, for whatever reason, a strong attraction to your offering and approach - an Affinity.

When working and thinking through a sales strategy on a potential engagement, identifying everyone's I-A-A is helpful in informing your action plan.

A typical scoring of these I-A-A characteristics might be 4-3-2. Each is rated on a scale of 1 to 5.

In this example, the 4-3-2 rating reveals that you are dealing with a person who has significant influence on the ultimate decision, who moderately likes your approach or solution, but has virtually no authority to make the ultimate final decision. This indicates your action plan requires a focused effort to educate that person of the value and benefits of your approach. Remember, the first number in the I-A-A rating convention indicates the amount of Influence they have. In this example, it is a lot!

If they become favorably inclined regarding your offering's benefits, you need to help and encourage them to communicate that enhanced appreciation of your approach to the EIC ultimate decision maker - perhaps by offering some tools or support documentation.

Do not stop before following through on that last part. If someone becomes an Advocate of your approach and does not communicate it to the EIC ultimate decision-maker, you have not accomplished anything.

The Approach-to-Business (ATB) of EIC Decision-Makers

Any meaningful sales success must deliver value and a lasting set of benefits to the client, as well as relevant rewards (beyond just your sales commission) for you and your firm. Such relevant rewards might include a long-term and highly satisfied client, an impressive case study, a testimonial, some referrals, and lucrative follow-on business.

Three things facilitate the achievement of this compound success: 1) a high degree of match between compelling need and offering value, 2) the Management Styles and ATB business personalities of the decision makers and decision influencers, and 3) the culture of the client organization. This third factor is largely driven by the second.

It's not likely you will be able to ask your clients to subject themselves to a battery of personality tests before you provide them a proposal or quote. So, salespeople need a quick way to assess EIC ATB business personalities and know how to deal with each.

To accomplish this categorization, I devised an Approach-to-Business (ATB) classification system, using simple observation, for quickly determining the exhibited business-personality types of client executives. It has been tested in practice, and formally with other salespeople from around the country, through talks, training programs, articles, and published blogs. Almost universally, salespeople quickly recognize the following ATB business-personality types within their own experience, sales pipeline, and client base.

And just for clarification:

An ATB business-personality is different than a psychological personality. An ATB Business-Personality describes the approach and behaviors an EIC will exhibit in evaluating alternative approaches to addressing their POG.

You would be correct if, after reading the next few pages, you concluded that the ATB categorization of client EICs would be most helpful in selling service-heavy offerings like professional services, banking, consulting, or information technology support services.

It's Not the EIC Title, It's the ATB Business-Personality

After about ten years in my own consulting business, I conducted an in-depth analysis of my client data. My intent was to discover the common factors that created a mutual, multi-dimensional client-salesperson success.

With those ten years of data, I analyzed industry type, executive title, organization size, business structure, ownership type, type of offering, and deal size - attempting to tie specific factors to mutual buyer-seller economic success. I found no direct correlation to success of any of those factors. However, when I sorted by business-personality of the Executive-in-Charge, the correlation became clear and, in retrospect, obvious.

My conclusion from that analysis:

The best predictor of a deal's long-term mutual success is the ATB business-personality type of the client EIC that is responsible for the specific deal. It's not title, or position, or industry - it's the ATB personality type.

This is so because executives must drive success. Executive personality sets the culture - and an organization's culture drives success.

The salesperson does not have the authority to affect change. The Navigational salesperson can only assess, analyze, diagnose, advise, recommend, propose, and guide. So, even before the engagement begins, understanding the business-personality of the EIC, the prime influencer of the client's organizational culture, is important.

Type 1: The StuMP

StuMP is an acronym for **Stu**ck in the **M**ud **P**erson.

StuMPs are people who will never change. They will never endeavor to improve their company's situation, and never engage or implement offerings that promise to do so. No matter how much evidence is presented of their need, the benefits that might accrue, and the success stories of people like them that have realized those benefits, they remain stubbornly unmoved.

StuMPs have a limited point of view and do not move far from it. Even if you, the salesperson, are convinced beyond any doubt that they need your help and could reap enormous value from your offering, your belief is irrelevant. StuMPs are simply disinclined to attempt and embrace change – and improvement initiatives just seem too risky.

What I am going to say next, will draw down on me the fire and hatred of sales managers everywhere.

Salespeople should not try to convince or educate StuMPs, because StuMPs really do not care.

Politely walk away. Do not persist. Unsolicited proposals will simply frustrate you, while bemusing them. It is futile. Persisting will only result in a lot of wasted emotional and physical energy, time, and build enormous personal frustration.

No matter how convinced you are of their need or the benefit that could be derived from what you offer, you are wasting your time trying to convince a StuMP. If you are lucky, one of your competitors will waste *their* time and energy, while *you* work with higher probability EICs.

Type 2: Takers

Takers know how to take. They take great notes, your time, your materials, your ideas, your concepts, and turn them into their own. Takers use your materials surreptitiously, under the radar, to try to do things themselves or suggest your approaches to your competitors' salespeople to force a price war.

Credit or compensation for your ideas? What ideas?

These prospects are expert at appropriating concepts, ideas, and tools - often asking during preliminary discussions if they can have copies of some of your key implementation documents "*to review with their people*".

Do not go there.

Politely decline by saying:

"I am only showing you these as examples. Every client situation is different, and it would be risky to attempt to apply these to your business until we have had a chance to engage, evaluate your specific situation, and tailor them appropriately."

This type of buyer is a particular curse when selling offerings that have a significantly higher consulting service component in them.

Type 3: The Opportunist

Opportunists want to purchase the minimum, bare bones package of offerings. Their hope is that purchasing the minimum level might be just enough to generate great results. Their expectation is "first class" results from an "economy-level" investment.

In these circumstances, follow-through to success is rare, since they do not have the expertise required to execute.

Quite often the Opportunist will start many small projects simultaneously, or in quick succession, as their opportunistic attempts start and stutter to a stall. They will lose interest quickly if results are not immediate or significant, or if it seems like too much effort.

For high service content offerings (law, engineering, design, construction, software development, information technology, consulting, training et al), Opportunists will almost universally inquire about purchasing just small starter, kick-off or "train-the-trainer" projects and try to seduce you into a scope-creep trap with the promise of bigger deals to come.

Type 4: Boss-Made-Me-Do-Its (BMMDIs, *pronounced "Bim-Me-Dees"*)

BMMDIs are the political hangers-on of the corporate world. They provide lip service and public support for an improvement initiative but rarely exhibit sincere enthusiasm. This is particularly prominent if the implementation of your offering has the likelihood of revealing weaknesses in their own capabilities, department, or function.

They may engage, feigning commitment, but only long enough to minimally satisfy the EIC. If the EIC's attention goes elsewhere, the effort will die on the vine – as will success.

BMMDIs have no personal commitment or belief in your solution.

They may even engage in "Lipotage™" – lip service in public, followed by indifference, or worse, verbal sabotage in private. The word "Lipotage" was coined and trademarked by my friend and colleague Bob Phillips and his co-author Larry Johnson in their book "Absolute Honesty", AMACOM 2003.

A particularly hopeless combination is a BMMDI project manager with an Opportunist EIC.

Type 5: The Terribly Troubled (TTs)

TTs really need help fast and are willing to quickly commit to addressing their serious problems. Their level of pain is high, as is their motivation to fix the problem quickly. They may research alternatives but will decide quickly. To them, every challenge is a compelling need. They are typically in a rush to get started and consequently may miss some alternatives – but they _will_ move forward.

Spend quality time with these prospects to ensure they understand what will need to be done (deliverables), what will be required for success (commitment), the time that will be required to see the improvement they desire (scope), and how you will work with their team to fix the problem (collaborative approach). Use exceptional levels of reassurance to ease their antsy-ness, discomfort, and encourage their patience.

The good news is, they typically have a high sense of urgency. It just needs to be managed for both your benefit and theirs.

Plan and sequence the problems they are facing. Bring calm, organization, and reassurance to the deal.

Type 6: Frustrated Drivers (FDs)

FDs can be very intense and quick in studying alternatives. Often, these are EICs that have inherited a family business or taken over the reins from an overly controlling or "old-fashioned" leader – perhaps even a StuMP.

They may have been waiting a long time for the opportunity to take the helm of the corporate ship, tighten the rigging, and straighten things out. Their drive and motivation are high. They usually have a good understanding of the organization's weak points, the resources and commitment needed to close performance gaps revealed in the pre-engagement discovery or assessment.

Upon commitment to your solution, they will drive for quick, visible results. They want to make their mark.

Establishing well-defined, clear goals, benchmarks, check points, milestones, and progress measurements will help FDs satiate their sense of urgency. Communicate frequently, clearly, and succinctly. Emphasize speed, drive for quick traction, and show measurable results.

Type 7: Sincerely Growth-Oriented (SGOs)

SGOs are committed to growth for the long term. These are clients that readily recognize that their organization and business have root cause issues to resolve and long-term challenges to meet. As such, SGOs demonstrate a sincere and strong desire and commitment to improve.

An ideal type of client, they understand and are motivated by performance excellence, thriving on achieving goals and constantly improving basic business processes. They are the best-of-the-best clients, intellectually, emotionally, and financially. If you consistently deliver high value to them through your offerings, SGOs will remain loyal for a long time and continue to reward you with new business and referrals to their EIC peers – inside and outside their company.

Type 8: Don Quixotes or DQs (aka Dreamers)

Imagine Don Quixote, the idealist and self-imagined white-knight savior. At times DQs may appear out of touch with reality. These Dreamers are lofty in their vision and motivation, perhaps even narcissistic and charismatic. Impulsive, easily distracted, and occasionally misdirected, they struggle to remain focused.

Based on their history of failed past "programs-du-jour" and organizational reputation for impulsiveness, Don Quixotes are typically challenged in generating organizational enthusiasm, buy-in and support. Their grandiose visions of the corporate future are rarely realistic or realized. They speak with unbridled enthusiasm but show little interest in getting deeply involved in the details of execution. They rarely get their hands dirty in implementation and do not follow-through. Client Dreamers, or Don Quixotes, rarely worry about such details.

In the words of General Colin Powell, "A dream does not become reality through magic; it takes sweat and hard work."

Do not look to this Don Quixote ATB type for heroic effort, effective leadership, decisions, details - or to earn any medals for bravery.

Business Personality to Profit: The Impact of Client ATB

According to our research, in terms of the highest long-term economic value for all concerned, Terribly Troubled (TTs), Frustrated Drivers (FDs), and Sincerely Growth Oriented (SGOs) generated the most meaningful successes by an order of magnitude over the other ATB types.

Remember, these three ATB business personality types, the Terribly Troubled, Frustrated Driver and Sincerely Growth Oriented, are highly motivated to move the needle of change and drive for improvement in the way things are done within their firm. Your offering, therefore, needs to be presented in the light of making that happen.

My own research revealed that these types, over the long term, generated more than 20 times the total revenue and 10 times larger individual deals, than the other EIC ATB types.

When you get in front of an EIC and the executive discussions begin, do not become so focused on the problem at hand, that you forget to observe the telltale signs of a business personality, namely the executive's ATB.

Reading the executive's approach to business (ATB) is as important as establishing trust. Correctly reading an EIC's ATB helps the salesperson identify and use language that will resonate in communications and proposals. Keep your eyes and ears open for the signs of your client EIC ATB. Walk their walk. Talk their talk.

While successes are very much related to a client's ATB characteristics, understanding an EIC's Management Style and the I-A-A of decision-influencers reveals additional valuable information. Most salespeople learn, early in their careers, that an early and accurate personality read of a client, can make a huge difference in the success of a client engagement.

Understanding people and what makes them tick and behaving congruent with those personality characteristics in your dealings with them, enhances trust.

Quick Reads of Management Styles and ATB Traits

Here are a few simple and easy-to-observe tips for quickly reading EIC types:

- If you enter an EIC's office, with no one else participating in the discussion, and Key Performance Indicator (KPI) charts and project schedules are on the wall, you are likely be dealing with a Director ATB type.

- If the EIC insists on asking many other people to participate in a Discovery Meeting, you might be dealing with a Harmonizer.

- If your Discovery Meeting is with an EIC that speaks in grandiose terms of a future and never shuts up long enough for you to ask questions, you may be dealing with a Don Quixote or Energizer – particularly if you can't establish any follow-on actions or commitments.

- If in the EICs office you observe many books, engineering degrees and process charts on the walls, and lots of sketches on the whiteboard, you may be dealing with an Analyzer.

- If you observe impatience and a furrowed brow on the face of the EIC you may be dealing with a Terribly Troubled.

- If you observe severe intensity on the face of the EIC, and the discussion is enthusiastic (with the EIC leaning forward), you may be dealing with a Frustrated Driver.

- If you have a calm, and obviously sincere discussion with a successful EIC you may be dealing with a Sincerely Growth Oriented individual – the best of the best client.

As Yogi Berra, the great New York Yankee catcher is purported to have said,

"You can observe a lot, just by watching."

*****

Chapter 9: Solution Formulation

In this Chapter …

The Objective of the Solution Formulation Stage

Strategizing the Win: Making the Time to Think

The Discussion Summary: Your Solution Proposal Roadmap

The Objectively Targeted Solution (OTS): What a client wants vs. what they need

Connecting to the Client's Vision

Solution Formulation Checklist

A Reality Check

The Objective of the Solution Formulation Stage

The efforts of the salesperson and their support team during this sales stage, must be dedicated to architecting an economically sound, bounded, relevant, and thorough solution for the client to consider and ideally buy. By meeting the client's challenges, overcoming their barriers, or providing a pathway to a meaningful growth opportunity, the solution must clearly be perceived by the client as providing meaningful value.

Solution Formulation involves crafting an approach to meeting the client's needs, which may at times, require a tailored blending of capabilities, skills, talents, and assets - yours, your internal team's, your alliance partners', and the client's. As the lead salesperson, you must compose, orchestrate, and conduct a solution symphony

- an offering, proposal, and implementation plan that both the client's ultimate decision maker, the EIC, and your internal management team can approve.

Strategizing the Win: Making the Time to Think

Salespeople, as a class, are an action-oriented lot.

Ask any salesperson, and you will likely discover they prefer to be out and about chasing down and meeting with prospects and clients, rather than sitting at their desk doing the computer equivalent of paperwork, shuffling administrative tasks, or just thinking.

I have found that many salespeople, even some of the highest performers, are notoriously delinquent at filing their expense reports, terrible at written communications, criminally undisciplined at keeping their CRM pipeline management system updated, and continually grumbling about the time demands of in-office administrative obligations. In their eyes, if an activity is not perceived as directly and positively impacting their ability to talk with a prospective or current client, it simply doesn't deserve priority status.

It is as if there are only two alternative universes: doing something constructive *outside* of the office or doing something non-productive and restrictive *inside* the office. In the salesperson's mind, the former helps them succeed, the latter restricts their success. They perceive activity and motion synonymous with progress.

The truth is the best place to navigate their success is between their ears. That's the place where the most productive action plans originate. Keeping with the Navigational Selling™ theme, captains, navigators, and sailors don't just jump on the ship, set the sails and head out to sea. They plan and prepare for every journey.

Strategic thinking during the Solution Formulation stage increases sales productivity, saves time in the long run, produces the highest degree of success, and, because it is inclusive of Discovery, delivers the highest perceived value to the client.

So, make the time to think through your best action plans and find someone to help you do that.

The Buddy System: Two Brains are Better than One

You may find that formulating an opportunity strategy alone, in the solitude of your office or favorite coffee shop, is comfortable. But is it effective?

I am a firm believer that two good minds are better than one. The additional perspective and attention to detail keeps you honest and improves outcomes. Having an established "buddy" system produces the best results. In such an arrangement, you and a peer mutually review each other's target account strategies and solutions.

Be selective - pick someone who is insightful, experienced, detail oriented, damned smart, and not afraid to tell you what they think - and why.

In the early days of computer programming, development teams adopted a "buddy" system to validate and speed up software coding. The process was called "code-reading". One person would hand a printed copy of the code to a buddy, then read aloud the code instructions they had written to perform a software function. The "buddy" would critique it, pointing out gaps, alternative ways to code a specific operation, or fundamental flaws in the algorithm. It significantly improved the early discovery of errors in code, sped-up debugging, and accelerated the production of fully functional code blocks.

An opportunity-review buddy can have the same positive impact on a salesperson's productivity. I highly recommend you find someone internal to your organization to be your opportunity review buddy. If you need a buddy that does not work for your firm, because there is no one that fits the bill internally, you should exchange formal client confidentiality agreements with that person – or otherwise assure that the information you share will not be used to the detriment of either your firm or your target opportunity client. And do not share unnecessary target client proprietary information.

If you have an important proposal to win with a first-time client, find a buddy and schedule a target account strategy and solution formulation work session. It will not only help you, but also continually refresh your mind with all the things that need to be aligned when proposing.

The Discussion Summary: Your Solution Proposal Roadmap

The solution proposal is carefully crafted from the raw information you gleaned during the Discovery step. Proposals should clearly comprehend any issues, management style observations, or considerations any decision maker or decision influencer may have revealed during Discovery.

I liken the client's review of a proposal as similar to a look at a high school class photo.

Most people when they search their high school class photo, look for themselves first - glossing over all other classmates with, perhaps, the exception of their high school sweetheart. (Just sayin'.)

The client's key decision makers and decision influencers must be able to easily identify and recognize themselves in your solution proposal. It must, therefore, incorporate their needs, their issues, their challenges, their management styles, and their desired outcomes.

The Sales Game is Won or Lost in Discovery

If you have not done a good job in the Discovery phase, how in the world will you be able to craft a solution and formulate a tailored proposal that meets the needs of all those involved in the client's decision?

It is nearly impossible to Discover absolutely everything. However, the more detailed the information you capture, the greater your probability of success. Your solution-proposal must provide enough insight, that when the client reads through it, decision makers and influencers are struck by two reflexive and important thoughts:

> First Thought: "*Great! They have included the things that are important to me, my role, and both my personal and business needs and goals.*"

> Second Thought: "*Wow! These guys are good! They are comprehensive and thorough. I can trust them.*"

These combined thoughts will implant within the mind of the reader, that the solution offered is both *low risk* – and more importantly in *their best interest*.

Don't Bother Proposing If…

If you have *not* done a good job in the Discovery phase, do not bother to formulate a solution until you have a substantial amount of the important situational information understood. Those key pieces of information include:

- the degree to which your scoring of the *qualification criteria is validated* through Discovery and confirmation of the client's perception,

- the client's *decision-making process* (its steps, timing, authorization levels and functional contributors),

- the client *decision makers and key decision influencers*, and the degree to which they will effectively execute their roles in the decision process,

- their *Management Styles, I-A-A, and ATB* (detailed in Chapter 8),

- their business, personal, and role-related *needs, and goals*, and how they will be impacted by addressing their problem, opportunity, or gap,

- close alignment of the significant positive *value-quotient* they will realize by addressing their POG with your approach, and

- their perception of *your firm's ability to deliver* what they need.

At this point in the sales process, it is worthwhile to pause your headlong rush to deliver a proposal, to assess what you truly do and do not know.

How do you do that?

With three tools, your thorough client-validated Discussion Summary, your personal Discovery Meeting notes, and the checklist above. Use these three tools, to test what you know and do not know.

If, after comparing your Discovery Meeting Notes and Discussion Summary against the checklist, you are missing key pieces of information, think like Detective Columbo – the shrewd television detective whose famous catchphrase was *"Just one more thing."* Contact your client Advocate or EIC, and open the conversation by asking, *"Could you answer just a few more questions before I begin to craft a proposal for you and your team to consider? I want to be sure I haven't missed anything."*

Then ask the important questions that fill in the gaps.

Storytime: All Clients Don't Really Have Precisely the Same Motivations. Do They?

While working with a client through a sales pipeline review, the chief salesperson for a particular target market (a new hire) began to review the sales strategy worksheets for each of his major pipeline opportunities.

After the fourth such worksheet, I noticed that the client decision criteria were all precisely the same – in the same order of importance. So, I asked how that could be. It seemed remarkable to have multiple clients using precisely the same decision criteria listed in identical order – even if they *are* in the same market segment. Had he asked each client EIC and received precisely the same response?

He confessed that he had not specifically asked the question of the decision makers and influencers at these companies. Rather, he relied on his deep industry knowledge and experience. He was confident that without asking, he knew how they would make their decisions.

I hope you recognize the intellectual arrogance and Discovery sloppiness of such a statement. Ultimately, despite his in-depth industry knowledge, claimed insights, and the stuffed Rolodex of contact names he had compiled over 30+ years in the industry, he did not succeed.

Moral of the Story: Assume nothing. Confirm everything.

End of story

The Post-Discovery Test Question

If you have confidence that you have discovered all the essential information needed to propose a strong solution, prior to actually sitting down to write the proposal, you can test the probability of its success by asking the following question of the client EIC.

If I provided a proposal that covered the objectives and needs documented in the Discussion Summary, what if any barriers would remain to get it approved?

An enthusiastic, encouraging response confirms a strong, emotional, but not binding commitment on the part of the client. This is the time for a handshake and immediate move to crafting a proposal. A hesitant, negative response provides the salesperson an opportunity to elicit additional or overlooked decision considerations or test the perceived value of what you have discussed.

By this time in the process, you and the client should have already aligned around the perceived magnitude of the value the client will receive from your solution, and a close estimate of the financial commitment required on their part to receive that value.

There should be no surprises when the client sees the proposal. No one likes surprises.

The Objectively Targeted Solution (OTS): What a Client Wants vs. What They Need

Good salespeople must be recognized as experts in their field, by both the client and the firm that employs them. Such expertise reinforces the *Trust Formula* and facilitates the client decision-making process through open, collaborative, and creative dialogue.

A salesperson that is not an expert in their field, will struggle to craft sound and creative solutions. Yet, even solutions offered by the most experienced and creative salesperson, cannot ignore what the client believes they need. Talented salespeople must learn how to blend an *Objectively Targeted Solution* (OTS) with what clients say they explicitly want.

An Objectively Targeted Solution (OTS) is a solution crafted from the combination of the salesperson's expertise, creativity, and objective problem assessment efforts. Those efforts reveal what is necessary to solve the client's root problems, overcome their real challenge, or help them capture their unrealized opportunity.

It is not uncommon that a creative, well-crafted OTS is *not* embraced by the client, even though it is diagnostically sound and in their best interest. Here are some reasons for that reluctance:

- they don't understand the OTS,

- they don't perceive enough value in the OTS,

- they are looking only to overcome symptoms, not root causes,

- they are laboring under a preconception of what they "think" they need, and your OTS appears to be a distraction and off-target,

- they have been convinced (by an internal influencer, advisor, or competitor), that a faster fix is available, one that requires less financial investment and commitment of their personal time, or

- they believe they do not have the time or funding for an extensive evaluation effort, or investment in this one problem.

The simplest way around this dilemma is to incorporate within your solution, *both* what the client wants and what the client needs. However, that is not always possible for a few reasons:

- *Insufficient Funding.* The client does not have access to sufficient funds for both,

- *Dangerous or Harmful.* What the client wants is, unbeknownst to them, dangerous or harmful, or

- *Misdirected Solution.* What the client wants will simply not address the problem, overcome the barrier, or enable realization of the opportunity.

The skilled salesperson must anticipate such situations and develop approaches for handling each circumstance. Several such approaches follow.

Insufficient Funding

Insufficient Funding situations are typically handled in two ways - by dropping the price or fragmenting the deliverables into phases. Neither of these are necessarily the best or wisest approach.

The best way to overcome the insufficient funding barrier is *not* to drop the price or reduce deliverables. Rather, it is important to do a better job of communicating the disproportionate value to be gained by the client from the OTS. That approach is called *Value Quotient Clarification*.

Economically, the OTS should be able to deliver to the client a minimum of 3X its client-borne economic costs to implement. Emotional, political, physical, and social value contributions are tough to translate into economic impact – but deliver client value none-the-less. When considering how to overcome funding limit barriers, don't overlook these impacts on decision makers, decision influencers and other client stakeholders. Share those perspectives with the client.

If Value Quotient Clarification does not work, then the second best and acceptable way to meet the available funding barrier is to fall back to fragmenting the solution into affordable phases.

For example: In a project like a solar installation, the first phase might be a design and simulation project. Phase Two might be assistance in accessing credit. Phase Three might be the solar generation installation, and Phase Four, the implementation of battery backup systems to assure power continuity for power outage situations.

The final approach of dropping the price to overcoming the insufficient funding barrier should only be considered if the first two approaches have been unsuccessful. It should be the absolute, very last resort.

Dangerous or Harmful

Potentially dangerous or harmful situations likely to result from the client's preference for solution, need to be handled by either walking away, politely declining or communicating the dangers explicitly in writing and offering what is needed.

Doctors must first do no harm. Salespeople also should do no harm. Winning a deal that ultimately results in negative or disastrous consequences for the client is not a win – even if you receive your commission check. It's an ethical breach, self-destructive to your firm's brand image and reputation, a liability risk, and sometimes illegal.

Is your commission check for that sale really worth the risk?

Misdirected Solutions

A client may harbor pre-conceived notions of what they sincerely believe will solve the problem - and ask for it specifically. If the salesperson knows, based on both experience and science, that the client-requested solution won't work, there is an ethical obligation to explain and explicitly communicate that to the client.

A doctor would not be acting ethically if they only treated patients with what the patient requested as treatment. The doctor should only consider the option of requested treatment if there is scientific evidence that the treatment will help, and diagnostic testing reveals appropriate indication.

So, the third approach to dealing with the insufficient funding situation, is to decline the opportunity if the consequence to the client or the seller of accepting it, even at a lower price point, would be negative.

Connecting Your Solution to the Client's Vision

As we will see in the discussion of Proposals in the next chapter, promising achievement of a client's Vision is risky. On the other hand, establishing a dependency connection between your solution and the client's Vision is extremely helpful. Therefore, it is important to frame your solution in the context of the client's vision. The client must understand that connection, its implications, and the enabling power of your solution to achievement of their vision.

It is highly unlikely your solution will be able to deliver and achieve the client's complete vision – but it can and should enable its achievement.   Visions are amorphous, imprecise, and their achievement is largely out of the control of the seller. Achievement of a Vision is an unreasonable deliverable to promise. However, it is important to communicate how a client EIC's vision of their future will be enabled by, and depend on, the successful implementation of your solution.

In the SMB2B world, when communicating to the members of the client's decision-making team, you must explicitly connect the dots between your solution and achievement of the client's vision. Your words should inspire individual commitment and trigger positive personal emotional responses.

Everyone on the client's decision-making team should be able to connect the solution you have proposed to the ultimate achievement of the improved vision-of-the-future they desire. The proposal should establish and communicate that connection.

But what if the client doesn't have a Vision?

In that case you have two options, help them craft one, or ignore it completely and simply offer a solution unconnected to any bigger picture. If you elect the former, you can collaborate with the client to craft one, but not promise its delivery.

Assisting the Client in Crafting the Vision

Vision-painting is powerful. It must be used wisely and ethically.

Some of the most successful leaders in history had an uncanny ability to communicate a vision of the future to their followers. The most effective military, religious, political, sports, business, and community leaders who wish to garner the support and commitment of their followers, begin with a Vision.

Presidents Abraham Lincoln and John F Kennedy knew the motivational power of a vision. Lincoln created a vision of the preservation of the Union and Kennedy of being the first country to visit and explore the moon. But Bernie Madoff and Harold Hill also motivated their followers with a vision – with quite different motivations and impacts. Bernie Madoff created an investment scam based on wealthy investors desire for more money – aka greed. His scam collapsed, costing his investors millions. He was eventually indicted, found guilty and imprisoned.

But "*Who was Harold Hill*", you ask?

Storytime: Professor Harold Hill - The Unethical Spellbinder

Harold Hill was the fictional, phony, early 1900's music professor of Meredith Wilson's Broadway show, *The Music Man*.

Hill was a spellbinder.

His scam was to convince townspeople in small midwestern towns, that purchasing musical instruments (from him of course), and allowing him to shape their children into a Boys Band would preserve and protect the idyllic, safe environment of their lovely hometown. Involvement in a band would protect the town's children from the evils presented by the presence of the newly installed pool table at the billiard hall.

To trigger the scam, he crafted a rousing vision of the threats presented by the existence of a pool table in the community and delivered that message to a crowd of citizens in the town square. Responsible loving parents would never allow their children to fritter their time away hanging around the pool hall and being exposed to the evil habits and conversation of slumming pool players.

He then contrasted that negative vision with one of pure, healthy, and uncorrupted children making their parents proud by playing musical instruments and performing in a community band – a stark contrast to the horrible consequences of pool. You can go to YouTube and find a video of his 5-minute *"Ya Got Trouble"* sales pitch to the townspeople.

When the musical instruments were delivered, before he could be expected to actually train the band, he'd leave town in the middle of the night to avoid being revealed (and punished) as a fraud.

In the video clip, Hill's speech illustrates both the effectiveness and misuse of vision crafting. The clip is lighthearted and entertaining - yet delivers a powerful lesson on both the importance of vision-crafting in sales and its unethical use.

Moral of the Story: Honesty and ethics in communicating a vision are important and effective sales skills to develop. On the flip side, not delivering the outcomes a vision promises, can produce harmful and potentially illegal consequences.

End of Story

Vision Connecting Words

Here are some examples of vision-connecting words and phrases that might be meaningful to decision makers (EICs) and decision influencers:

Vision Connecting Words and Phrases Relevant to B2B Client EICs and Business Owners

- growth (both top-line and earnings),
- flywheel impact,
- leverage,
- increased economic value of the business,
- reward for all their hard work and investment of their time and money,
- development of key personnel,
- brand impact,
- reduced personal, physical, and emotional burden,
- ease of recruiting and retaining talent,
- asset leverage,
- reduced costs,
- reduced stress,
- family impact,
- legacy,

- productivity improvements,

- trust,

- team (or key individual) capability growth,

- cycle time / inventory turns, and

- cash flow.

Of course, not all words and phrases apply to all situations, but the higher the relevance to the vision, the higher the probability of a win.

Vision Connecting Words and Phrases Relevant to B2B Client Decision Influencers:

- increased bonus,

- opportunity for leadership,

- leading-edge technology learning opportunity,

- easier selling,

- recognition,

- personal growth,

- career enhancement,

- competitive advantage,

- opportunity to increase personal skills, experience, and capabilities,

- peer recognition,

- reduced pressure,

- high-value learning experience,

- team support,

- collaboration, and

- visibility.

Storytime: Leveraging Early-Adopter Client Pioneers

I worked with a client that had developed a truly innovative software offering. Few potential clients within the target market had such a solution, and the productivity and economic benefits to clients were significant. Eventually all companies in the target market segment would need to install such a productivity enhancement solution to remain competitive in their markets.

The key decision influencer and implementer within the typical client company was likely to be the client's IT manager, though the ultimate approval authority would likely remain with the client's division EIC.

While not a selling feature, being one of the first technologists to implement this type of solution would provide the IT manager with a significant boost in career experience. As the need and benefits of this software innovation grew in the marketplace, IT managers with that experience would be sought after by other companies wanting to realize the same set of benefits. The open-market value of the IT implementer would be significantly enhanced.

On successful system deployment, my client let it be known they were looking for early adopters to share their experience in technical forums and trade shows. The software company would pay travel and lodging for the IT manager's participation. The suggestion, however, had to be held in abeyance until a client company had made a commitment and complete successful installation. To offer the public exposure opportunity prematurely ran the risk of tripping the wire of ethical breach.

Moral of the Story: A breakthrough learning opportunity may resonate with decision influencers for reasons of their career enhancement, but those *individual* benefits may not add to the value received by the client firm.

End of Story

Your solution must imply that it will enable achievement of a relevant vision – both to EICs and decision influencers. The solution must be perceived as an important stepping-stone in achieving that vision. The words and phrases above can crystallize a vision and make it personally relevant.

Remember: Act ethically in all cases when identifying and communicating "resonating" vision motivators for individual decision makers and decision influencers.

The Solution Formulation Checklist

When formulating a solution, here is a helpful checklist:

☐ Does the solution include a *clear, common understanding between you and the client*, of the approach and what the client will consider success? How will you and the client know when that success has been achieved?

In some cases, success may simply be that the product you proposed is delivered to their door. In other cases, success may include that the product is delivered and installed. In yet a further extension of the definition of success, it may include an in-situ operational test prior to the final invoice being paid.

In my early career in engineering, when we procured automated equipment, we would not consider implementation a success until the equipment was tested on our manufacturing floor and had proven its ability to achieve its targeted production rates with consistent quality.

Only then would we pay the final invoice.

The definition of success varies widely by product or service. But more important than what it includes, is whether what it includes is mutually understood and agreed to by you and the client – in writing.

☐ Have you included in the solution, the considerations and needs of all the key decision influencers and decision makers? Have you expressed those considerations in the words and styles they will resonate with?

Remember that each of the key decision makers and influencers may have a different ATB, Management Style, title, role, I-A-A, concerns, and other explicit and implicit considerations. They need to see themselves and their considerations in the proposed solution.

☐ Have you explicitly articulated the Value Quotient?

In the automated equipment example cited in our first checkpoint above, the economic component to the Value Quotient is relatively straightforward to calculate. Typically, an anticipated economic benefit projection must be calculated and approved by the client's management team - before the request is approved for funding.

In contrast, emotional, social, physical, and political benefits can only be described qualitatively. Nonetheless, they should not be left out or ignored.

You may ask, "*How in the world can a salesperson discern the degree of each of these non-economic value quotient factors?*"

First, you can *observe closely and listen carefully* to the words the client decision makers and influencers use.

If during the Discovery phase, some of the decision-making team expressed frustration with the continual work-burden placed on them by old, slow, and unreliable equipment, then the elimination of those emotional, physical, and social discomforts should be included in the solution description.

Second, the salesperson can ask directly – the way a nurse a or a doctor might when they ask you if you are in pain.

Medical staff typically ask a question like, "*On a scale from 1 to 10, how would you rate your current pain level?*"

In assessing the *Emotional* contribution of the client's value quotient, the salesperson might ask, "*On a scale of 1 to 10, with 10 being the highest, how strong are your feelings about how the problem is personally impacting you?*".

In assessing the *Political* impact of the decision, the salesperson might ask, "*On a scale of 1 to 10, how politically-charged is the need to find a good solution?*"

Of course, decision makers and decision influencers will not likely share their internal feelings with you unless they trust you. They must feel you are asking in order to find an optimum solution. So, we revert back to the Trust Formula (Chapter 5).

The salesperson must have established a deep trust with the decision makers and influencers to be able to elicit the deeper hidden emotional, social, and political impacts associated with the client's need to solve a problem, meet a challenge, or avail themselves of an opportunity. Trust is the foundation.

In formulating your proposal, you must be careful to include the social, political, emotional, and physical points of the value quotient in such a way that they resonate with those relevant decision makers, while also being careful not to violate any privacy, confidentiality, or trust.

☐ Milestones: Have you and the client agreed on the timing of the project and its major milestones? If so, those milestones must be included in the proposal.

☐ Team / Roles / Expectations: Have you and the client agreed on the roles, contributions, and expectations of both you and members of the client's team assigned to the project or deal?

☐ Pricing: Have you included a clear explanation of the product prices and service fees? Is the payment schedule clear? Are the invoicing schedule, payable due dates, and cancellation fees explicit?

A Reality Check

I am not so naïve to believe that, as you read through this check list, you are not overwhelmed by the thought of considering all these details for each opportunity in your sales pipeline. The recommendation will likely elicit something like, "*He's nuts! It's impossible to invest this much effort in every individual opportunity.*"

If you think that, you might be surprised to know I agree.

Such recommendations are intended for opportunities that: 1) represent a major client opportunity, 2) are extremely competitive, 3) are needed to save a long-term client relationship, 4) offer high leverage, or 5) are deemed crucial for some other reason.

It is unlikely that all of this will be required if, for example, a current client requests you to extend your service contract for something that has already been delivered and achieved its objectives. In such a case, the checklist can be significantly reduced. However, to capture meaningful changes in the client's situation that might require adjustment or addition, you might consider doing a re-Discovery.

On the other hand, the opportunity for a first big win of a highly visible, highly leverageable deal in a new target market, compels you to do everything you can to win. That will not likely be accomplished with a simple price and delivery quote. If this is the situation, use the checklist.

*****

Chapter 10: The Proposal

In this Chapter …

Quote vs. Proposals

Contents of a Good Proposal

The Client Situation Summary

Statement of Work and Deliverables

The Approach (optional)

The Client's Expectations of Success (optional)

Responsibilities of the Client

Key Personnel Bios (optional)

Pricing & Fees

The Signature Block

Increasing Sales Productivity - The Correct Way

A *Proposal* is the formal documentation of an offer to work with the client to achieve their objective or goal, utilizing the products, services, and capabilities of the salesperson's firm. If the proposal is signed by both the client and the salesperson's EIC, it is binding. While typically not as complex as a Contract, a proposal should have a standard yet flexible format, and in its standard form, be reviewed by an attorney so that it can be re-used and tailored as needed.

A well-crafted proposal is _not_ intended to act as a hard-sell document. It should not be used as your last chance to promote and make closing arguments to convince the client of the brilliance of your solution. Rather, the proposal should be considered a final organizing document that compiles and delineates the specifics that have _already been identified in Discovery, documented in the Discussion Summary, and confirmed with the client_.

Ideally, proposals organize and memorialize what you and the client have already reached a mutual understanding about. A proposal summarizes what they need, the products and/or services that will be delivered, the client objectives and desired outcomes of the delivery and implementation of those products and support services, and the cost.

A proposal should trigger no surprises.

Based on thorough Discovery, collaboration between the client and the salesperson, and previous agreement regarding needs and approach, at this point the proposal should be moving forward - not stalled by a challenge in the final authorization loop. If it _is_ challenged, the salesperson missed something or someone important during the Discovery stage.

Every extra minute the salesperson invests in building trust, discovering the value quotients of the client's decision makers and influencers, understanding the client decision-making process, and pre-testing the client's response to the solution as it will be articulated in the proposal, will save hours of re-work, and grease the skids of approval.

It's only when the salesperson receives an affirmative response to the post-discovery question identified previously, and again below, should they take keyboard in hand and formulate a proposal.

"If we provided a proposal that covered the objectives and needs documented in the Discussion Summary, what barriers would you anticipate to signing it?"

After an answer of "_none_" to that question, the ultimate decision maker's signature should simply be an administrative act.

Quotes vs. Proposals

In a misguided and false belief that it saves time and speeds the win, some companies and salespeople will request the bare minimum from their internal support organization in crafting an offer to a client. That request results in a single-page quote that only offers the _lowest price possible_ and _fastest delivery_.

Such an approach is common among piece-part and component manufacturers that view the act of sales as a repetitive two-step dance: 1) receive an RFQ from a purchasing manager, and 2) respond quickly with a quote for the fastest delivery and lowest price possible. This one-page quote routine (OPQR) has worked well-enough and generated enough success for many older, established businesses to thrive.

But we are not talking about this type of business in this book. In Navigational Selling™ we are talking about businesses that need to sell complex, service-intense offerings, that address significant client POGs, with multiple decision makers and influencers in the loop. It is an environment characterized by:

- multiple decision-makers and technical decision influencers within the client organization,

- offerings that have a significant variation associated with their delivery, requiring varying degrees of tailoring, customization, implementation, integration, and service,

- clients who have matured to the degree they understand and may require consideration of more factors than just price and delivery, and

- other considerations that might include quality audits, environmental considerations, inventory management, reliability and integrity of the supply chain, an approach to implementation, systems integration, track record of the implementation team, collaboration in solution development, and more.

These considerations are impossible to incorporate into a single page quote. Moreover, incorporating such considerations as a proposal instead of a quote, may strongly differentiate your offering.

Storytime: Breaking the Chains of Old Habits

A client that produced custom precision metal parts wanted to find a way to grow their business faster in the highly competitive Midwest market. That region was awash with suppliers of metal parts, mostly servicing the automotive 2nd tier supplier market. The client was frustrated with the too frequent cycle of "quote and lose" to a larger competitor. They wanted to find a way to break through.

By transitioning to a proposal format for major opportunities, instead of a one-page quote, they broke out of their old paradigm and differentiated themselves. They won - against numerous larger, better established, tough competitors. Their proposals added considerations such as case studies, design concepts, quality assurance, key employee resumes, and clarity about the process they would be using to assure collaboration, progress, and design integrity along the way.

Shortly after the engagement, I received this unsolicited email comment.

"Wanted to let you know that we just won a HUGE program that alone will increase our annual revenue by 20%. We incorporated numerous techniques from the previous proposals that we worked on with you. This was an extremely competitive situation with 10 bidders and ultimately, "we knocked their socks off". Not sure we would have won this had we submitted this proposal using the same approach we used prior…"

Moral of the Story: Well-crafted proposals within a price-and-delivery habit market can differentiate and impress the toughest of clients.

End of Story

Given the complexity of a typical multi-person, multi-personality, multi-management style, multi-need, multi-role, client decision process, orchestrating winning solutions takes thought and testing before firing off a simple price-and-delivery quote.

Competitive Reality: Avoiding the Hard-Sell in a Proposal

Regarding restraining oneself from hard selling in a proposal, you would be justified in questioning how it is possible when, at times, competition is so intense. This could occur when a client has informed you that they have put a problem solution out for bid or have started discussions with several providers to assure they look at all their options and select the best.

The strictest form of a bidding process is in government contracts. In such a process there is typically a requirements document, a call for proposals delivered to all interested bidders, followed by a formal question-and-answer session to which all interested bidders are invited. Such a process is employed in an attempt to provide a level playing field for all bidders, assure ethical behavior, and provide ethical and legal cover for government employees.

But we are not addressing government contracts. Rather we are selling to B2B companies, who largely have a less complex and less rigid vendor assessment and selection process than government entities. This allows ample time and access to individual decision-makers for pre-proposal questioning and discovery.

In such a case your competitively advantaged position and solution will have been established before the client receives your proposal. The strength of that position will be built on the following foundational factors:

- the depth and effectiveness of your *Discovery* process, including the *Discussion Summary*,

- your thoroughness in conducting, analyzing, and sharing the results of any *Client Self-Assessments*,

- how well you have established *Trust*,

- how well you have *Qualified* the opportunity,

- how well you have understood the *Decision-Makers* and *Decision-Influencers* (their needs, personalities, approaches to business and management styles),

- the strength and credibility of your *Referral*,

- your ability to deliver *Insights* on the client's challenge, exemplified in original articles and talks produced by *Thought Leaders* in your firm,

- your communication and explanation of clear, relevant *Differentiation*, revealed during the Discovery stage, that positions your solution as the *RPQL* (Relative Perceived Quality Leader) in your field,

- your demonstrated historical successes with challenges similar to that of the client - validated through *Case Studies*, *References*, and *Testimonials*,

- your bullpen of experienced *Technical and Service Talent*,

- your *Methodology* for solution delivery, and

- your primary interest in resolving the *client's POG vis-à-vis your own self-interest*,

In essence, you must collaboratively architect your winning solution before producing and delivering your proposal, whether it's a multi-vendor evaluation bidding process, or an individual journey. If you have done a good job on this list, there is no need for a hard sell within the body of the proposal.

Contents of a Good Proposal

Not all proposals follow the same formula and incorporate the same content. As a guide, you might consider incorporating, as appropriate to the situation, the following proposal components:

Part 1: The *Client's Situation Summary*, which accurately reflects the challenges, problems, or opportunity the client needs to develop, and their implications,

Part 2: A *Statement of Work*,

Part 3: *The Approach*, (optional)

Part 4: *Establishing Success Expectations*, (optional)

Part 5: *Responsibilities of the Client*,

Part 6: *Key Personnel Bios*, (optional)

Part 7: *Prices & Fees*, (prices for the product components of the solutions and fees for the service part), and

Part 8: *Approval*.

Part 1: The Client Situation Summary

The Client Situation Summary is a brief statement of the client's problem, opportunity, or gap (POG). It should allude to the negative impacts of the situation and elicit the thought in the mind of the client decision makers, "*This salesperson truly understands our challenge and its implications - almost better than we do!*"

Its purpose is getting all readers to the same level of understanding about the nature of the POG and its implications. It should not over-state the POG, appear hyper-critical, and never point fingers or assess blame. It must be diagnostic, coolly objective, and spot-on.

Including the Client Pre-Engagement Self-Assessment in the Situation Summary

It is appropriate and helpful to include the results of any client self-assessment in the Situation Summary. This reveals the extent of the client's need and reminds them of the gaps they self-identified during Discovery.

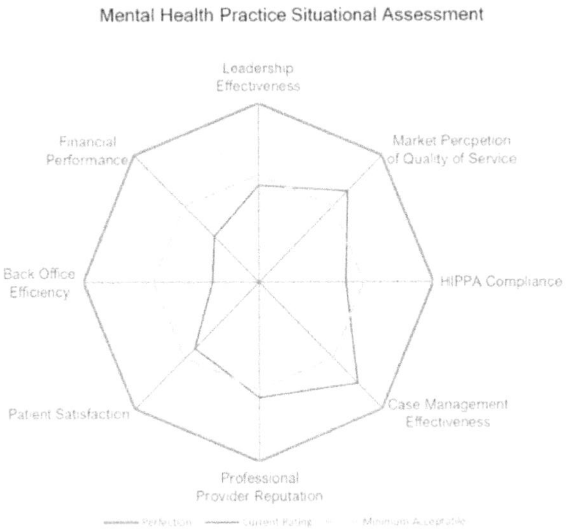

Mental Health Practice Situational Assessment

Figure 19: Mental Health Client Assessment in Situation Summary (redux)

The Implications If Problems or Opportunities Remain Unaddressed

In stating the client challenges in the Situation Summary, it is important to clarify the possible negative implications of the situation if it remains unresolved.

Implications might include:

- the potential or likelihood of the client's competitor gaining market share while the client struggles with the challenge or leaves a problem unresolved,

- continued negative financial impact on the revenue or expense lines,

- stubborn quality issues that do damage to the brand's reputation,

- skilled employee recruiting difficulties because of a weakly perceived brand or market position,

- employee and key-talent turnover,

- legal or liability issues,

- cash flow struggles,

- degradation of return-on-assets, inventory, or investment,

- and more.

Simply stating the problem without implications is not enough. Even worse is stating a fact, without explicitly identifying it as a problem and explicitly communicating any negative implications.

Storytime: I Asked You if You Were Going to Turn Left

A single friend of mine from a small midwestern city brought a date to a mid-week symphony performance. Leaving the concert hall, the streets had little traffic. Working his way toward the freeway, he stopped at a red light, needing to make a left turn to enter the on-ramp of the freeway once the light changed.

His date quietly asked him, "*Are you planning to make a left turn?*"

To which he replied, "*Yup.*"

He was in the right of two lanes that both curved onto the on ramp. The light changed. He turned left, admittedly unaware another car had moved into place in the lane to his left, just far enough back to be in his blind spot. Cutting the turn a bit short, thinking he had freedom of turn, he immediately hit the car on his left.

After the exchange of insurance cards and phone numbers, on getting back into the car, he apologized and asked his date, "*Did you see that car before the light changed? I didn't.*" To which she replied "*Yes.*"

Completely embarrassed, he patiently asked, "*Might I ask why you didn't tell me?*"

In response she said, "*But, I did. I asked you if you were planning to make a left-hand turn. Didn't I?*"

Moral of the Story: If there is a potential negative consequence or implication of a situation, communicate it explicitly and directly. Don't expect a client to perceive and immediately understand a hidden or implied meaning.

End of story

Returning Clients

Working with repeat clients can be a challenge and a delight. Consultants, doctors, and auto mechanics may be visited on numerous occasions by the same client, needing to address the same problem. While service-intense businesses may feel good about a trust-based client relationship that keeps them coming back, sincere specialists wonder at times, why the client is never able to avoid the same recurring issue.

Helping a client overcome a challenge the first time is the salesperson's purpose. However, assuring a solution sticks and continues to produce the outcomes it was intended to, is ultimately the client's responsibility.

A returning client struggling with the same problem and repeatedly needing help will not enjoy being confronted by a product or service who can't help but say I told you so! *"If only you had followed our guidance and done what we recommended, then you wouldn't keep having these same problems and needing to call upon my help. It is costing you money, wasting both our time, and risking (fill in the blank). I hate to say it, but I told you so."*

Storytime: Exasperation is <u>Not</u> a Salesperson Virtue (even if it is justified)

> I know a salesperson who, after the fourth time a client approached him with the same problem, attempted to help by pointing out, that the recurring nature of the problem pointed to a lack of accountability, discipline, and follow-through within the firm. The missing accountability ingredient, a characteristic of the culture of the firm, rather than the technical solution, was the problem. Until that was addressed the challenges would recur.

> He delivered the message with an intensity borne of 10 years of frustration in working on and off with the client on the same problem again and again. The client EIC disagreed and took umbrage at the overly intense, critical message delivered in the presence of their whole executive staff.

> The message, delivered in an impassioned attempt to garner increased commitment, backfired. Given the client firm used a consensus decision making process, and just about all were incensed at the criticism, project approval was postponed indefinitely. The firm decided to use a DIY approach.

> *Moral of the Story:* A fine line exists between a clear *<u>Objective</u>* Situation Summary, and a clear *<u>Critical</u>* Situation Summary. The difference is in the delivery. The line must not be crossed. Being right does not trump being diplomatic. Being diplomatic does not trump being honest and clear.

End of Story

Part 2: Statement of Work and Deliverables:

A *<u>Statement of Work and Deliverables</u>* is precisely that. It describes the products and services to be provided by the salesperson's firm. It includes: the stand-alone products that will be delivered, the expert stand-alone services (engineering or technical expertise, diagnostics, analysis, design, etc.), and the product-related services (tailoring, configuration, installation, integration, testing, and training).

If, for example, you are selling automated manufacturing equipment or software (both tangible deliverables), your statement of work might include planning the integration and checkout, project management, coordinating the internal and vendor efforts to assure correct installation, training, and preparing an operational and maintenance manual.

A Statement of Work and Deliverables tells the client what they can expect from the supplier. Anything not in the statement of work yet is still required to make the effort a success, is the responsibility of the client's team. The client needs to be apprised of any supplemental needs or requirements, and they must be explicitly delineated within the proposal in the *Responsibilities of the Client* section.

Here are some Navigational Selling™ definitions, the distinctions of which will be helpful in crafting the *Statement of Work and Deliverables* sections of your proposals.

A *Deliverable* is the generic term for something you promise the client will receive from doing business with you. Deliverables can take several forms: delivery of a product, accomplishment of an objective, achievement of a milestone, reaching a measurable goal, or realization of an outcome.

An *Objective* is some general improvement the client wishes to realize. An example might be, "Reduce operating expense." The objective can be considered accomplished if expenses are reduced after the deliverable is deployed within the client organization. If the specific amount of an Objective is stipulated, an Objective becomes a Goal.

A *Goal* is a quantified, specific, target Objective. The accomplishment of a Goal can be confirmed if measurable conditions are achieved. Let's say, "*Reduce operating expenses by 10% in the coming fiscal year 2022, as compared to 2021.*"

Goal achievement is highly dependent on pre-contract agreement between the client and the seller about the starting points.

Milestones are easily identifiable achievements on the path to accomplishing either an Objective or a Goal.

As an example, assume you have sold a piece of customized, automated capital equipment to a client. The equipment is designed to reduce manufacturing costs. In such a situation, it is not uncommon to have agreed-upon milestone payments; 25% on project kickoff, 25% on a successful operation demonstration of the equipment,

25% on equipment delivery to the client site, and the final 25% on functional prove-out on the client's shop floor.

In this case, the final 25% may also include proof of having achieved the Goal, such as, "Demonstrate an assembly rate of 2500 parts per hour with a part quality acceptance factor of 99.5% on the buyer's Boise, ID factory floor."

An *Outcome* is a future state. Outcomes can be tangible (a product or service successfully delivered), or intangible-emotional (stress relief) or physical (a better night's sleep). The only Outcomes that are reasonable to offer are those whose achievement can be objectively determined. Examples of tangible outcomes include delivery of an Offering, and achievement of an Objective, Goal, or Milestone.

A *Vision* is a situational construct that incorporates tangible, behavioral, and emotional elements. In a Vision, objectives, outcomes, goals, milestones, deliverables, effective behaviors, and emotional fulfillment are all achieved. Clients, Owners, EICs, employees and other stakeholders all win. A Vision represents an ideal future state.

Vision crafting is a valuable skill for selling and generating client enthusiasm and buy-in. Promising the delivery of a Vision in a proposal can easily become over-selling and should be avoided. Wildly optimistic visionary promises, with no basis in fact, can be fraudulent.

Vision will be addressed again later in this chapter in Part 4 of the Proposal: The Client's Expectations of Success.

A *Success* is a mutual client-salesperson acknowledgement that all the conditions (deliverables, milestones, outcomes, objectives, and goals) stipulated in the Statement of Work have been achieved.

A *Contract* is a formal, comprehensive legal document which incorporates the conditions and deliverables described within a proposal. A signed Proposal may be a pre-cursor to a Contract. The proposal is considered a meeting of the minds on intent of the engagement, and the contract is the binding document which incorporates the points of agreement in the proposal, as well as Terms and Conditions (T&Cs). In some cases, a contract may even define the jurisdiction for any disputes.

Some clients may require complex, attorney-drafted contracts. While for others, the signed Proposal is sufficient to begin work. Other times T&Cs are defined as part of the client's purchase orders, and acceptance of the Purchase Order by the seller implies acceptance of the client's T&Cs.

The more complex the problem, offering, deliverables, risk, and consequences – the higher the degree of consideration for using an attorney-drafted formal Contract rather than relying solely on the Proposal. Commonly, the larger the client the more complex the contract. In the SMB2B world, formal, attorney-drafted contracts are rarely used unless the Proposal is a large investment.

The key to engagement success is achieving clarity and agreement with the client about which measures you will use to define that success, their definitions, and the measurement methods that will be used to determine their achievement.

Types of Proposal

The Statement of Work typically defines the type of proposal being offered, of which there are six:

- Tangible Deliverable-Based proposals,
- General Objective-Based Proposals,
- Milestone-Based Proposals,
- Goal-Based Proposals,
- Retainer Proposals, and
- Combinations of the previous types.

The Tangible Deliverables-Based Proposal

A typical deliverable-based is designed to deliver a quality product that meets all specifications in the time required. Depending on the product's complexity, software for example, the proposal may include services such as tailoring, configuration, installation, integration with existing systems, data migration from older systems, documentation, in-situ testing to assure its operation, and user training.

The General Objectives-Based Proposal

A general Objectives-Based proposal might offer to deliver products and services to help the client achieve a specific objective, such as, "*an increase in year-on-year sales and earnings each of the next three years.*" In this case, success can be measured by asking just one yes/no question at the end of each fiscal year; *"Are sales and earnings higher this year than last?"*

The Milestone-Based Proposal

Milestone-Based proposals typically support the achievement of an Objective and assure the client that progress is being made toward their ultimate Objective or Goal. Progress and accomplishments, essential to overall achievement of Objectives, are Milestones.

For example, our initial general sales and earnings objective (above) might be re-stated to include Milestones:

"Increase year-on-year sales and earnings each of the next three years, through organization-wide sales training and the implementation of a cloud-based CRM system."

With that restatement, progress to reaching the client's Objective can now be measured against key independent Milestones that might be stated as:

- 36-members of the sales team are trained in the new sales process by March 15th,

- the CRM is installed and operational,

- 100% of sales support, customer service and marketing staff are trained in the use of the CRM by April 15th, and

- a new sales forecasting system discipline and quarterly update process is implemented.

Achievement of these milestones is easily tested by answers to just a few questions.

- Is the CRM system implemented and operational?

- Has the sales training been completed for the entire sales team?

- Has the sales training been completed for the sales support, customer service and marketing staff?

- Is sales forecasting being done quarterly using the new forecasting system?

The Goal-Based Proposal

A Goal provides more specificity to an Objective and might be stated as: "Increase sales by 10% to $12,100,000 at 38% margin in the coming fiscal year ending December 31."

This approach is bounded in time, quantified, specific, qualified by the margin condition and, presumably achievable from the recorded current revenue level of $11,000,000. The challenge with this type of deliverable is that so much of its accomplishment is out of the hands of the seller and relies upon the client's competencies.

In a Goal-Based Proposal it is critical to have absolute agreement between the seller and the client on the starting point, the finishing point, and the role and shared responsibilities of the client's team in achieving them. These clarifiers form the basis for accountability and for the financial verification of accomplishment of a goal-based proposal.

The Outcome-Based Proposal

An Outcome is a future state. In our sales and earnings situations, the Outcomes achieved in the future state might encompass:

- the firm's sales process is more efficient and effective,
- sales goals are more frequently achieved,
- sales costs are reduced,
- forecasting is more accurate,
- inventory turns are improved by reducing inventory investment requirements based on more precise and accurate forecasting,
- higher margins provide opportunity for additional new product investment,
- salesperson turnover is reduced,
- market share is increased, and
- the economic value of the client's business is enhanced such that more suitors inquire about the possibility of acquiring it.

Each of these Outcomes is objectively determinable – but such a collection of Outcome data will be difficult to keep track of and establish a starting point for. This complex set of Outcomes approaches Vision stature – so be careful how much you promise and commit to in your proposals.

The Retainer Proposal

The retainer proposal simply delineates the services that will be provided on request of the client in exchange for a set monthly or annual fee. This most common in professional services such as Law, Consulting, and on-demand Coaching.

We've used a client's sales function in the proposal type examples of the last few pages, but the same approach and considerations would work equally well for a client's operations improvement POG. Once improvement is envisioned, quantified, and planned, the specifics will vary by the type of offering and proposal.

Again, more important than how you state your deliverables, objectives, outcomes, and statements-of-work is that you and the client agree about its dimensions and specificity.

Part 3: The Approach (optional)

Remember, in Navigational Selling™ the salesperson is the Navigator. The Navigator plans the journey and plots the course - the Approach.

Most suppliers of service intense B2B business solutions have formulated a standard yet tailorable process for delivering their solutions. Some firms and clients may call this an Approach. Others may call it a process or methodology. Often these processes, approaches or methodologies make use of tools unique to the solution-delivering firm, or the nature of the kinds of problems their clients commonly need resolved.

Through the Discovery and Solution Formulation stages, a solution provider's unique approach may have been a strongly differentiated selling point important to the client. If this is the case, adding a paragraph, slide, process flow graphic or timeline within the proposal to explain the solution approach, acts as a reinforcing and reassuring reminder to the client. It assures that one of the client's important considerations in making their selection of your firm as solution provider, will be applied to the specific POG resolution offered by the proposal.

I have seen "Approach" sections added to a wide range of business proposals – from small stamped-metal parts, to software, to consulting services to recruiting.

Depending on the engagement's complexity, and/or inexperience of the client with this type of project, this section may promote a common understanding between the two teams (the client's and the seller's) so that the choreography of the engagement is coordinated and goes smoothly.

As such, some clients may require that the proposal include a detailed Approach and path through which you will lead your client in achieving their objectives.

You may also elect to use the Approach section if there is something unique and meaningfully differentiated about your Approach that will reduce risk for the client, increase the speed at which the outcomes will be realized, or provide reassurance. Additionally, an Approach section that highlights *Milestones*, will provide reassurance to the client that there will be visible checkpoints along the way by which they can see progress.

Part 4: The Client's Expectations of Success (optional)

A *Success* is a mutual client-salesperson acknowledgement that all the conditions (deliverables, milestones, objectives, etc.) stipulated in the Statement of Work have been achieved. A Success will trigger the emotions associated with accomplishment, reward, validation, stress-relief, and joy.

A Win-Win Success means both Client and Seller win. The client, the salesperson's firm and the salesperson should all feel the engagement was rewarding. But what is included in the *Client's Expectations of Success* part of the proposal, must only be the Successes that apply to the client. If you begin to include win-win considerations that reek of self-interest, the Trust Formula begins to degrade significantly and immediately.

The difficulty in defining and validating success will vary greatly over the range of proposal type. Validating the Success associated with delivering a stand-alone product (no service needed) is much easier than validating the success of achieving a client's Vision.

Figure 20 illustrates the increasing degree of difficulty of achieving and validating success over the range of Proposal Type.

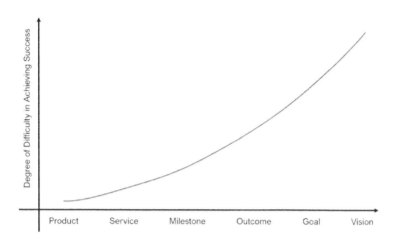

Figure 20: Degree of Seller Difficulty in Validating Success Over the Range of

Deliverables

At the extreme right of the chart of the *Client's Expectations of Success* is the achievement of a Vision. A client-centered Vision, at its inception, is communicated by the seller in imagery - and defined by the behaviors an EIC hopes to see within their organization as indicative of the realization of that Success. Vision achievement is also realized in the feelings the EIC experiences when they observe the desired behaviors working well in practice.

Here's a somewhat extreme example. Achievement of a Vision of successful democracy might be validated through an observation that a high proportion of eligible citizens are voting, elections are honest, and parliamentary rule is working for the benefit of the country and its people.

In a B2B business context, to validate the successful achievement of a Vision, a business owner might need to observe:

- an increasing market value of their business, as suitors bid-up the price they are willing to pay for its acquisition,

- a smoother and higher win-rate sales process,

- a more rapid new product development cycle,

- a significantly reduced employee turnover,

- and more.

You can see how an unbounded Vision, articulated in a proposal can be near impossible to deliver and validate.

Promising the achievement of a Vision is to be avoided.

What counts more than any specific proposal type, is establishing an agreement and mutual understanding between the client and the salesperson about the Client's Expectations of Success.

Keep Success Client-Centric

We will discuss Win-Win success in the next chapter. But, for the moment, it is important to note that in crafting the Client's Expectations of Success section of the Proposal you must include only client-received benefits and value. Including any Seller-based benefits will erode the trust formula by injecting a degree of seller self-interest.

Only factors applicable exclusively to the client, should be included in the Client's Expectations of Success part of proposals. Those dimensions of success realized by the seller in a win-win, should be leveraged by the selling organization, but not waved in front of the client.

Part 5: Responsibilities of the Client

To deliver the value proposed to the client, complex solutions of the nature we are discussing in this book require close collaboration between a client's internal team and the salesperson's team. If the salesperson's firm is required to deliver a complex piece of automated equipment to a client's factory on Saturday, and have it checked out and running for first shift Monday morning, at minimum, someone within the client's organization has to be there to open the doors and turn on the lights. Collaboration in complex solutions is essential.

Because collaboration is critical, client responsibilities must be made clear. The proposal needs to document the specific expectations and responsibilities of the client regarding their role in achieving the ultimate success of a proposed solution.

Responsibilities of the client organization might include:

- accessibility to systems and passwords,
- facility or office access,
- assignment of a Project Manager and specialist team,

- assignment of a project or deployment team and the specific roles each participant will play,

- temporary office space, parking permits, security access,

- approval of project-related expenses,

- availability of key personnel or client organizational services (facilities, IT, HR),

- participation in periodic (daily, weekly, or monthly) progress work sessions,

- executive access (to address those rare occurrences when project manager authority is insufficient to overcome barriers), and

- invoice payment authorization, per the terms stipulated in the proposal.

If one thing is certain, it is that one cannot possibly identify all the potential circumstances that will require client collaboration. It is important to include as many items as have come up in the past or in similar circumstances. More importantly, it is essential to establish a trust-based relationship with the EIC, for just those times when a unique situation arises.

Part 6: Key Personnel Bios (optional)

Clients want to know their investment in this proposal is in experienced and capable hands. Brief bios of the seller's personnel involved in the delivery of the *Statement of Work and Deliverables* may be included in a proposal.

Caution: It is important to avoid what may be a bait-and-switch perception. If during discovery and assessment you brought in your "heavy-hitter" to help seal the deal, and then offered a relatively green recruit to execute the project, the impact on the client might trigger an erosion of Trust.

It is critically important to avoid the perception of a bait-and-switch with regard to key execution personnel.

Part 7: Pricing & Fees

If you are a small manufacturing firm, your negotiations with procurement specialists within large corporate customers can be brutal. More than ever, they seem to be driven by a nearly sadistic combination of corporate edicts that might include threats of sourcing overseas, demands for cost and price reductions by some per cent annually, periodic audits of your cost structure, threats to reduce the number of suppliers by 20% annually (to keep everyone on their toes), and driving to 60-day (or longer) payable policies – all while achieving the lowest piece-price possible.

These selling conditions define a prototypical "price-driven" market – though I have heard it described in other NSFW terms.

Sadly, some small B2B firms feel they can never do anything meaningful about these challenges. So, year after year they eke out marginal success by squeezing their selling prices and margins, repeatedly trying to sell to the same hard-nosed customers, continually targeting the same markets and agreeing to be victimized by the same abusive, big brother, bullying procurement practices.

There are ways to beat these challenges. Some of the solutions are quick and some take time to develop. But if you take no risk or action, there will be no improvement to your situation.

I refer you back to an earlier story in this chapter, the Midwest metal parts stamping firm. They overcame this type of situation and differentiated themselves against massive competition, by breaking with convention and employing a proposal format to respond to an RFQ, vis-à-vis their typical price and delivery quote.

They proved it could be done – with great rewards.

Assuming you have decided to use a proposal format for selling into important client opportunities, what should the pricing section consider?

The pricing section should not be used as a last-ditch effort to argue about the value the client will receive from your product/service. By the time the client receives the Proposal, the *Value-Quotient* from the client's perspective should already be clear.

The pricing section of a proposal should simply state pricing for the products and services necessary to deliver the anticipated value to the client, and any associated fees relating to the deployment of those products. This means you and the client should already have agreed on what will be delivered, the estimated value it will provide, and the approximate costs they will see in the Proposal. Anything more than a 20% variation from the estimate discussed in pre-proposal discussions should be clarified with the client before delivering the proposal.

There are three approaches to fees to be considered: Fair-Elastic Pricing, Fixed Pricing and Contingent Pricing.

Fixed Pricing

The easiest offerings to package and price, are products requiring little to no associated services.

Fixed Pricing means that the price for what is promised to be delivered is fixed. It does not mean that premium pricing can't be justified based on quality, reliability, brand name, technical performance, or delivery.

(P.S. Fixed Pricing is *NOT* Price Fixing which is illegal.)

Fair-Elastic Pricing (Value-Pricing)

Fair-Elastic pricing means increasing the fee or price for a service based on the anticipated increase in value perceived or received by the client. If not considered as a reasonable pricing alternative by the seller, it might be classified as lost opportunity and gross undervaluation of what you provide. At its extreme other end, it can flirt with price-gouging.

Research from the Profit Impact of Market Strategy (PIMS) data base reveals that product and service-related businesses that are perceived as Quality leaders, can sustain 15% higher prices than their competitors with lower Quality reputations.

The increased value perceived and received by clients working with relative perceived quality leaders (RPQL) justifies higher prices – as long as the basis for that perception is in a dimension relevant to the client. Being the highest performance car in speed and handling is probably not relevant to a retired great grandpa in Florida.

Thorough *Discovery* will almost assuredly reveal variation between different client needs such that that fees will have a high probability of variation. In B2B service-intense sales, you do not need to charge the same fees to all clients.

The Robinson-Patman ACT is a federal law passed in 1936 to outlaw price discrimination. An amendment to the 1914 Clayton Antitrust Act, its intent was, and remains, to prevent "unfair" competition. Here is an excerpt.

> "*A seller charging competing buyers different prices for the same* "**commodity**" *or discriminating in the provision of "allowances" - compensation for advertising and other offerings - may be violating the Robinson-Patman Act. This kind of price discrimination may give favored*

customers an edge in the market that has nothing to do with their superior efficiency. **Price discriminations are generally lawful, particularly if they reflect the different costs of dealing with different buyers or are the result of a seller's attempts to meet a competitor's offering.**

Robinson-Patman claims must meet several specific legal tests:

- *The Act applies to (products and) commodities, **but not to services**, (my emphasis added) and to purchases, but not to leases.*
- ***The goods must be of "like grade and quality."***
- *There must be likely injury to competition (that is, a private plaintiff must also show actual harm to their business).*
- *Normally, the sales must be "in" interstate commerce (that is, the sale must be across a state line.)*

I have bolded the phrases that apply to the types of Seller-Client transactions we are talking about here.

- We are discussing differentiated offerings not commodities – offerings which will likely require varying degrees of tailoring and associated services to meet a client's specific needs,

- It is unlikely any two clients, even if they compete with one another, will need precisely the same combination of offerings in the precise same proportions, and

- Higher quality, highly differentiated products & services, that deliver premium value to clients over their commodity counterparts, are not commodities.

Note: I am not a lawyer. If you have any doubts or questions, you should consult with your attorney.

While tripping over a potential violation of the Robinson-Patman Act is unlikely in Navigational Selling™ situations, based on its emphasis on thorough Discovery principles, you may still want to consider moral and ethical considerations as your boundaries to value-pricing flexibility. What is legal in pricing to similar customers is not always fair.

I recommend the concept of "Fair-Elastic Pricing" be employed in proposal pricing and fee-setting. Fair Elastic Pricing seeks fair value exchange. Fair-Elastic Pricing does not condone opportunistic price gouging.

Navigational Selling™ pricing is all about fair value exchange. RPQL-based price premiums are fair. Price gouging is immoral, unethical, unfair, and in certain cases illegal.

Here are some factors, guideposts, and circumstances around the concept of Fair-Elastic Pricing. For charging premium fees, both you and the client should recognize any of the following situations:

- multiple important dimensions of value, beyond just economic, will be received by the client,

- there is a unique capability, talent, or experience match between what you are offering and their need,

- there are unknowns that cannot be assessed in the time available before the engagement must begin, and premium prices will mitigate the risk for both parties,

- there is value synergy, by including multiple outcomes and offerings within a single package, aka a larger scope,

- the engagement will require on-demand, exclusive access to the salesperson's team for extended periods, obviating the seller's ability to engage other clients,

- extensive tailoring of the engagement will be required,

- there will be time and travel requirements for geographically dispersed locations.

In summary, in Fair-Elastic Pricing the rule is simple:

In Fair-Elastic Pricing, first establish with the client the magnitude of the long-term value that will accrue to the client from success, then set a rational value-based fee.

Contingent Pricing

Contingent pricing sets the seller's fee based on the magnitude of the economic (cash) benefits and results achieved by the client because of the engagement.

Some franchised, cost-savings-based consulting practices, for example, have contingent pricing as their primary source of fee-setting. Their sales argument is that there is no risk to the client. However, such contingent-fee-based offerings do not always win for the seller, however.

Such an arrangement requires that before the engagement is executed both the salesperson's team and client can analyze and objectively agree on current client cost/spending levels – and use the same basis for evaluating cost reductions post-engagement. This early analysis permits the salesperson's firm to decline taking the engagement if the opportunity is not lucrative, but also requires the salesperson to expend a lot of effort before finding treasure.

Agreeing to contingent fees is ill-advised for the following reasons:

Control of the Factors of Success: Salespeople, assess, analyze, advise, and guide, but have no direct managerial control of client activities and priorities. Agreeing to a fee based on the multiple execution factors required for success, over which you have no direct control, is risky at best.

Fair and Equal Treatment: Would the client ask the power company to accept contingent fees for the electricity they use during their course of their business, and pay only if the product that electricity was used to build sold well and became profitable? Nope.

Could the firm find and keep employees if they paid them solely on achievement of objectives? How would they live in the interim?

No Remuneration for In-Process Effort Delivered: Being asked to defer compensation until savings are realized, is basically asking you to work for a reduced fee, eliminating your possibility to engage other full-fee clients within the same time window.

Avoid clients wishing to negotiate contingent pricing.

Part 8: The Signature Block

Ultimate decision makers vary in title from client to client. Contracts are only binding if signed by the person who has the ultimate authority to commit the resources of the company to its execution – the EIC. In a true 50:50 partnership, either partner may sign. In a sole proprietorship the officer of record, typically the sole proprietor themselves needs to sign.

Storytime: Reading the Fine Print

> A consultant I know took on an assignment as a temporary Chief Marketing Officer for a small healthcare products company. Arriving on the first day of this engagement, he found three documents on his desk – all of them

requesting substantial authorizations to issue payment checks for marketing expenditures, totaling hundreds of thousands of dollars. The only explanation accompanying those requests was that they were routine contractual obligations for joint marketing promotions to be paid to several of the firm's large independent retail distribution outlets.

The consultant asked to see the contracts before simply signing the requests.

Reviewing the contracts, he discovered that none had been authorized by any officer of the company – invalidating them. And, in fact, one of the contracts had been signed by a person that was not even an employee of the firm and never had been. Rather he was an independent, outside sales rep, with absolutely no authority to commit the firm to such an obligation! Another contract had an automatic-renew clause that took effect if a re-negotiation didn't take place by a certain date – and that date had passed.

The discovery of the invalidity of the contracts saved the client a lot of money, and for sure, disappointed some salesperson (and their executive) somewhere.

Moral of the Story: Be sure you have a signature from the right people (EICs) with the appropriate authority to commit the client's resources before charging ahead.

End of Story

For The Flipp-Berger Group, Inc.:	For DewDrop Consolidated Inc.:
Gerard Flipp, Jr. President ___	Ms. Joan Lopes-Reardon, PhD, CEO ___
Date: _____	Date: _____

Proposal Formats

Some SMB2B firms have used Word documents to craft proposals, others prefer PowerPoint slides. Word allows for clarity of description. PowerPoint encourages a more succinct use of words and graphic representation. but may require more pages if you elect to include all the parts described above.

A typical proposal using Word should require no more than four or five pages - in PowerPoint eight to ten pages, depending on which proposals sections you feel the situation warrants.

Increasing Sales Productivity - the Correct Way

I am aware that to some experienced salespeople all this Discovery, Qualification, Solution Formulation and Proposal detail may seem like overkill. I can hear protests of, "*I don't have that kind of time. This is all going to slow me down! It's not necessary. I've been selling for a long time, and I've never had to do all this stuff before.*"

In response, let me caution.

Any sales productivity enhancement you wish to achieve, will be most effective and long-lasting if you find ways to speed the process of discovering all the client-relevant needs and working through the details, vs. looking for increased productivity by skipping those details.

Find a way to do the right things faster to speed up your success, rather than skipping the right things.

I will leave it at that.

*****

Chapter 11: Follow-Through & Winning

In this Chapter …

Follow-Through

The Expectancy Theory of Motivation

Dealing with Client Reluctance

Expectancy Questioning

Win-Win Winning vs. Just Winning

The Biggest Barrier to Winning

Follow-Through

Follow-Through means moving a proposal through to signature and beginning a client engagement. It is the signing of the proposal, quote, or contract that marks, as Winston Churchill may have put it, "*the end of the beginning*" of an engagement.

A Win is not a verbal OK - even if it is accompanied by a handshake. A Win is not a promise to do it next quarter. Rather, a Win is an actual signature by someone in the client's firm with official title and explicit authority to commit the client organization to a contractual engagement. It includes a starting date, after receipt of any agreed-to kickoff payment.

If you have executed well on all the sales stages to this point, you may still not be all the way there. You should not presume you are. You may only be 70% of the way. If, on the other hand, you overlooked key parts of the sales process to this point, you may not even be 25% of the way to a win and EIC authorizing signature, even if you prematurely delivered a proposal the client said they would consider.

Having delivered a proposal with poor preparation throws it out of your hands. There is little to do but wait and follow-up. The longer the time span between today and when you delivered the proposal, the less likely it is that the proposal will ever result in a Win.

Do not rush to the proposal stage before you have what you need. It may be difficult to hold back, but the faster you drive to deliver a proposal the more likely you will have missed something important. So, the last effort you must engage in, is motivating the client EIC to commit – as witnessed by their signature.

The Expectancy Theory of Motivation

The Expectancy Theory is a motivation theory first proposed by Professor Victor Vroom of the Yale School of Management in the 1960's. While technology and automation have made lightyears of progress since then, human nature has not changed much.

The Expectancy Theory defines the power behind motivation as deriving from three factors:

1. the probability that an action taken by an individual will lead to the accomplishment of the intent and objective of the action,

2. the probability that the accomplishment of the intent and objective of the action will produce a reward, and

3. the reward will be relevant to the individual taking the action.

In formula form it looks like Figure 21 below:

$$Motivation = (p)\ Action \rightarrow Accomplishment + (p)\ Accomplishment \rightarrow Reward + (p)\ Reward \rightarrow Relevant$$

$$(\ where\ (p)\ means\ ``probability"\ and \rightarrow means\ ``leads\ to"\ )$$

Figure 21: The Vroom Expectancy Theory of Motivation

Underpinning each factor is the client's belief and trust in you, your firm, your approach, your abilities, your honesty, and your intense commitment to their success.

Storytime: Wait! Did you Actually Read That?

After a year-long engagement, the client of a consultant I know, asked him to offer a follow-on proposal that encompassed a much broader set of needs for the client – spanning multiple departments. At the EIC's request, the consultant met with the EIC the day after delivering the proposal. He expected to be questioned about the approach he had proposed, since most of the added effort would encompass work in an area quite different than the last proposal – yet still within the scope of his expertise.

After a brief hello and taking a seat, the consultant was shocked to see the EIC immediately turn to the last page of the proposal and affix his signature.

The consultant couldn't help himself and said, "*Whoa! Aren't you going to read it? Ask any questions?*"

The EIC responded, " *Not necessary. I know you, your capabilities, experience, intelligence, and dedication to our success. And I know what you have done and helped us accomplish so far. So, let's get on with it.*"

Moral of the Story: Trust is the most powerful client motivation to trigger a Win.

End of story

Dealing with Client Reluctance

I have always been amazed at the reluctance of some prospective clients to address their POGs – even those who are in deep trouble and in desperate need of a remedial effort.

It struck me one day that their reluctance might be born of simple fear. So, I asked a few clients about that.

I discovered that the fear was real and born of a concern that attempting to change the status-quo in their firm, might, despite their good intentions, instead completely crater their current cash generation machine - as weak, shaky, and inefficient as it might be. Fear is a powerful force, trumping reason, opportunity, and hope. Fear is, in its extreme form, paralyzing.

So, as much as Trust is a primary ingredient in selling any offerings, reassurance is needed as well.

I have found that getting to the root of client reluctance can be addressed methodically by addressing the three factors within the Expectancy Theory of Motivation equation of Figure 21. In other words, clients will not sign a proposal if any of the three factors are not compelling – both emotionally and logically.

The three negating factor beliefs are:

1. they don't trust (believe) that the *Action* proposed in the document will *Accomplish* the goal (whether it be overcoming a barrier, achieving an objective, or realizing an opportunity),

2. they don't trust (believe) that a significant enough *Reward* will be realized if the actions proposed in the proposal are *Accomplished*, and

3. they don't trust (believe) the *Reward* will be meaningful and *Relevant* enough to warrant the risk and cost associated with the efforts described within the proposal.

If this circumstance arises, your most powerful sales super-powers are patience and inquiry. Not pressure. Not closing tricks. Rather, patience and inquiry.

Every client situation is slightly different. The range of circumstances, skills and capabilities of clients' management teams vary widely. Each culture is unique. Their market circumstances are different as is their financial situation.

Your challenge, therefore, is to build enough Trust, and provide enough Reassurance, to convince the client that your offerings and experience, validated successful in other circumstances, will work as well in their unique environment and circumstance, and deliver the outcomes they so desperately need.

Building Trust and providing Reassurance are invaluable ingredients in producing compelling proposals, executing successful engagements, and building a market leading client experience.

Gentle, supportive, and reassuring inquiry works much better in reinforcing trust and creating a win-win, than closing through semi-transparent trickery.

Research conducted by the Huthwaite Group and published in Neil Rackham's book *SPIN Selling* indicates that using closing techniques to trick a client into signing creates negative consequences in the long run.

Clients who have been tricked into signing on the dotted line are less likely to be happy, less likely to recommend you to others and less likely to re-buy from you and your firm.

Knowing this, your goal must be to reassure and build trust and agreement that the offerings you are recommending are in the client's best interest – not to squeeze out a signature by any means possible.

I can honestly look back and recognize that every proposal I offered that died on a client decision-maker's desk or received no response (even after numerous follow up calls), failed because I did a poor job of some important part of the selling process – mostly Discovery.

Expectancy Questioning: Increasing Your Odds of a Win

If you followed the optimal path through Discovery and Solution Formulation stages, you asked and received a positive response to the test question:

"As it stands now, considering what we agreed would address the issue, if I delivered a proposal tomorrow what hesitancies might you have to approving it? If you have concerns or reasons for hesitation, how best should we address them to eliminate any delay in moving forward?"

So, between an initial positive response and any new reluctance there are only a few possibilities: a) something changed, b) you missed something important, or c) both.

What's needed at this point is polite, unemotional inquiries, aligned with the Expectancy Theory, not trickery.

Along that line, I offer a series of questions below, framed to reinforce trust, provide reassurance, discover previously unrevealed barriers, and ultimately motivate the client to provide a final signed authorization to proceed.

Some people might call this handling objections. That conjures up the image of a clever, move-for-move chess game in which you and the client engage in a play-by-play win-lose match. If you stymie the client, (excuse the mixed metaphor of chess and billiards), they may have no choice but to sign the agreement. You may believe the client is signing the agreement happily, but that is not likely. If you tricked the client with some clever word-work, the signature you get is simply starting the relationship on bad footing.

Note that the questions below are framed as open-ended, to elicit specific information that can impact and accelerate the decision in a positive manner – and to be directed to the EIC.

Yes/No questions are instinctual in this situation, however taking extra time to frame questions in an open-ended form, will provide you what you need to build trust, reassurance, and commitment with the client.

Action Will Lead to Accomplishment Questions:

Q1. It appears we have reached a point where there remains some reluctance to proceed. What do you perceive as the risk associated with the proposed objectives, recommended offerings and deployment plan we defined?

Q2. How might we increase the probability of success? How might the approach be modified?

Q3. How have the original objectives changed?

Q4. What other circumstance have changed? Funding? Team buy-in? New people involved? Other more important priorities?

Accomplishment Will Lead to Reward (Desired Outcomes) Questions:

Q5. How has your perception of the likely benefits and value of implementing the recommendations shifted since we formulated the plan?

Q6. What gaps do you think might remain when the implementation is completed?

Q7. What adjustments do you feel would improve the total scope and impacts of the outcomes?

Q8. Within your organization (both management and the execution team), whom do you think might not feel that the outcomes and rewards for completion would be relevant and worth the effort? What might we do to improve that perception?

Relevance of the Reward Accruing to the EIC and the Firm Questions:

Q9. How meaningful do you perceive the ultimate benefits of implementing the recommendation?

Q10. What other types of benefits do you think we should design and integrate into the recommendations?

Q11. With whom in the organization (management and implementation team), do we need to reinforce the relevance of the benefits and value of implementation?

Such questioning should reveal the root cause of reluctance with enough specificity to be addressed.

The Biggest Barrier to Winning is Your Former Self

The enemy of a successful proposal approval is your former self – your former self who, before crafting the proposal, did an inadequate job of the qualification, discovery, solution formulation, and proposal preparation steps described in the preceding chapters (6,7,8,9 and10) within Part 2 of Navigational Selling™.

It may be the "you" who did not prequalify the account and opportunity well enough to know that your service offering would not appeal to the prospective client or appear to deliver relevant and meaningful value. Or the "you" that did not understand the buyer personality types and frame your proposal, or adjust your communication and behavior, appropriately. Or the "you" that did not ask and get good answers to the important questions.

We, and I include myself because my track record has never been 100%, are our own nemeses.

That is why this section on Winning is short. Closing tricks do not work in the long term. The research proves it. The only thing that does work consistently is highly disciplined qualification, discovery, and solution formulation behaviors.

A Win-Win should, by its nature, be the shortest segment of any sales journey if you have Navigated the Client journey well.

Win-Win Winning vs. Just Winning

The first thing to clarify is the definition of a good Win.

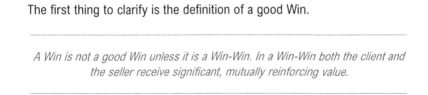

A Win is not a good Win unless it is a Win-Win. In a Win-Win both the client and the seller receive significant, mutually reinforcing value.

A bad Win is a contract or proposal signed, without regard to the ultimate success of the undertaking or the ultimate receipt of value by the client. A good Win for the client should, at minimum, provide significant progress towards, if not complete achievement of the client's objectives.

Referring to the concept of Value Quotient (Chapter 5), depending on the specific circumstance, to be considered a good Win for the client, they must experience a degree of benefit in any or all factors of the value-quotient formula - not solely economic.

- economic (the primary benefit motivator in most B2B settings),

- emotional (reassurance, satisfaction, confidence, security),

- physical (stress relief, a better night's sleep, lower blood pressure),

- social (the respect, recognition and appreciation of workmates, employees, or industry peers), and

- political (a higher level of trust, respect, and visibility through all layers of the organization).

Furthermore, each of those benefits must not be overwhelmed by their corresponding costs.

On the other side of the ledger, a good Win for the seller, may provide any, or all, of the following benefits:

- follow-on business,

- a trusted long-term client relationship,

- a case study,

- a testimonial,

- referrals to new clients,

- penetration of a new market,

- product or process changes that may be leveraged to other opportunities or markets, and of course,

- revenue and profit.

In all cases, an honest salesperson must strive for a good Win-Win, not just a Win or Close.

A Quick Aside for EICs and Sales Managers: When interviewing candidates for a new sales position within your company, ask them to describe several of the most significant Win-Wins, not just the "biggest deals" they closed. Their answer should incorporate client, business, and personal wins. The answer will be indicative of their pre-disposition to a Navigator Mindset.

The second thing to recognize is: if you have done everything perfectly to this point, a pre-win win (a client EIC's signature on the proposal) should not present a challenge or be impacted by a delayed response. But life being what it is, and repeated perfection being a near-impossible goal vis-à-vis reality, there may be many instances when a proposal does not meet with immediate client approval in the form of a signature by their EIC.

A baseball analogy may drive this point home. Arguably, the most productive hitter in the history of Major League Baseball was Ted Williams of the Boston Red Sox, whose career spanned 1939 to 1960. But even Ted Williams, who won the American League batting championship six times in his career, only had a batting average of just over .400 in his best year (.406 to be precise) - and a career average of .344. This means that he was successful at bat between 34% and 40% of the time.

The point: Not all your delivered proposals will result in a Win. Life intervenes, circumstances change, and your client's organizational responsibilities shift. Expect it.

Through it all, keep in mind:

Your noble purpose in being a salesperson is to improve the client's situation. Achieving that improved situation is the client's motivation and objective in working with you. Just Winning the deal, is not. Letting your personal drive and goal to Win the deal, overwhelm the achievement of the client's drive and goal to achieve their objective, is poison.

I recognize that the former statement is an idealistic view that may run contrary to the most hard-nosed sales managers in the B2B marketplace, but I stand by it. Living by it reinforces your reputation, personal brand, and builds trust with former clients - also increasing the probability of referrals and long-lasting repeat business.

Seller Success: Don't Leave Your Winnings on the Table

In the previous chapter we established that a win for the client is your primary objective. We also stated that creating a win-win is crucial. Win-Win means that both seller and client must benefit.

As a salesperson, you must remain vigilant to capture 2nd, 3rd, and 4th levels of success, those other components of success most relevant to your personal professional success and your firm's reputation and brand. These "other" success treasures are not to be listed or anticipated in client discussions. Rather, they should be kept in mind and leveraged. Examples of these are illustrated in the 2nd, 3rd, and 4th levels of success in the following milestone-based success example.

A Milestone-Based Seller Success Example

Situation: A salesperson for a CRM software firm that also does sales training, has offered to install a CRM system, configure it, and tailor a 1-day sales training program - delivering the training and manuals to 25 people at the client's annual sales meeting in Tampa, FL on February 15th.

Expected Deliverables: These are clearly stated in the details of the signed engagement agreement between the salesperson's firm and the client. These might include: the number of people to be trained, the specific content of the material, the location and time, the system installation and configuration of the CRM, and its testing.

The client's Vision of Success is a future where salespeople have doubled their win rates, never need to request price reductions to win business, smoothly assist clients through their own buying process, client returns and conflicts have virtually disappeared, and the firm's sales recruiting process is highly effective and productive in finding great talent.

Client's Expectation of Success: The salesperson's firm does precisely what the proposal stipulated. The CRM is configured and set up, the training program is created and delivered, customized user manuals are produced (both in binders and online), and training is delivered to 25 salespeople in Tampa on the 15th of February. The milestones have been achieved, the invoice submitted, and promptly paid.

The 1st Measure of Win-Win Success Accruing to the Seller

The client is pleased. The basic win is Revenue earned, commission paid, and earnings appearing on the bottom line. In addition, a new client has been added, market share has increased, a trusting relationship has been established, and the potential to generate additional business has improved.

The client received what they contracted for, and the salesperson and their firm were appropriately rewarded.

The client sees the success in the behaviors of their sales and customer service team and their firm's steadily increasing four and five-star ratings.

Good, for sure.

A 2nd Measure of Success Accruing to the Seller

After realizing the 1st Measures of Success, has the salesperson left any winnings on the table? There may be more to seller success than the paid invoice (for the firm) and the paid commission (for the salesperson).

Consider a second level of possible Seller success.

In addition to realizing all the benefits in the 1st Measure of Success, the client provides glowing post-training reviews from the attendees and testimonials that can be quoted on the seller's website and in the seller's promotional materials.

Additionally, since the program has been tailored, the firm may have developed new concepts it can leverage into future engagements for other clients, *(if you retained the rights to original material)*.

Better success, no doubt.

But wait, there could be more. There could be another achievable level of success.

A 3rd Measure of Success Accruing to the Seller

In addition to the 1st and 2nd Measures of Success, it may be possible to garner a referral to another, larger client with twice the number of salespeople needing to be trained.

Even better success!

A 4th Measure of Success (accruing to the Seller)

Nine months after the CRM is installed and training has been delivered, having already experienced the mutual client-salesperson benefits of the first three levels of success, the salesperson receives an unsolicited email from the client's EIC. It seems that the client's sales success has improved by 35% since the Tampa training. She attributes it almost completely to your program.

Soon afterward, the salesperson and client EIC meet at a local conference. The salesperson thanks the EIC for the email and asks, "*How are things going?*"

To which she replies, "I am so glad I ran into you. You would not believe how the work you did with us has continued to pay off and yield amazing results. We are on track to double our revenues without having to add any additional salespeople."

"In fact, I was going to call you this week. We just acquired a competitor, and we need you to train the combined sales teams. The total number of salespeople and sales managers will be just under 50 – and we are considering including the Customer Service teams. Would you be interested in doing that?"

The salesperson replies, *"Certainly!"*

The firm has a documented, quantified, verifiable case study of the value delivered to the client, a return client, and a larger follow-on engagement.

In this case you have achieved multiple levels of success; specific client-relevant milestones and deliverables that evolved into a quantifiable economic value quotient for them - and more. This additional information can help you in promoting, selling, thought leadership, competitive positioning, value pricing, new service development, differentiation, discovering a new market and so much more!

So, we should smile and be proud, right?

OK, do a victory lap. But please, do not leave important pieces of information undiscovered.

By asking a successful client the question, "*What did this success mean to you, your business, and your team?*", another opportunity is created. You have an opportunity to discover other components of the Value Quotient, namely the additional benefits meaningful to the firm's team and business success.

A deal Won and delivered should be a win-win for both the client and the solution-delivering firm. But "winning" can have a long tail – both generating and delivering benefits to the seller over time after an engagement has ended. They can only be exploited if the salesperson pays attention to the client and keeps in contact.

Remember, a Value Quotient has economic, emotional, physical, political, and social components of both benefits and costs. Digging a bit deeper helps you discover those contributing factors.

I once provided sales training to a small group of software salespeople, and when I asked the success question, I discovered they thought they learned a lot and "*it was fun*". Prior to hearing that, even though I incorporate humor into my training programs, I never thought of that long-term, memorable emotional component as value delivered.

Why does post-engagement questioning about the client's definition of success have value to you?

Because it typically reveals successful behaviors and activities that can, and should be, repeated. After a successful engagement, don't just run home with your commission check and feel you have extracted the last nugget of gold from the mine. There is probably more rich ore.

****

Part 3: Adoption and Evolution

Too large a proportion of sales training that is periodically conducted by SMB2B firms has weak sticking power. Because things don't stick, they don't take hold and produce anywhere near the magnitude of the improvements originally intended.

Some salespeople will pick up and internalize a few tidbits that they apply to their daily efforts, but most will only vaguely remember important pieces of content. That is, unless the new behaviors, practices, disciplines, tools, and techniques are integrated into the business processes of the firms with which they are employed, automated where appropriate and, most importantly, rewarded.

Only when Sales Managers and EICs behave in the following manner will the sales troops adopt, comply, and benefit. Sales Managers and EICs must:

- adopt, exemplify, and consistently use their new process disciplines and vocabulary in their daily conversations,
- ask to see the tools in action,
- establish checkpoints to assure the process is being adopted and used,
- automate the processes,
- set the behavioral compliance expectations, and
- implement reward systems that encourage the correct behaviors.

Training is only the beginning of any committed effort to improve. And like the military, training must be repeated regularly so the behaviors needed in specific extant situations become second nature and well honed.

Part 3 of this book discusses the challenges associated with both Individual and Organizational Adoption of Navigational Selling™.

Chapter 11: Individual NavSell Process Adoption is for Salespeople

Chapter 12: Organizational Level Process Adoption is for EICs

Chapter 12: Individual NavSell Process Adoption

In this Chapter …

Salesmanship Skills

Foundational Disciplines

Personal Discipline

Measurements & Metrics

Coaches, Buddies and Accountability Partners

Sales Goal Setting and Sanity-Testing

Creating an Account & Opportunity Repository

Assessing Your Starting Point for an Individual Sales Improvement Journey

The Two Paths to Individual Performance Improvement

Final Word on Individual Sales Improvement

In every major personal challenge, from war to losing weight, the first battle is always a battle of the mind.

Growth means change.

Change, even if it is a change for the better, is least traumatic if it is synthesized slowly and methodically. In this way, pain and trauma are minimized and the adjustments are experienced with less stress. In this chapter, we will discuss how to realize sales improvements to receive the greatest impact, in the shortest time, with the least amount of trauma.

The first thing to recognize is that there are two groups of things that need to be improved to realize enhanced and more effective sales results. The first group is basic Salesmanship Skills, steps and concepts reviewed in Part 2, Chapters, 5 through 11. The second group encompasses the Foundational components that must be in place for the seedlings of the first group to flourish.

This chapter will focus only briefly on Group 1, sales skills, steps, and concepts. These were covered in great detail in Part 2. The majority of this chapter will instead focus on Group 2; the *Foundational* items that nourish the Group 1 items.

Group 1: Salesmanship Skills

The sales skills and techniques that NavSell practitioners and process adopters will find most productive follow. They are listed below in order of importance and impact. Each item is accompanied by a reference to the place within this book that covers the specific topic in detail.

- selection and *Focus* on the most lucrative target markets for each offering (Appendix C),

- embracing *Sales Call Planning Disciplines* - establishing meeting objectives, setting agendas, suggesting attendance, and requesting client homework (Chapter 7),

- crafting *Discussion Summaries* (Chapter 7),

- using *Client Assessments* to reveal the severity and implications of explicit and hidden client POGs (Chapter 7),

- *Listening Before Selling* (Chapter 7),

- asking the client to share their *Decision-Making Process* and *Decision Criteria* (Chapter 4),

- improving *Opportunity Qualification* using the six criteria and those ratings informing your *Action Planning* (Chapter 6),

- improving *New Business Development* activities (Appendix D),

- learning to *Read People* - client decision-makers and decision influencers (Chapter 8),

- using *Proposals instead of price and delivery Quotes* for big deals (Chapter 9),

- always behaving in a way to continually build and reinforce the *Trust Formula* (Chapter 5),

- sealing the deal using the *Expectancy Theory of Motivation* instead of closing tricks (Chapter 10), and

- committing to a *Navigator Mindset* (Chapter 5).

Yup, that's a lot to process, and you won't be able to embrace everything at once. So, as you work through the book, feel free to pick and choose those concepts and techniques that resonated most with you.

Group 2: Foundational Disciplines

The following pages, we'll review concepts that have not yet been covered to this point - yet have critical importance in an individual's adoption and practice of Navigational Selling™ principles. Those concepts and foundational principles are:

- committing to *Personal Discipline* in both your professional sales and personal lives,

- implementing *Measurements & Metrics* to monitor new and improved sales behaviors,

- using *Coaches, Buddies, or Accountability Partners*,

- formulating and sanity-testing annual *Sales Goals*, and

- using a CRM or other simple *Pipeline Management System* to track opportunities through the four sales stages.

Personal Discipline

Discipline is a matter of mind over everything else. Those whom many judge the most successful, talented, and creative people in the world, have come to that stature through a high degree of personal discipline.

As this book is being written, Phil Mickelson, the professional golfer, established a PGA tour record by becoming the oldest person to win a major tournament at the age of 50. The number of putts he practices, attempting to sink 100 in a row from a circle 3-feet away and around the hole from 10 points of the compass, is legendary.

Tom Brady, former New England Patriots quarterback, now with the Tampa Bay Buccaneers, who has led both teams to a total of seven Superbowl wins and seems to defy the ravages of age and the physical brutality of the game, is tremendously disciplined in his diet, physical conditioning regimen, and practice routines.

Randy Newman is a music composer. He has written songs and musical scores or many memorable movies, from the "Toy Story" franchise to A Bug's Life, Monsters, Inc. and The Natural (a baseball movie). He has won 12 Academy Awards and been nominated for an additional 93. Mr. Newman has a highly disciplined daily routine for his creativity.

Closer to home, *the* most productive salespeople I have had the pleasure of working with over the last 30 years, all demonstrated impressive levels of personal discipline as their foundational super-power.

Discipline is an essential ingredient to repeated accomplishment – including becoming a great salesperson.

Discipline is not genetic, nor culturally inherent. That fact underlies the training that new recruits receive in military basic training to become high performing individuals and units. Few will argue that the group of new recruits showing up for basic training in the Marine Corps all have the same starting point – physically, emotionally, intellectually, or genetically. Yet they learn discipline – which grounds them all, permitting higher performance both as individuals and as a unit.

While the thought of rigorous discipline may strike fear into the heart of many a salesperson as having the potential for wasting valuable time and restricting creativity, it produces the reverse effects, by increasing efficiency and productivity.

What if you are *not* in a salesperson role?

I have found, in general, that the higher the technical expertise and experience level of an individual in their non-sales specialty, (accounting, engineering, psychology, law, computer science, etc.) the less likely the person is to be a natural salesperson. If this category of individual fits you, this is no cause for despair. I can assure you, all the skills essential for sales success, can be learned quickly by embracing the structure and rigor of a proven sales process. It is particularly easy for the technical, process-oriented specialist, to get their arms around – if they have the personal desire and discipline to embrace them.

The concepts of Navigational Selling™ can help you improve your sales game. But only if you mix them with personal discipline, so that each important word in its vocabulary, each tool, approach, and technique is coated and permeated with the power of discipline.

To continually improve their game, salespeople must practice personal discipline. It is a must to become consistently successful and requires practice and honing.

But you need not go it alone.

Coaches help.

Buddies help.

Accountability partners help.

Amazon, which has quite a collection of books about how to achieve more through higher levels of personal discipline, can also help.

In the end, _you_ must be the one to improve your personal behavioral disciplines. If that is not accomplished, all the buddies, coaches, accountability partners and books in the universe will not help.

Success achieved without personal discipline is just luck - and nothing to either be proud of or count on.

What about natural talent, you ask?

There are many naturally talented people in the world. And we have all seen stories in the press of highly visible, extremely talented sports and entertainment figures falling prey to their lack of personal discipline.

You can never just count on luck to save you in any but the fewest of circumstances. And you can never depend on just natural talent to provide long term consistent performance.

I will leave it there.

Measurements & Metrics

Goals are objectives that have been quantified. Progress toward goals, therefore, must be measured. In the world of sales, there are two types of measurements of interest: outcome and behavioral.

The use of _Outcome Metrics_ is the primary way most salespeople measure success. Total revenue delivered, the dollar value of sales booked this quarter, or the total commissions earned are outcome metrics. _Outcome Metrics_ are typically dependent on other things – sales behaviors most notably.

As an example of outcome metrics and their dependency on behaviors, let's talk about body weight.

If I want to lose weight, for example, I can measure my weight every day and track it religiously in a diary. My weight, however, is an outcome metric dependent on my behaviors. Unless I improve my behaviors (the amount of exercise I engage in, the number of desserts I consume, and the number of alcoholic beverages I drink) the outcome metric, my weight, will remain unchanged.

Behaviors are *Independent Variables*. They depend solely on my will power and personal behavioral discipline, assuming my health is sound. If I measure my behaviors (the independent variables on which my weight depends) and they trend in the right direction, my weight (the dependent outcome metric) will trend in the right direction – down.

Sales metrics and measurements are no different.

We are certainly interested in our outcome (dependent) measures of success. Bookings and the sales commissions they produce pay the bills. But the only way to consistently generate them is to adhere to consistent high-quality sales behaviors (the independent variables) on which those outcomes depend.

Figure 22 offers a comprehensive example for monthly tracking and measurement of both your behavioral (independent) variables and outcome (dependent) variables. It includes both sales and new business development related activities and behaviors.

You may say, "That's crazy! I don't have the time for that."

It's not. And you do.

One hour a month at most - less if you have an automated CRM configured for producing the report.

One hour a month is not an outrageous thing to suggest for keeping yourself aware of whether your sales behaviors are producing the results you want. For 15 years I produced a monthly report for my accountability coach, which included a table like what you see in Figure 22. It kept me on my toes and focused on the right things. If at any time my outcomes were lagging, I could guarantee it was my lagging behavioral disciplines.

Look at the measurement and metrics being tracked (Figure 22).

As of May 31, 2021	2021 Goal	Current YTD	Mo-Mo Change	Comments
New Business Dev Activities:				
Networking Activities:				
# LinkedIn Connections	2,500	1,472	+15	In selected target markets; decision makers
# Referral Source Meetings	24	8	+2	Complementary service
# Referrals Given / Received	24/24	13/8	2/2	Shared ideal client profiles
# Networking Events/Meetings	24	9	+1	"What do you do?" response prepared
Thought Leadership Activities:				
Articles / Blogs produced	24	6	+2	In Intra-Market Network vehicles
Talks / Webinars Delivered	6	1	0	To Intra-Market Network audiences
# Referral Source Alliances	4	2	0	Mutual confidentiality; Complementary
# Researched Account Targets	20	5	+1	In selected lucrative target markets
Sales Process Behaviors:				
# New Target Client Discovery Mtgs	12	3	+2	Pre-Qualified through research
# Current Account Re-Discoveries	24	9	0	Account Management
# New Opportunity Discovery Mtgs	24	4	+2	Objective, Agenda, Attendance, Homework
# Client Assessments Conducted	20	8	+1	Implications questions
# Discussion Summaries	20	6	+6	
# Proposals Delivered (>$25K)	24	5	+5	
# Proposals Delivered	24	2	+1	
Sales Pipeline Health by Stage	Target	Current	Last Mo	# of accounts and opportunities
# Pre-Qualified Targets Accts	25	15	12	Measure of accts prequalified YTD
Qualification	13	14	18	Current # accounts in this stage
Discovery	12	12	15	Current # accounts in this stage
Solution Formulation	15	8	12	Current # accounts in this stage
Follow-Through	10	12	12	Current # accounts in this stage
Success Rate	Target	Current	Mo-Mo Change	
New Client Wins > $25K	18	6	+1	From new first-time clients
New Opportunity Wins > $25K	18	9	+2	From Current clients

Figure 22: Salesperson Behavioral and Outcome Metrics Tracking

There is one additional consideration to remember about measuring behaviors. The behaviors must be done well, with rigor and correctly. There are correct ways to do certain physical conditioning exercises and incorrect ways. The incorrect ways do not produce the results intended - and may even result in personal injury. The same is true for sales behaviors.

For example, consider the production and delivery of Discussion Summaries.

To refresh, *Discussion Summaries* are the messages sent to a client EIC (or ultimate decision maker) within 24 hours after a Discovery Meeting has taken place. The Discussion Summary confirms what was heard and any follow-on action items agreed to.

Poorly crafted, weak content, typographical and content errors, or the failure to identify action items are worse than sending no Discussion Summary at all.

Salespeople must not fool themselves by thinking they can check the box on "sent a Discussion Summary" if it is poorly crafted. Producing Discussion Summaries is an independent and a success-producing behavior which enables sales. They must be written well, and the client's response recorded each time they are crafted and sent.

Similarly, the number of Discovery sales calls is an important number to track. However, the number of Discovery sales calls made is only as productive as those with a specific mutually agreed-upon Objective and Agenda, and attendance by more than one individual in the client's organization that is associated with and knowledgeable about the client's POG.

When tracking behaviors, be honest – you can only give yourself credit for those times the behavior was executed with care and discipline.

Don't have the time to track behavioral and outcome metrics?

Make the time. It is worth it to keep yourself on track with the right success-dependent behaviors.

Coaches, Buddies and Accountability Partners

In Chapter 9, Solution Formulation, we suggested finding a buddy, coach, or accountability partner with whom you can review and test your account and opportunity strategies, chew over specific challenges, and garner tips and insights to help you improve.

In seeking out a coach, buddy, or accountability resource consider whether they:

- are experienced, insightful, and smart,
- are accessible and responsive in times of emergency,
- can put themselves in the position of the client,
- will only act and respond in what they sincerely believe is your client's best interest,
- can be trusted to keep your and your client's information confidential,

- can be a resource for people, tools, and information (recommending meetings, referrals, books, tools, or approaches), and

- will be with you for the long haul.

Tiger Woods has a swing coach. Phil Mickelson, referred to earlier in the book as an example of incredible professional discipline, has a swing coach too. I have a business coach, and joined an accountability group several years ago.

No man is an island. No salesperson should be either. Being an island is just not necessary and hinders your competitive strength.

Sales Goal Setting and Sanity-Testing

The bottom-line measurement of your success is the achievement of your sales goals. Independent of where and by whom they are set, a salesperson should test the sanity of their goal, and re-test on a quarterly basis.

Achieving your total sales goal may be further complicated by the establishment of sub-goals by offering. While your total sales goal for the year may be $2,500,000, that number may be comprised of three or four sub-goals, one for each of three specific offerings and, perhaps, a fourth for a new offering that is planned for launch in the first quarter of the year.

Each offering in your goal has its own range of sales dollar-value. Not all offerings will deliver equally compelling value to all clients, meaning that all offerings will not be equally easy to sell and deliver - or provide you with equal financial rewards. Whether an offering takes a long or short time to sell, the selling of it consumes your most valuable asset – your time.

So, how do you decide where to focus your time and energy?

Time Allocation

The speed with which an opportunity is identified, landed, and executed can vary widely. All engagements take time to qualify, propose, win, and execute. As a result, your earning potential is dependent on:

- the number of days a year you have available to sell,

- the time it takes to qualify, win, assure a deal for an offering is successful and the client is pleased, and

- the price a client is willing to pay for the offering.

To trigger your thoughts about the revenue and earnings achievable from your suite of offerings, let's run a calculation. Here are some planning factors:

Factor 1: Weeks Available in the Year

Assume 52 weeks a year, minus 2 weeks of vacation, minus another week for holidays (Christmas, Thanksgiving, New Year, 4th of July, etc.), and another week for miscellaneous personal needs. That leaves a total of 48 weeks.

Factor 2: Hours per week Available to Sell

Assume 48 weeks x 40 hours/week x 75% (the % of time of your workweek that can be allocated for selling and executing) = 1,440 hours. Therefore, the total hours available to sell to achieve your revenue goal must be less than 1440. (The 75% availability factor recognizes the reductions of available time created by administrative obligations, such as meetings, training, travel, client emergencies, computer systems challenges, etc.)

Factor 3: Annual Revenue Generated per Offering

The annual Revenue Generated per Offering = Revenue per Offering Deal x the number of Offerings sold/delivered.

A simplified short example:

> Assume your sales goal is $750,000.
>
> You have only one offering with an average selling price (ASP) = $10,000
>
> The number of deals needed to achieve your $750,000 goal = $750,000 / $10,000 or 75 deals.
>
> You must sell 75 of these deals over the course of the year to meet your goal.
>
> Let's say that, on average, it takes 20 hours to sell one of those offerings (identify, target, call, meet, qualify, discover, propose, and win).
>
> (20 hours to sell) x (75 deals) = 1500 hours to achieve your goal in a year
>
> With 1440 hours available and 1500 hours required, you are just under 100 hours short.
>
> At best, with the selling time available, you can book and execute 72 deals, or $720,000. The numbers do not allow the achievement of your goal. It is close, but there is no safety factor to cover the unexpected.

You have several choices:

-    reduce your goal,

- become more efficient at selling,

- increase the average selling price,

- sell additional offerings, or

- a combination of the above actions.

Setting realistic achievable goals is important. Achievability testing is required.

Figure 23 below illustrates an Excel spreadsheet model that can be used to test revenue goal achievability, based on the time you have available for sales and your offerings' average selling prices.

The life of a salesperson is a time management balancing act.

A Sanity Check Walk-Through

The sales goal sanity test spreadsheet in Figure 23 is modeled with:

- four standard offerings

- two of those offerings can be customized at selling price premiums,

- two different types of service offerings,

- eight major current accounts, averaging annual revenue of just over $110,000 per account, all requiring Account Management,

- 35 other accounts of lesser revenue value averaging just over $11,000 per account annually,

- there are no new offerings being anticipated for the year, and

- time availability measured in days vs. hours (48 weeks x 5 days/week x 75% available to sell)

- there are small across-the-board price increases that will need to be put in place in all existing accounts.

The goal is to generate $2,500,000 of revenue from this salesperson's account portfolio. The plan in Figure 23 maps a path to $2,615,670 (if nothing goes wrong).

Sales Goal Planning Sanity Check	Unit Sales Price	# Opportunities	Gross Revenue $	Sales Days (ea)	Sales Days (total)	Comments
Suite of Base Offerings:						
Offering A (standard)	$ 145,000.00	2	$ 290,000.00	7	14	
Offering B (standard)	$ 12,500.00	7	$ 87,500.00	4	28	
Offering C (standard)	$ 85,000.00	3	$ 255,000.00	7	21	
Offering D (standard)	$ 7,500.00	10	$ 75,000.00	4	40	
			$ 707,500.00			
Custom Offering (incl installation service):						
Offering A (customized)	$ 175,000.00	2	$ 350,000.00	5	10	
Offering C (customized)	$ 125,000.00	1	$ 125,000.00	5	5	
			$ 475,000.00			
Service Contracts						
Type A	$ 12,500.00	4	$ 50,000.00	2	8	
Type B	$ 20,000.00	3	$ 60,000.00	3	9	
			$ 110,000.00			
Current Account Management		Pricing Actions				
Major Accounts (8 major accounts)	$ 890,000.00	1.80%	$ 906,020.00	2	16	
Other Accounts (35 other accounts)	$ 246,000.00	2.50%	$ 252,150.00	0.5	17	
Expanded Penetration (New Opportunities)	$ 27,500.00	6	$ 165,000.00	5	30	
			$ 1,323,170.00			
	# New Deals	38				
	Days Available	180				
	Days Needed	198				
	Workload %	110%				
	Total Revenues	$ 2,615,670.00				

Figure 23: Time Allocation, Revenue Forecasting and Sanity-Testing Tool

Achieving this plan will require:

- a successful price increase introduced to all current accounts,

- successful expansion of business opportunities within current accounts,

- a bit more than $1.1 million of new business generated from 38 new deals.

The model also illustrates that the number of sales days required will be 10% higher than what is available, 198 vs. 180. So, this salesperson has a problem.

What the plan does *not* consider:

- To achieve the 38 new deals in the plan, what number of opportunities will need to be identified, qualified, and proposed?

  A 100% win-rate is unrealistic - unless the firm is a monopoly, and the compelling need of clients is extremely high. So, the hours associated with attempting to sell new deals will need to be increased to account for the time spent on dead-end and lost opportunities. The salesperson is already at 110% of available time. The plan does not comprehend any sales losses.

- This plan assumes that New Business Development activities (identified in Figure 29) are being largely managed and executed by someone else in the organization. Alternatively, one might inflate the hours required for selling an offering by adding an allocation for New Business Development time – but that gets rather complex.

The point of sanity-checking is that our planning eyes are always larger than our available time stomachs. So be realistic in goal setting.

This time/planning conundrum leads to the need for balance. Dropping less productive offerings is one solution. Increasing prices is another. Finding bigger deals is a third. Looking for fewer, larger, and more complex deals makes the number of wins required less, but typically increases the time required to find and secure those deals.

Storytime: He Just Couldn't Believe It

While working with a large wholesale distribution firm with more than 100 salespeople, I was surprised at the desire each salesperson had to continue to request expansion of the number of accounts assigned to them. They were jealous of house accounts, because the commissions of house accounts (those managed by regional warehouse managers) did not load into the commission plan of the outside sales team members. They were living under the assumption that the more accounts assigned to them, the more commission they would earn. Easy money.

The number of accounts assigned to some salespeople exceeded 100. By my thinking, I could not see how these outside salespeople could manage that many accounts over the wide geographic areas of the inland Northwest that were their territories. So, I suggested that they measure the amount of time spent with their accounts vs. the amount of commission earnings being generated.

Several months later, one senior salesperson who had been with the company for 40 years approached me at a regional sales meeting and said he did what I had suggested. He was shocked to realize that some of the accounts that required the most support (and his time), were producing miniscule contributions to his earnings.

He informed me that he fired a dozen or so of them, by giving up control and assigning them as house accounts to be handled by the distribution centers.

He then said, "*I couldn't believe it. Now I have more time to work on the more productive and faster growing accounts and I can already see the impact on my check!*"

Moral of the Story: Assure your time is allocated to those opportunities, offerings and accounts that will produce the highest return.

End of Story

There is no correct model. But knowing how to iterate your plan until you find the right combination of offerings, sales process times, accounts and efficiencies is a habit that should be revisited semi-annually and lead to appropriate adjustments in business mix.

A blank Excel form of this sales goal planning model is available, along with other tools from this book, in The Navigational™ Selling Workbook, available from The QMP Group, Inc. Send an email to QMP1@QMPAssociates.com to learn more.

Creating an Account & Opportunity Repository

Accounts and Opportunities

Salespeople have a lot of information to keep track of current client accounts, target accounts, key people at those accounts, sales opportunities, NBD activities, referral sources, alliance partners, appointments, teammates, internal administrative obligations, and most importantly, their promises and action plans. Customer Relationship Management (CRM) Systems are designed to make organizing, tracking, and managing all that information easy and accessible.

CRM data maintenance is typically the last thing a field salesperson wants to do. Data entry makes salespeople feel like clerks. After all, they are salespeople. They are top-of-the-food-chain professionals. Rain makers. Masters of their territory universe.

It is no surprise then, that salespeople put off working in their CRM. A common feeling is that it takes too much time to keep current, it sucks their energy, and it doesn't do much to help them win. They will use it and comply with management requests to "fill it out" if they must, but it's substantive contribution to their ability to win a deal, from their perspective, is not compelling.

Salespeople want to be on the road, sitting across from a customer, doing a standup sales pitch, or be out networking. Many I have met and worked with, feel a CRM system is largely administrative nonsense. They need to be in front of customers, creating relationships with prospects and golfing with executives of their biggest customers. They should not be wasting time two-finger typing words into a computer that will never contribute anything meaningful to their commission check.

I get it. I can see their point, but a salesperson must keep track of things.

There are many alternatives for managing your sales pipeline, from rather pricey CRM applications to a simple Excel spreadsheet. I have used many versions across the whole spectrum, have helped clients install massive mid-6-figure systems that resided on mainframes (back in the day) and even designed my own to share with clients.

They all seemed to have one shortcoming or another.

This book is already too long to delve into the details of how to make CRMs helpful to field salespeople, so I will be brief in my thoughts on sales pipeline management in the last few pages of this chapter.

Sales Pipeline Management

An experienced Salesperson may have 200 or more client firms in their CRM, considering their current prospect list with past clients, current clients, industry targets, primary referral sources and possible speaking venues. That is a lot to keep track of. A CRM system helps – if you have the discipline to use it.

A good CRM system will:

- track and remind you of needed action items, deliverable dates, and follow-ups,

- act as a database repository for contact names, email addresses, phone numbers, discussion notes, proposals, documents, hyperlinks to website URLs, LinkedIn profiles, research, and whatever other on-line information you wish to have quickly available,

- store client and opportunity-related documents, such as discussion summaries, communications, emails, proposals, and assessment results,

- link to on-line websites and other client-relevant pages,

- be quickly accessible and easy to use by cell phone and tablet,

- keep track of opportunities by sales stage,

- improve and facilitate sales forecasting, and

- provide near instant visibility (the ability to view, at-a-glance), a large swath of your opportunities and move them along the sales path.

My preference is SmartSheet™ configured in the card mode. It meets all the CRM needs of an SMB2B. It does not do marketing automation.

Figure 24 offers a configuration of SmartSheet™ as a scrum-board, pipeline management system that follows our Navigational Selling™ process.

Figure 24 Scrum Type Sales Pipeline Management Tool

How a Scrum Sales Pipeline Works

In its simplest form, a scrum CRM (or sales pipeline) tracks your activities with accounts, target market network venues, alliances, referral sources and opportunities through the stages of your sales process.

Referring to Figure 24 note the progression possible for accounts and opportunities from left to right.

The first five columns in our example help the salesperson manage and keep track of their activities with the primary sources of New Business Development generated leads. Those columns are Venues, Alliances, Referral Sources, New Target Accounts and Current Account Re-Qualifications.

Once the lead turns into an Opportunity from any one of those sources, that Opportunity enters and is processed through the four-stage process of Navigational Selling: Qualification, Discovery, Solution Formulation and Follow-Through/Win. In any scrum-based system, the salesperson can simply drag and drop the opportunities to the next stage as they warrant.

Scrum is a quick way to see the condition of a sales pipeline and note potential bottlenecks and low points. It is a visual tool that helps you see the health of your sales pipeline at a glance.

Clicking on any of the boxes reveals the details of that account or opportunity, as in Figure 25 below. This snapshot shows an expanded ExampleCo account with attachments and comments from the same SmartSheet™ tool configuration. While not shown in Figure 25, I have configured my accounts to collect 20 pieces of account data, making it useful for sales analytics.

That data comprises market segment, decision-maker management styles, ATBs and I-A-As, date the account was first logged, next action item, date last contacted, last action taken, source of the opportunity, the offering being considered, the next action to be taken, and has key documents attached for quick access (emails, proposals, discussion summaries, etc.)

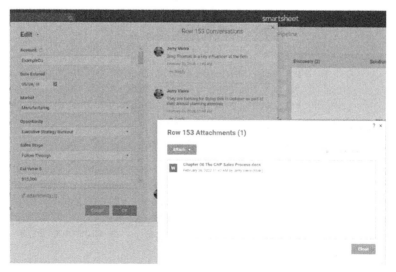

Figure 25: Sales Pipeline Account Profile Using SmartSheet™

A critical function of a CRM is its ability to notify the salesperson of any committed actions through an email. For SMB2B this type of CRM is more than adequate - and with extra user subscriptions can be shared with other members of your team.

To craft an appropriate strategy and action plan you will need multiple pieces of information:

- the six opportunity Qualification ratings,

- the relevant decision makers' and influencers' (names, titles, Management Styles, I-A-As, and ATBs) for the specific opportunity,

- the Discussion Summary, highlighting the client's POGs,

- the decision-makers' and decision influencers' value quotients,

- the client's decision-making process,

- your competitive position, and

- your actions to date.

The SAP Sheet

For purposes of discussion, we will call a *Strategy-and-Action-Planning Document* the SAP-Sheet. The SAP Sheet enables to view all the information regarding a single opportunity on one screen – or on one large sheet of paper.

There are several approaches to developing the SAP Sheet:

- craft your own SAP Sheet using Excel or Google Sheets,

- use an SAP Sheet that maps a specific sales methodology, (that SAP Sheet is typically designed by the creator of that sales methodology using the vocabulary, concepts, sales stages, and techniques unique to it), or

- configure your CRM to create your customized SAP sheet.

In each case, the challenge is finding a way to automatically populate the sheet from the CRM. Without the capability to automatically populate an SAP sheet, the salesperson is relegated to double entry of information – once to feed the CRM beast and the other to populate the SAP Sheet. Independent of how it is populated, the SAP Sheet can be affixed to the account in the CRM as an attachment or as a call-up screen tab.

SAP Sheets represent a wonderful mechanism to quickly determine which key pieces of information are still missing before a proposal is formulated. The SAP

Sheet is essential for reviewing an opportunity strategy with your Buddy, Coach or Accountability Partner.

Implementing CRMs and SAP Sheets

If you are a sole proprietor, or the only salesperson at an SMB2B firm company, you may not need to pay more than $200 a year for a single-user license of an on-line CRM, or pipeline management system subscription. Then you can build your own scrum-configured pipeline management system and SAP Sheet using Google Sheets or Excel - or use a Navigational Selling™ SAP Sheet, available from the QMP Group, Inc. on request with proof of book purchase.

Assessing Your Starting Point for an Individual Sales Improvement Journey

There are two approaches to identifying your best starting point for an individual sales skills and process improvement journey: a) the Quick Fix Table, and b) the in-depth sales effectiveness self-assessment.

The Two Paths to Individual Performance Improvement

A salesperson's personal improvement journey need not wait for a corporate program of change.

There are many prescriptions in the pharmacy of sales improvement – but like Alice in Wonderland, you won't know which to take, or in what proportions, unless you understand which you need most.

Formulating a personalized improvement plan that will give you the fastest and longest lasting impact, requires an honest diagnostic assessment of your strengths, weaknesses, and most urgent and important improvement objectives. Once you assess what you need to improve, then you can stroll the aisles of the pharmacy, and select which of the following behavioral recommendations will be needed to improve your game.

The Quick-Fix Guide

The Quick-Fix Guide is shown in Figure 26. To use this table simply look at the topics listed in the left most column, Personal Sales Challenge/Symptom. When you find a topic that applies to your situation, look at the corresponding information in the right-hand column. You will see the Navigational Selling™ concepts, Chapters, and

Appendices that apply. You can read those sections and decide which techniques or tools you want to weave into your current approach.

Additionally, you might also consider working from the Index of this book, where quick access to key words and phrases are available. In the first paragraph of this book, Note to Readers, I promised to try and make the "gems" available, accessible, and easy to find. This Quick Fix Improvement Guide, along with the Index, Table of Figures and Glossary of Terms are my efforts to keep that promise.

Personal Sales Challenge/Symptom	Helpful NavSell Technique
Difficulty loading front-end of pipeline	• Follow New Business Development Disciplines: your approach to networking, developing referral sources, formulating alliances, engaging in thought leadership, doing target account research Appendix D). • Map and leverage your target Intra-Market Networks (Appendix D) • Re-visit Target Market Focus selection criteria (Appendix C)
Low Win Rate	• Re-evaluate and adjust Target Market Focus (Appendix C) • Improve discovery of client Decision-Makers' Value Quotients (Chapter 5) • Improve sales tools: case studies, testimonials, references (Appendix D) • Use 6 Opportunity Qualification Criteria: (Chapter 6) • Improve Discovery methods; Use Discussion Summaries: (Chapter 7) • Use Trust Formula-based action plans (Chapter 5)
Low Sales Productivity	• Use Sales Call Planning disciplines: pre-qual, objective setting, agendas, attendance, homework (Chapter 7) • Sales Call Planning and Discussion Summary disciplines (Chapters 7, 8)
Missing Things in Proposals	• Improve Discovery techniques: reading people, discovering decision-making process, Discussion Summary disciplines (Chapters 3, 6, 7, 8)
Price-based Competition	• Value Quotient discovery and development (Chapters 5 & 9) • Client self-assessments (Chapter 7) • Improve Target Market focus (Appendix C)
Too much Administrative Time; Not enough selling	• Build time allocation sales plan & sanity check (Chapter 11)
Weak Client Advocates	• Improve I-A-A (Influence, Authority, Affinity) assessment and people evaluations during Discovery (Chapters 7, 8) • Revisit understanding of what a Client Advocate is (Chapter 8) • Craft action plans based on Trust-Formula (Chapter 5) and Opportunity Qualification Criteria (Chapter 6)
Knowing the best way to say things and ask questions	• Answering the "What do you do?" question (Appendix D) • Phraseology examples throughout book

Figure 26: Salesperson Navigational Selling™ Quick-Fix Improvement Guide

The Individual Sales Process & Skills Effectiveness Assessment

Those readers wishing to take a deeper diagnostic dive into their strengths, weaknesses and process shortcomings can avail themselves of the nine-dimension Individual Sales Process & Skills Effectiveness Self-Assessment shown in Figure 27, below.

Figure 27: NavSell Individual Sales Process & Skills Effectiveness Self-Assessment

The nine dimensions of individual sales skills and process excellence shown in Figure 27 are rated and compiled from 27 specific behavioral attributes. Those 27 behavioral attributes are consolidated into the nine dimensions, making the diagnostic easier to read at a higher level. But to understand which specific behavior modifications will have the greatest positive impact on your performance, you will need to review and understand the 27 sub-scores that contribute to each of the nine dimensions.

Reading the Assessment Graph

The outermost solid green line is the border of perfection. The yellow-dashed line represents the minimally acceptable level of sales skills and process capability. And the solid dark blue, irregularly shaped polygon, depicts the results from an anonymous assessment-taker's personal perception ratings of their own skills.

"Whoa!" you might say. *"Who would be crazy enough to rate themselves low – and reveal their incompetence to the whole world?!"*

There are two answers.

First, there is no reason to reveal the results to the whole world.

If a salesperson wants to improve their game, they can simply take the assessment and improve those skills with a coach, a buddy or alone with this book. If you have the will to improve, there are private, quiet, personal ways to accomplish that goal.

Secondly, if you are sincere in your desire to improve your sales game, you must know where to start, which areas need the most help and specifically what you must do to get the greatest lift in the fastest time. And as all self-improvement programs require, you need to be honest with yourself.

If you cannot be honest with yourself, you have three choices: a) continue to underperform your potential, b) bet on Lady Luck, or c) like Brady, Mickelson, and Newman, work your butt off at improving.

The list below shows the 27 sub-characteristics, their meanings, and what they evaluate, as well as their associated graphic dimension.

Dimension 1: Personal Discipline

- *Personal Behavioral Discipline* – the degree to which the salesperson exhibits consistency and discipline in their personal and business behaviors.

- *Pipeline Management* – the degree to which the salesperson manages their priorities, time, client contact relationships, commitments, and sales opportunities in an organized and automated way.

- *Measurements & Metrics* – the degree to which the salesperson regularly measures their behaviors and performance to assure steady improvement and priorities.

Dimension 2: Target Market Focus

- *Ideal Target Market* – the degree to which each of the offerings the salesperson sells, has clearly identified high client value-received target market segments.

- *Ideal Client Profile* – the degree to which the ideal clients (those that will received the highest value quotient for each offering), have been described and can be determined quickly through discovery.

- *Differentiation Match* – The degree to which the offering's differentiated strengths have been identified, validated with potential client testing, quantified and are able to be clearly demonstrated to prospects during the sales process who fit the ideal client profile.

Dimension 3: New Business Development

- *Intra-Market Network Networking* – the degree to which the Intra-Market Network (IMN) has been mapped for each major offering and is being leveraged by the salesperson.

- *Thought Leadership* – the degree to which the salesperson is actively seeking, delivering, or participating in talks, blogs and webinars that discuss the target market clients' major challenges.

- *Alliances* – the degree to which the salesperson has established cross-referral alliances with trusted partners in the primary target markets.

Dimension 4: Qualification

- *Target Account Research* – the degree to which the salesperson is researching new potential target accounts using publicly available or private data base subscriptions to discover information about the client to help pre-qualify and focus their time investment and sales efforts.

- *Clarity of Qualification Criteria* – the degree to which the salesperson consistently qualifies an opportunity well, before quoting, proposing, or engaging the rest of their sales support team in the sales effort.

- *Use of Assessments* – the degree to which the salesperson uses some form of tailored assessments to reveal a client's issues, problems, opportunities, or gaps (POGs) and their impacts on the health of the client's organization.

Dimension 5: Discovery (Client Needs)

- *Sales Call Planning* – the degree to which the salesperson is effective in planning and preparing for Discovery meetings with new clients.

- *Questioning & Listening* – the effectiveness of the salesperson's questioning and listening skills in revealing important information with respect to the client's challenge, decision process, people involved, and needs.

- *Discussion Summary & Validation* – the degree to which the salesperson records the key information revealed in a Discovery meeting, summarizes them for the client, and confirms the accuracy of that summary with the client before proceeding with their sales effort.

Dimension 6: Discovery (Client People & Decision Process)

- *Reading People* - the degree to which the salesperson can read people-types (Management Styles, Influence-Authority-Affinity, Approach to Business) for inclusion in the approach they will take to offering a solution.

- *Understanding Individual Value Quotients* – the degree to which the salesperson comes to understand the needs, motivations, and perceptions-of-value each member of the client's decision-making team will want to see in a proposed solution.

- *Client Decision Process* – the degree to which the salesperson understands the client's decision-making process, who will be involved, how long it will take, and who will have the authority to give final approval to any proposal or contract.

Dimension 7: Solution Formulation & Proposing

- *Inclusiveness* – the degree to which the salesperson's proposals are inclusive of the client team's business, personal and emotional needs. This includes the ability of the key decision makers and decision influencers to see themselves and their needs reflected in these proposals and illustrates the effectiveness of the salesperson's discovery skills.

- *Pre-Agreements* – the degree to which the salesperson and the client's EIC (ultimate decision maker) reach tentative agreement on the content and approach for any solution prior to a proposal being prepared.

- *Proposal-to-Win Cycle Time* – The degree to which the time between delivery of a proposal and final acceptance by the client (in the form of the client EIC's signature on a proposal) is less than 30 days.

Dimension 8: Crafting Winning Sales Strategies

- *Formulating Account-Level Strategies* – the degree of the salesperson's skill at researching and formulating approaches to enable engagement with a new client prospect.

- *Formulating Opportunity-Level Strategies* – the degree to which the salesperson is able to craft differentiated, high value quotient opportunity-level proposals that win.

- *Competitive Success* – the degree to which the salesperson is successful in winning head-to-head competitive opportunities.

Dimension 9: Account Management

- *Currency* – the degree to which the salesperson keeps in contact with, and stays current on the people, situations, and industry issues, of existing clients.

- *Expansion* – the degree to which the salesperson is able to expand penetration within existing accounts.

- *Balance* – the degree to which the salesperson is able to effectively allocate time and priorities to the optimum balance of new and current account activities.

By understanding the specific performance strengths and weaknesses within each dimension, appropriate improvement efforts can be initiated through understanding and practice of the concepts within Navigational Selling™.

As with other assessment tools, this one can be accessed with an email to QMP1@qmpassociates.com. Remember to specifically ask for the Navigational Selling™ Individual Sales Effectiveness Assessment.

The Salesperson's 4A Role

Salespeople can be considered by a client as anything from an irritant to be shunned or a godsend to be embraced as a savior. Those salespeople who are considered the latter behave in a highly supportive and enabling role.

The Salesperson most appreciated and respected is the well-informed helper. That role of helping typically includes:

- objectively *Assessing* the client's POG,

- expertly *Analyzing*,

- *Advising* in the best interest of the client, and

- *Assisting* in the selection and deployment of the selected solution and assuring client realization of its intended value.

Those roles are the 4A functions of a Navigational Selling™ Mindset.

The "A" that does not exist is Authority. A salesperson is not an officer or employee of the client company and therefore has no authority to make unilateral decisions or enforce rigor in the client's decision process or deployment.

A salesperson can assess, analyze, advise, and assist. The client Executive-in-Charge makes all the ultimate decisions. The salesperson only owns the power to influence through each of the 4As.

Leading through influence implies a need to use the powers you have beyond authority. The sources of this magic power are your abilities to:

- listen carefully and intently, politely question for clarification,

- respect, understand and integrate the ideas of others,

- empathize with the client's situation,

- agree with reluctant and skeptical members of the client's team that assumptions should be tested, and data-driven conclusions drawn - changing approach when it becomes apparent it is needed,

- adjust quickly and give credit for adjustment to those who suggested it,

- collaborate, manage, and facilitate productive discussions and working sessions,

- demonstrate your solution expertise and insights with modesty,

- discover and respectfully reveal things others have been missing for long periods of time,

- spotlight and openly recognize other's accomplishments and sublimate your own, and

- above all, be honest.

Solving the technical problems associated with an opportunity in the area of a salesperson's expertise is rarely the major challenge. Dealing with the personal motivations, skill gaps, and understanding the agendas and fears of the client's decision makers and decision influencers, while making meaningful progress, is.

A Final Word on Individual Sales Improvement

There are many approaches to selling. I strongly encourage salespeople to read as much as they can about client-focused sales techniques.

Sales books suggest many approaches. Some are helpful and insightful. Some, IMHO, are terrible - harkening back to pushy, objection-handling, closing-driven techniques of the 1930s. Recent research has proven that those slick closing approaches have a long-term negative impact on customer satisfaction, a client's willingness to buy (and re-buy), and their inclination to recommend you to others. How would you feel if a friend introduced a pushy salesperson to you?

Unconstrained sales objectives-setting creates situations like the not-too-distant-past Wells Fargo scandal, wherein the win was all that counted, and ethics or legality were sacrificed on the altar of the growth gods.

Questioning and listening, instead of, and certainly before, pitching, have been popular for the last 30 years. Reading client personalities and adjusting accordingly is also helpful, but few salespeople remember, or know how, to do it effectively.

"Challenging" is in vogue these days. It has been made popular in the research-based book "*The Challenger Sale*" by Matthew Dixon and Brent Adamson, (Penguin Books 2011). It has a lot of merit.

Above all, I believe there is one over-riding principle that should color all the positive sales techniques and process disciplines for any approach to lead to peak performance. That is to assist your client.

All of the components of Navigational Selling™ strive toward the end goal of building *Trust* with your client:

If the list of high-payoff essentials identified at the beginning of this chapter is simply too much to keep in mind at the start, I suggest tattooing three simple imperatives on your arm.

- I will *build TRUST with the client* through every recommendation I make and everything I say and do.

- I will conduct an extremely *thorough Discovery* process.

- I will make my primary motivation a sincere desire to *assist the client navigate their journey to achieve their goals*.

*****

Chapter 13: Organizational Level Process Adoption

In this Chapter …

To Executives-in-Charge

Just Training Is Never Enough

The Recipe, Blueprint, and Conditions for Implementation Success

Culture: Reinforcing the Foundation

Market Strategy & Focus

New Business Development

Sales Process Techniques & Tools: Adoption Priorities

Measurements & Metrics

Analytics

Dealing with Slow Process Adoption

A Final Word Regarding Organizational Implementation

To Executives-in-Charge

This final chapter is addressed specifically to Executives in Charge (EICs) of SMB2B firms who need to improve the performance of their sales organization. Included in this group of readers are Business Owners, Division General Managers,

CEOs, Vice Presidents of Sales, and Vice Presidents of Marketing & Sales Organizations.

This chapter deals with formulating a rapid impact program for implementation and adoption of relevant techniques and tools at the organizational level. Chapter 12, _Individual NavSell Process Adoption_ dealt with the independent implementation of techniques and disciplines at the individual salesperson level. You will notice a great degree of overlap between this and that last chapter. I have tried to approach this one, from the unique perspective of the EIC.

The challenge for any EIC after committing to an initiative to improve sales performance, is assuring the long-term stickiness of the disciplines, techniques, process steps, tools, and behaviors that have been embraced – and assuring that they achieve the intended results.

You may feel at this point, that if you have read Chapter 12, nothing more is necessary. You wouldn't be completely off base. However, Chapter 12: Individual NavSell Process Adoption, encourages individual diagnosis of shortcomings and individually tailored improvement plans. Chapter 13, in contrast, deals with organizational level adoption issues and challenges, and addresses such issues as: the role of Culture, setting priorities for the adoption of the most productive techniques, what to do when organizational level adoption stalls, and the allocation of task assignments between New Business Development and Sales.

If you have slogged through this book to this point, the sheer number of concepts may seem overwhelming. So, let me reassure you on a few important points.

First, to achieve significant improvement, you need not consume the whole process enchilada at once - complete with all the tools, techniques, approaches, and ideas. Many can stand on their own, and still deliver immense value. This means the adoption of just a few of the techniques can stimulate huge improvements in sales productivity, time management and the quality of the proposals your sales team delivers.

Second, the few, best, high-reward techniques will be different for different business circumstances and offering types. You will need to carefully assess and select which to put in your sales process tool kit, and the order in which you introduce them. This chapter highlights the specific techniques, behaviors and approaches that have commonly produced the greatest impact with real-world clients. Many of the stories in earlier chapters illustrate their application and results.

Third, some of the techniques that follow have the power to enhance the effectiveness of any sound sales methodology, including what you may already have in place in your organization. For example, sales call planning approaches, target market attractiveness assessments and selection criteria, and leveraging the intra-market network (to mention a few concepts introduced in other chapters) are universally applicable to any service intense SMB2B business sales process.

Just Training is Never Enough

One final thought about committing to a sales performance improvement initiative.

Training alone isn't enough to generate meaningful and lasting improvement. It is only a beginning.

If you train your sales team once and expect some magic productivity-flywheel to suddenly appear and begin to spin, it will not likely happen. Even if, in a perfect world, the Navigational Selling™ sales methodology was adopted in total and practiced religiously, there remain other critical conditions that must exist in your firm to realize significant, long-lasting success.

The Recipe, Blueprint, and Conditions for Implementation Success

The long-term success of any sales improvement program requires a handful of enablers. Those enablers are:

- a *culture of performance excellence*, which encourages individual discipline, expectations setting and accountability,

- meaningful *client-centric value quotients*, (one for each offering),

- a sound, *focused competitive target market strategy* for each offering,

- *high-leverage New Business Development activities*, (this is not tactical marketing),

- the adoption of a few *high-productivity sales tools and techniques*,

- hands-on *coaching, supervisory, advisory, or buddy-based support* for each salesperson, and

- individual and organizational level *measurements and metrics*, to assure the right behaviors are being practiced and results are being achieved.

In this final chapter, we will touch on each of those essential enablers. Rather than repeat what has already been said earlier in the book on any of those subjects, you will be referred to the Chapters, Figures and Appendices that apply to the specific recommendation. So, be prepared to bookmark or dog-ear the pages that are being referred to, or those that you judge will be particularly germane to your specific business situation.

Culture: Reinforcing the Foundation

I mention Culture first because it affects everything an organization does. In the Navigational Selling™ Marketing & Sales Engine model, culture is the lubricant of an organization's Marketing & Sales Engine.

Another way to understand the role of culture is to consider it the soil that nourishes success. If an organization has a nutritious culture just about any "seed" of a good initiative can take root and grow. On the other hand, if an organization has a dysfunctional culture, it is the equivalent of soil devoid of nutrients. In such a case, no initiative, however strong the genetic seed of the idea, will flourish.

A business is a living, breathing, socio-economic organism. Just as a society cannot escape its culture, a business organization cannot escape the overarching influence of its corporate culture, either. Neither can an animal escape its inherited, learned, and evolved DNA-driven impulses, instincts, behaviors, actions, and reactions. Those characteristics may be able to be bred out, but such genetic modifications cannot be expected to show results overnight. It is the same with business organizations. Nonetheless, it is important to assess, recognize deficiencies, and begin work on the cultural adjustments necessary for success.

In my unofficial survey of over a hundred client engagements, a firm's culture is the single most important nutrient promoting its health and survival - and culture is primarily driven by the CEO ATB type, discussed in Chapter 8: Reading People.

My guess is that your corporate house is already built. The foundation of that house, its values, processes, employees, management processes, markets, clients, ethics, products and services, brand position, financial status, and much more is already in place. Therefore, it is completely impractical to assume anything like a greenfield starting point exists.

An EIC wanting to implement a new process improvement of any kind will need to deal with the reality of integrating a new approach, set of disciplines, expectations, and vocabulary into an already established corporate culture. The less the employees of your firm are experienced in change management, the more difficult it will be. Moreover, change by edict is a tough row to hoe.

It may seem counterintuitive, but those companies with the highest degree of strict established norms, expected behaviors, processes, and disciplines already in place, find process change implementation the easiest.

Why?

The existence of norms, expected behaviors, processes and in-place disciplines, are evidence of a culture of accountability – and accountability will be essential for rapid adoption and shakeout of any new process.

What I am saying here is …

The Culture of the firm is the biggest predictor of successful change.

Assessing the strength of your firm's culture

Most organizational assessments we use, include a dimension for organizational culture. If that cultural dimension is scored low by most individuals in an organization, that is the place to begin any initiative, no matter the process or technique being implemented.

The checklist below in Figure 28 suggests the existence of a solid, performance-based culture. It is a long list but worth a quick review to understand what the genetic rungs of a healthy cultural DNA helix look like – and how that might compare to your current situation. The definitions of each term are available in the *Glossary of Terms* at the end of this book.

If you would like to score your internal corporate culture, rate each of the listed characteristics, on a scale between 1 and 5, with 5 being the highest. Rate the degree to which you believe your organization exhibits each specific characteristic. A perfect score is 85, which represents a highly productive corporate culture.

The degree to which these organizational characteristics exist and garner high ratings, provides the first indication of an organization that can accomplish great things.

☐ Ownership   ____
☐ Accountability   ____
☐ Expectations Setting   ____
☐ Goal Setting   ____
☐ Alignment   ____
☐ Measurements & Metrics   ____
☐ Absolute Honesty   ____
☐ Teamwork   ____
☐ Open Communications   ____
☐ Ethics   ____
☐ Sense of Urgency   ____
☐ Focus   ____
☐ Quality   ____
☐ Decision-Making   ____
☐ Training   ____
☐ Key Process Discipline   ____
☐ Mentorship / Coaching   ____
                    Score Total   ____

Figure 28 Organizational Culture Effectiveness Score Sheet

A few of these characteristics carry more weight than the others. With respect to sales process improvement, the most important and enabling cultural characteristics are:

Discipline

For a salesperson to succeed they must exhibit a significant degree of personal discipline and reliability. For a sales organization to succeed it must also exhibit disciplined and consistent behaviors – the right behaviors.

Focus

Closely related to discipline is focus. Multi-tasking has been proven to reduce effectiveness in all the tasks being multi-tasked. Multi-tasked activities produce less than optimum results. The sales role requires the ability to focus-on-demand and immediately kill distractions.

Expectations & Accountability

As you work through sales process change, you will likely conduct training, ask your team to do some new things, expect behavioral change, hold them accountable for changing their behaviors, and expect them to comply.

As a leader, you must exemplify the desired behavior and hold your people accountable. You will need to set clear expectations (supported by the training), set up checkpoints to observe compliance, and reward evidence of the new desired behaviors.

Ethics

If your sales team is going to succeed, ethical behavior is essential in all dealings with clients, peers, employees, and internal support staff. Use the Client-Salesperson *Trust Formula* (Figure 12 Chapter 5) to judge your organization's understanding of trust-building behaviors.

Absolute Honesty

Absolute Honesty is a cultural imperative that requires direct, open, and honest communication between employees and bi-directionally up-and-down throughout the organization. It implies data and fact-driven information exchange.

The Simplest Motivator of Cultural Change

No argument, culture change is a challenge. Culture change cannot occur without three things. The first is executive commitment, demonstrated through personal behavioral example. The second is an incremental plan. The third, is best related in the brief story that follows.

Storytime: The Challenge of Culture Change has a Magic Potion

Some years ago, two well-respected world-renowned professors I know, began a research effort to discover the factors that make companies customer oriented. The professors wanted to establish clear causality between corporate cultural characteristics and the degree of a firm's customer orientation.

Many potential variables were identified that might account for the degree of customer orientation exhibited by a business, including something as seemingly far-fetched as the childhood backgrounds of the CEOs. The researchers considered that there might be a connection between the CEOs of companies that were highly customer-centric and their upbringing in poorer segments of society. They speculated that it might influence the CEOs to exhibit more empathy. The thinking was that such an empathy factor would trickle down to the people in the business and be realized and perceived by clients as a high degree of customer centricity.

After much data collection and processing, the professors found one prominent factor that predicted the degree of customer orientation exhibited by a firm.

---

*The companies that rated highly in customer orientation, **rewarded** their employees for customer orientation!*

You get the behavior you reward.

Moral of the Story: If you are embarking on a cultural change journey, start immediately by identifying, training, measuring, personally exemplifying, and rewarding the behaviors you want your employees and salespeople to exhibit.

End of story

Market Strategy & Focus

By far, the greatest impact on improving sales will be driven by the firm's Market Strategy.

I have experienced this repeatedly in our marketing and sales transformation breakthroughs with our client base. Simply stated, small market strategy improvements can generate explosive sales! By contrast, I have also experienced expensive sales training programs that resulted in little to no impact, because the market strategy was fundamentally unsound.

A caution to EICs reading this: Low or weak sales performance is often a symptom of a bad strategy, and not a symptom of a root cause deficiency in your sales process. While, to some degree any sales process can be improved, a perfect sales process cannot overcome a fundamentally unwise market strategy.

In Chapter 1, we recounted the somewhat fictionalized story of the Battle of Stalingrad, as portrayed in the movie, "*Enemy at the Gates*". The story captured the essence and foolhardiness of trying to capture an objective through a frontal assault – supported by nothing except fanatical officers, lots of well-trained brave soldiers, and no strategy.

Soldiers without a good strategy are casualties in the making.

How do you know if you have good offering-specific market strategies?

Market strategies are offering-specific. This means you should not expect one strategy to be the best for multiple offerings. A simple test of whether an offering-specific market strategy is sound can be determined by answering the following questions:

- *Is the offering's Market Strategy Focused*?

    A good strategy is focused on a target market in which clients experience a high value-quotient as a result of purchasing, deploying, and using your offering. Not every client receives the same level of value from your service. Those who perceive the greatest value are more likely to buy it, pay more for it, be happier with it, tell others like themselves about it, and return when they need more.

- *Does the offering deliver a Compelling Value Quotient to clients*?

    The value the client receives from the benefits delivered by your offering, must greatly outweigh the client's costs associated with buying and deploying the offering. Furthermore, both the benefits and costs are more than exclusively financial – including emotional, physical, political, and social components. This compelling value quotient must be supported by real-world data, case studies, testimonials, and references.

- *Does it leverage your Strengths*?

    The best strategies pit your strengths against your competitors' weaknesses in your primary target markets.

- *Is it differentiated enough to justify Price Premiums*?

    Price premiums must be supported by the degree of its unique value quotient compared to competitive approaches, including Do-it-Themselves and Do-Nothing options. Value Quotient is discussed in detail in Chapter 5: Pillar 5.

- *Does its Channel-to-Market deliver meaningful supplemental value to the client*?

    Your channel-to-market must be selected based on its capability to deliver supplemental value to clients as first priority, not simply *your* need to get product on the shelves. Supplemental value might be training, installation, updates, demonstrations, selection, service and more. From the client's standpoint it's all one transaction.

Appendix C: Market Strategy, covers formulating sound Market Strategy in detail, offering a 13-factor market attractiveness assessment tool for selecting the most lucrative markets to target.

If you do not have a good focused market strategy in place, an improved sales process won't make up for it.

New Business Development (NBD)

New Business Development (NBD) is the high-leverage activity associated with discovering and engaging with reliable sources of multiple, pre-qualified opportunities.

Its position in the Market Strategy-to-Sales continuum is depicted in Figure 29 below, and again in Figure 39 in *Appendix D, New Business Development*. Combined with a strategically sound and focused market strategy, the following NBD activities can produce an order-of-magnitude better return on investment than tactical marketing initiatives.

I strongly recommend that you review Figure 29. Notice the specific marketing and sales activities that are typically part of the four major functions of a marketing and sales organization: a) market strategy, b) new business development, c) tactical marketing, and d) sales.

Four New Business Development practices have proven to produce the greatest results for SMB2B:

- Leveraging Intra-Market Networks (IMNs),

- Thought Leadership,

- Alliance Development, and

- Target Account Pre-Qualification Research.

Brief descriptions of each follow. More detailed explanations can be found in Appendix D, New Business Development.

Leveraging the Intra-Market Networks of Your Target Markets

The Intra-Market Network (also known as the Market Ecosystem) is the communications and influence structure within a target market. It is comprised of that market's Venues (where participants in that market meet, live or virtually), Vehicles (what they read), Opinion Leaders, Primary Referral Sources, and the EICs associated with the offerings you provide.

The Intra-Market Network (IMN) is proven to be an order of magnitude more productive in communicating a value proposition than mass media. Mass media is the equivalent of a frontal assault. IMNs are the equivalent of a focused penetration initiative aimed at the neural communications network that naturally exists in a market.

The structure of an Intra-Market Network is shown in Figure 40, Appendix D.

Thought Leadership

Thought Leadership is the collection of coordinated activities associated with sharing and spreading relevant insights concerning some aspect of the client challenges that your offerings address. It comprises articles, blogs, webinars, talks, podcasts, and whitepapers produced by an expert in the field, preferably one of your most knowledgeable, and experienced employees or happy clients.

Those insights are intended for delivery to groups of client decision makers and decision influencers within the *Intra-Market Network*.

Thought Leadership is the least expensive and highest leverage expenditure that a service intense, SMB2B business can make.

The advantages of thought leadership webinars and talks are significant. How else can you (or a salesperson) gather groups of perhaps 100 industry influencers, executives, decision makers, and decision influencers in a room and capture their undivided attention for an hour?

The objective, of course, is not to blatantly pitch your products, (which will only assure you never get invited back to talk), but rather to share your insights related to common consequential challenges the clients in the audience are facing currently or will be facing in the near future. Such talks firmly position you and your firm as leaders in an industry, and cost you nothing more than a plane ticket, a hotel room, and a few meals.

Thought Leadership is discussed extensively in *Appendix D, New Business Development*.

Alliances

Those firms which offer complementary products and services to your type of ideal client, can represent opportunities for a steady stream of referrals to your salespeople.

Seeking alliances with those firms that offer complementary services *and* are perceived by your common clients as high-quality suppliers in their specialty, must be the objective. High Quality alliances, as perceived by your target client base, help your brand. No alliances are better than bad alliances.

Alliances are discussed more in *Appendix D, New Business Development.*

Account and Market Research

Thanks to the internet, numerous business entity data bases with lists of businesses to target, are relatively easy to discover and sift through.

Do not fall victim to believing that your firm needs to spend copious amounts of money to discover the names of new target clients or on tactical marketing initiatives to generate leads.

Storytime: Target Market Focus and Research Pays Off Big-Time

Early on in my consulting career, I worked with a product manager who after struggling to grow his revenues, finally succumbed to what the analytics revealed – that there was a much better opportunity to grow if he would only focus on one high-value-quotient target market instead of trying to be everything to everyone.

Seeing the wisdom of the strategic adjustment, mostly because nothing else was working, he immediately wanted to launch an advertising and promotional program aimed at that focused market – a frontal assault.

I asked him to wait.

Calling the national association of the target market industry, I was able to score an association membership directory. Total cost $95.00 for a hard copy.

When I received it, I handed it to the product manager and said, "*Here is the industry membership directory. Every one of your prospective clients is listed here. You've already had a few extraordinarily successful installations of your product with clients in this market, so you have some references and a couple of value-validating case studies. I suggest you start there.*"

The industry directory listed all the 5,000+ hospitals in the U.S. The information in that directory included names of each member hospital, their CEO, Chief Financial Officer, IT Director, Head of Nursing, Head of Physicians, other key personnel, as well as the number of beds, any medical specialties practiced, location, and more.

The national organization also promoted an annual conference, providing an opportunity to look into the heart of the issues EICs faced. Using the directory as a chart of the Intra-Market Network and Thought Leadership techniques, the business took off – without any advertising.

Moral of the Story. It is a reasonable expectation of your salespeople to do industry research through LinkedIn, Google, client websites, industry association membership lists, and other industry databases available by NAICS code and accessible online through many public libraries.

End of Story

Separate NBD from Sales If the Workloads Become Unmanageable

Figure 29 below, Sales and New Business Development (NBD) Task Map, illustrates the placement of responsibilities in a typical marketing and sales organization. It allocates common tasks to four functions: Sales, New Business Development, Tactical Marketing, and Market Strategy.

The portion of the chart to the left of the vertical dashed line illustrates the division of tasks commonly associated with both Sales and New Business Development. It is not unreasonable to expect all those tasks to be the responsibility of a salesperson, if there is no New Business Development resource on staff, or no internal Tactical Marketing function available.

I know of several large company salespeople who handle it all and succeed. They are disciplined, work hard, manage their time well, and stay focused on the most productive, high-leverage activities. On the other hand, if the workload becomes too overwhelming, then the tasks must be split, and resources identified to handle those tasks in the NBD column.

Figure 29: Sales and New Business Development Task Map

NavSell Sales Process Techniques & Tools: Implementation Priorities

The following Navigational Selling™ sales process techniques and tools are listed in decreasing order of potential impact on a sales process improvement initiative. As an EIC, if you are going to encourage the behavioral adoption of any of them, start at the top of the list and work down. The explanation of these activities can be found in Part 2 (Chapters 5 thru 11).

The recommendations that follow are those with the highest *overall organizational impact*. An EIC should want to see these sales behavioral recommendations adopted first.

Implementation Priority 1: Sales Call Planning aka Preparing for Discovery Meetings

There are three parts to this priority: Sales Call Planning, Discovery Meeting Agendas, and Discussion Summaries.

Discovery: Sales Call Planning

Sales call planning in the vernacular of Navigational Selling™ is the establishment of the following agreed-upon items, in collaboration with a prospective client and sufficiently in advance of any meeting to allow adequate preparation.

- *Objective* – the primary goal of the discussion,

- *Agenda* - the mutually agreed list of items to be discussed, and their order,

- *Participation* - who the meeting participants and contributors will be,

- *Homework* - what information the client will provide to assist the discussion, and

- *Logistics* – the time, date, location and expected duration of the discussion.

Discovery Meeting Agendas

Discovery Agendas demonstrate to the client a high degree of client-centricity, by showing respect for their time. Agendas typically follow this sequence:

- Personal Introductions & Background Sharing (if the first meeting),

- Client's Challenge,

- Approaches (various ways to overcome the client's challenge),

- Applicability (discussion of which approach discussed offers the most promise), and

- Next Steps (as appropriate)

Such an Agenda usually requires 60 to 90 minutes. The majority of time should be dedicated to the Client's Challenge. After all, *Discovery* is all about them and their POG, not you - particularly in the first discussion.

The benefits of the practice of pre-meeting Sales Call Planning and Agendas should be apparent:

- it minimizes the number of sales calls necessary to complete discovery of issues, and the client's decision makers, influencers, and decision process,

- it permits the client to reveal their challenges, barriers, and problems prior to the salesperson offering solutions,

- it permits time for both the client and salesperson to prepare appropriately for the meeting (particularly when combined with a pre-meeting phone discussion to outline the client's challenge, and

- it allows time and appropriate decision-influencer participation to enable in-depth qualification.

An Agenda produces the time efficiency needed to quickly get to the heart of the client's challenge, meet the client's key people who in one way or another will influence the decision, and involve the expert resources and sales materials you brought to the meeting. Dialogues for how to request the Agenda, participation, objective, and determine what to prepare is in Chapter 7: Discovery.

If nothing else changes in your firm's sales methodology, at a minimum, this will increase sales productivity, enable more comprehensive discovery, and improve the content of your proposals.

Discussion Summaries

Discussion Summaries are the second most powerful weapon in a salesperson's technique arsenal.

A *Discussion Summary* is a message, typically an email, sent to the client EIC within 24 hours of a discovery meeting. The message summarizes the Discovery Meeting conversation and the key points revealed during the discussion – capturing any mutually agreed, follow-on action items.

The standard form of a Discussion Summary follows:

- it *thanks the EIC*, and any other attendees that may have participated, for their time, their frankness, and any detailed information they were willing to share,

- it *empathizes with their business challenges*, while reassuring them that a solution can be found,

- it *itemizes the key points* of the discussion,

- it *requests a review* of the summary pieces of information you captured during the discussion and recorded in the message - and requests correction of those points that you may have misunderstood or mistaken,

- it *details any action items* that were decided upon during the meeting Agenda,

- it *thanks the individual again*, and

- it *promises a follow-up* call in a few days to assure they received and had an opportunity to read the message, hear any corrections or misstatements it contained, and answer any questions they may have.

A Discussion Summary delivers strong benefits to both the salesperson and their firm:

- it demonstrates to the client that the salesperson listened closely and well,

- it demonstrates to the client that the salesperson has adopted a collaborative quest to address client's POG,

- it demonstrates a desire on the part of the salesperson to understand, in depth, the details surrounding the client's POG, and shows a sincere effort to be accurate by asking for feedback as to the summary's accuracy, and

- it differentiates the sales approach from other competitor salespeople who do not make the effort or take the time to craft a similar message.

Discovery Meeting Planning and Discussion Summaries are by far the most valuable and easiest sales techniques and behaviors to implement. The Discussion Summary, along with an example, is discussed in detail near the end of Chapter 7: Discovery.

Implementation Priority 2: Ideal Client Profiles

Closely aligned with the power of formulating a sound market strategy is providing the salespeople with an Ideal Client Profile to use in pre-qualification efforts and account research.

Ideal client profiles not only describe the client problems whose resolution will provide client significant value, but also describe the personality types of clients and client cultural characteristics that will likely embrace your offerings and approach.

Ideal client profiles are very offering specific.

Implementation Priority 3: Qualification Criteria

Navigational Selling™ recommends six factors against which to qualify opportunities. Adopting and insisting on true, customer-revealed, qualification criteria assures that competitive advantages can be leveraged, and action plans are optimized. The six qualification factors are covered in detail in Chapter 6: Qualification.

For convenience, those factors are listed here:

Compelling Need - The Compelling Need factor rates the degree to which a challenge or problem faced by a client is critical, needing to be addressed immediately or soon, or there will be significant consequence for not doing so. Regulatory compliance, safety considerations or the need to meet bank covenants are just a few examples of needs that fall into a high Compelling Needs category. Research has shown that between 30% to 50% of a typical salesperson's pipeline is lost to "*No Decision*". This means that 30% to 50% of effort is wasted because the client never had a real and compelling need to begin with.

Match - Match rates the degree to which your service offering precisely meets the challenges presented by the client's Compelling Need.

Value Quotient - The client Value Quotient qualification factor rates the long-term value that will be realized by the client, of acquiring and using your solution to fix their problem or meet their challenge, compared to the costs borne by the client of implementing that solution. The Client Value Quotient is both a subconscious and conscious calculation in the mind of the client. It comprises both, the five perceived benefits (economic, emotional, physical, political, and social) divided by the five perceived costs (economic, emotional, physical, political, and social).

Competitive Advantage – The Competitive Advantage qualification factor rates the degree to which the client believes you have a competitive advantage over other alternatives. Do not forget that "Do it Themselves" and "Do Nothing" are legitimate forms of competitive solutions in the eyes of a client – whether they are wise alternatives or not.

Advocate – The Advocate qualification factor rates the strength of a key person within the client organization that loves your approach and offering. This person will promote you and your approach when you are not there, provide you inside information as to the progress of the decision, and maintain a steady internal force encouraging the client's selection of your approach. The higher the organizational position of your advocate, the higher the Advocate rating.

A quick note before we explain the last qualification factor – *Leverage*. The first five qualification factors are only valid from the client's perspective. When a salesperson communicates to an internal team how well an opportunity is qualified, they must have reason for believing the ratings are valid from the client's point of view.

Leverage - Leverage is the only Opportunity Qualification Factor that is valid from both the seller's and buyer's perspectives.

From the seller's perspective, Leverage estimates the degree to which a win of this opportunity provides any or all the following opportunities to you and your business:

- for more business,

- to enter a new industry,

- to add a new capability to an offering,

- to build a strong and impressive case study,

- to gain a strong testimonial,

- to tout an industry leading organization as a client, and

- for strong in-market referrals.

Adoption of the Navigational Selling™ Qualification Factor rating system assists salespeople, sales managers and EICs understand the reality and potential of any opportunity in the sales pipeline. It also assists in identifying the most important actions that should be taken to shore-up the company's position with a client for a specific opportunity.

Implementation Priority 4: Proposals not Quotes

Of the techniques we highly recommend organizations adopt, the switch from quotes to proposals will likely be the most difficult – particularly in organizations that have operated for many years using only the quote approach.

A story from Chapter 9: Solution Formulation, is repeated here for convenience and to make a point. The quote is from an EIC operating a metal parts company in the upper Midwest where the competition for automotive-based business is extreme. (Parentheses have been added or clarification.)

Storytime: Breaking the Chains of Old Habits (redux)

A client that produced custom precision metal parts wanted to find a way to grow faster in the highly competitive automotive supplier market of the Midwest. That region is awash with competitors, mostly servicing the automotive 2nd tier supplier market. The client was getting frustrated with the too frequent cycle of "quote and lose" against larger competitors. They wanted to find a way to break through.

By transitioning them to a proposal format for major opportunities, instead of a one-page quote, they broke out of their old paradigm, winning against larger, better established, tough and numerous competitors. Their proposals added such considerations as Quality, case studies, design concepts, key employee resumes, progress milestones, and the process they would be using to assure collaboration and design integrity along the way.

Shortly after the engagement, I received this unsolicited email comment:

"Wanted to let you know that we just won a HUGE program that, alone, will increase our annual revenue by 20%. ... This was an extremely competitive situation with 10 bidders and ultimately, "we knocked their socks off" (with our proposal). Not sure we would have won this had we (used) the same (quote) approach we used (in the past)... "

End of Story

Proposals permit you to tell you whole capability story as it relates to the solution you are proposing and differentiate you from other competitors trapped in the "Price and Delivery Quote Paradigm". One-page quotes, communicating only price and delivery only, do not allow differentiation on anything but price.

Implementation Priority 5: Buddies, Coaches and Accountability Partners

Every professional I know, from CEO to salesperson, could benefit from having a sounding board, whether that sounding board bears the title of Coach, Supervisor, Buddy or Accountability Partner. It helps to have someone with whom to test ideas, engage in creative problem solving, review documents created by the salesperson, vent, formulate sales strategies, provide encouragement, and guide through an improvement journey.

The highest performing professionals in the world have coaches. Tom Brady, famed quarterback for the New England Patriots and Tampa Bay Buccaneers and seven-time super bowl winner has a personal quarterback coach that he seeks guidance from when he is struggling. Most PGA professional golfers on tour have swing coaches. The most successful salesperson I know has a coach.

The best situation arises when the Sales Manager takes on the role of the Buddy and Coach.

As an EIC you must encourage every salesperson to have a buddy, coach, or accountability partner.

The role of the Buddy is discussed in Chapter 9: Solution Formulation and the Proposal and Chapter 12: Individual NavSell Process Adoption.

Implementation Priority 6: Insist On and Simplify the CRM Information Repository

Salespeople typically despise CRMs (Customer Relationship Management) systems. To salespeople they appear to be a time-suck, and to them, these kinds of systems provide little help in achieving their sales goals. They often see system-feeding as a distraction from what they really need to be doing and what motivates them – being in the field visiting with current and prospective clients.

But CRMs house important customer and sales data and are an invaluable asset of the firm. EICs must therefore insist that salespeople keep that CRM data current and secure.

The most effective sales team I ever worked with is large. Yet, in the past, it has experienced a high turnover rate in sales personnel. Without a CRM housing current account and opportunity information, a new salesperson would be at a severe handicap. It would mean they would need to recreate the account profile, account history, decision-maker information, as well as account, opportunity, and sales data.

In some SMB2B firms, particularly those with only one or two salespeople, some salespeople believe that the contact data of the clients they work with is their personal asset, not their firm's. Some have even admitted that they consider their closely held contact information as their insurance policy against being fired. And, in some cases, the salesperson feels that their contact list is the reason why they would be a valuable hire for another firm in the same line of business.

To EICs, let me state emphatically …

Account, client, and opportunity information gathered in the course of a salesperson's employment with the firm, is an asset of the firm, not the salesperson. That is why EICs must insist that account-level, opportunity-level and other important data is current, stored and secured within the firm's CRM.

There are two major categories of data within a CRM: *Client Account Information* and specific *Sales Opportunity Data*.

Two lists follow. The first list is our recommendation on the Account-Level data that should be recorded in a SMB2B firm's CRM, the second details our recommendations on the Opportunity-Level data that should be recorded.

List 1: Account-Level Data, Attachments and Links

- NAICS industry code,
- executive team names and titles,

- industry association participation,

- names and locations of operating divisions,

- annual reports,

- website links, and

- industry whitepapers and forecasts.

List 2: Opportunity-Level Data, Attachments and Links

This list comprises information about the specific offering that is being sold and includes:

- product or service offering,

- value of the opportunity to your firm,

- sales stage: qualification, discovery, solution formulation, follow through,

- disposition: won, lost, no decision (no decision is the default if there is no definitive response, one way or the other, from the client by 90 days after proposal is delivered),

- EIC, ultimate decision maker, name, management style, ATB, I-A-A,

- decision influencers: name, expertise, and

- advocate: name, reason for the advocate's preference

Attachments : These are key documents essential to a win:

- *Discovery Meeting Agendas and Presentations*,

- *Client Organization Charts*,

- *Discussion Summaries*,

- *Client Self-Assessment* results, and

- *Proposals*.

Encouraging CRM Use

Getting a sales team to use and keep their CRM account, pipeline, contact, and opportunity records current is a huge challenge. That is primarily because most salespeople don't feel that a CRM is a personally useful tool. To them it is simply an administrative overhead chore, necessary only to keep the higher ups happy. I have found it not uncommon to see salespeople keep two systems – one of their own devising and the corporate sanctioned one.

Here are a few suggestions to encourage and realize compliance in the use of your CRM by the sales team.

Minimize the Number of Sales Steps: By minimizing the number of sales steps (or stages), salespeople won't have to continually access the system just to move opportunities along the process. Navigational Selling™ has only 4 stages: Qualification, Discovery, Solution Formulation, and Follow-Through/Win. A scrum-based CRM allows opportunities to be quickly "dragged and dropped" along the stages of a sales process.

Set Expectations and Reward Inclusion of Important Attachments: These comprise Discussion Summaries, Proposals, Client Assessments, client Organization Charts, and Sales Call Planning Agendas. If you want people to use good sales call planning, discovery techniques, and create a track record of account activity for the support team to use in their roles, documentation helps. You might even consider rewarding the behaviors. If documents are attached to the CRM, it's easy to measure and verify individual adoption of good sales behaviors and assess the quality of those documents.

Publicize Examples of Adoption: Have individual members of your sales force share with the rest of the team how the CRM helped them win a big deal or stop a competitive threat. Research has revealed that adoption, use, and visibility of new approaches by de-facto opinion leaders within a group, is extremely effective in accelerating the adoption of a new process, tool, innovation, or technique.

Conduct Major Opportunity Reviews: Holding major opportunity reviews in which salespeople discuss their major open opportunities and/or progress in penetrating target accounts, creates learning opportunities for the other sales team members. If you have a sales team – more than 100, it's a bit difficult and could take weeks. That is not reasonable. But, if you think Opportunity Reviews would be a helpful learning technique, break the groups into smaller numbers – no more than six participants at a time. Your sales managers should lead the reviews.

Note: Personally, I do not like calling these sessions "reviews". They should be working sessions. When a salesperson comes out of such a gathering, they should feel that it was worth their time, that they learned something, received valuable advice, and that they will be helped by implementing suggestions and techniques that they heard about during the session.

Move Account Ownership: This is a bit heavy handed, but if a salesperson is continually negligent in keeping important account and opportunity information current, as an EIC you have a responsibility to protect that company asset. Transfer that account ownership to someone on the sales team who has more rigorous discipline and good sales behaviors in their genes.

Implementation Priority 7: Measurements and Metrics

In your organization, acceptable sales results will be the direct result of your sales team's discipline in adhering to sound sales behaviors. Identifying those success-enabling behaviors, and continually monitoring and measuring the team's adherence to them, is critical to the firm's success.

Tracking and measuring personal sales behaviors, especially the critical antecedents of success, is an important discipline to develop. Remember we want to focus on behavioral independent variables as much as outcome success variables. The enabling sales behaviors are the precursors of success. See a more detailed discussion of individual metrics in Chapter 12.

As a starting point, from the list of *enabling sales behaviors* below, select those behavioral metrics you think are the precursors of sales success and are most needed in your organization.

- the number of high-quality *referral sources and alliances* developed,
- the number of external *referrals received and provided*,
- the number of *in-target-market event venues attended* (leveraging the intra-market network for networking),
- the number of *in-target-market event venue talks* delivered, and blogs published (thought leadership),
- the number of *self-assessments* taken by clients,
- the number of *sales call planning process cycles* executed (objective, agenda, attendance, and homework),
- the number of *agenda-driven discovery meetings*,
- the number of *discussion summaries*,
- the number of *LinkedIn contacts*,
- the number of *coach, buddy, or accountability-partner working sessions*,

- a semi-annual *self-assessment of sales skills* (reading people, qualification, questioning & listening, revealing client decision-making process, identifying client decision influencers and decision makers, and POG identification), and

- a self-graded *quality of proposals*.

It's easy for a salesperson to track the number of Discovery Meetings they conduct in a month, the number that generated a Discussion Summary, the number of pre-discovery Agendas they offered to prospects and the number of pre-meeting client Self-Assessments that were taken. If your sales team perfects and tracks these behaviors, your business will achieve a higher level of success. If they fail, they will likely be able to track that failure to something on the list that was overlooked or intentionally thought not necessary.

Salespeople can also grade themselves on their effectiveness in many of the other behaviors like Questioning and Listening, People Reading, and the capture of client decision-making processes.

Implementation Priority 8: Analytics

A periodic analytics activity is the most commonly missing function in most marketing & sales organizations. Yet, in our experience at The QMP Group, it has produced the greatest breakthroughs for clients. Breakthroughs do not occur with every client and every time an analytics exercise is conducted, but often enough so that analytics discipline should be in every SMB2B business arsenal.

Here are several examples and impacts, of some basic analytics we have conducted in the past:

- More than one thousand new installations of software offering in a new market in roughly 2½ years. Prior to the analytics effort, there was only one installation in that market. Analytics revealed a significant unmet need, an extremely high client value quotient in meeting that need, and many potential clients across the country with the same need.

- A compound annual growth rate of 55% for 6 consecutive years, from roughly $1.7M up to $30M,

- A jump in target market deal size from $22K to $1M+

- A jump in average selling prices from $1,000 to $4,000

All those breakouts were triggered by some basic historical sales analytics, digging into the anomalies the analyses revealed, testing the root cause of those anomalies with clients, and executing a slight course correction of the market strategy. It is important to note that in none of these cases was there a need to expand the level of marketing expenses by any significant amount. A re-focus of the existing budget covered expenditures that were needed.

A sales and marketing analytics exercise can answer many questions and provide insights for adjusting strategy. Here are examples of information that could be revealed through in-depth inquiry and an analytics exercise:

- Which group of customers is receiving the highest value-quotient from our offerings? What is special about those clients? How many more like them are there that have the same challenge?

- Which of the market segments we serve are growing the fastest - independent of the magnitude of sales they are generating? What is driving that growth?

- Which sources are producing the most and best-prequalified leads for our sales team and why?

- What behaviors are our most productive salespeople exhibiting that others are not?

- Which territories are selling the most and growing the fastest? What can our other sales territories learn from that success and how can we put in place and encourage a regular best-practices sharing?

Not having an analytics process is like fixating on the distant mountaintops and never noticing the gold at your feet.

Shortcuts

Salespeople are always looking for a smarter way to do things. Sometimes that results in skipped steps. Their objective in skipping steps is to increase their productivity and bandwidth – enabling them to spend more time on the road meeting additional client prospects. But in truth, that is an unwise approach to productivity.

The most effective way to increase productivity is to get more efficient and effective in the execution of the critically important sales behaviors, rather than skipping those behaviors altogether.

You wouldn't want a pharmaceutical company to skip steps in the production of a critical drug in a search for productivity enhancements. You wouldn't want your airline pilot to skip steps in the pre-takeoff checklist. If you value the ability to attract and win the best clients, insist that your salespeople stick to the checklist of productive sales behaviors.

As an EIC, please don't search for productivity in shortcuts. Rather look for productivity in your sales team learning to be more effective and efficient at the right behaviors.

Personal Behavioral Metrics vs. Outcome Metrics

It is common to want to measure your progress by the amount of money you make, your sales and profit.

It is also common to monitor your health by stepping on the scale in the morning. But gaining weight is not necessarily a measure of ill health if you are adding muscle mass as a result of regular workouts. Being under weight. Being underweight is not always a sign of being healthy either.

My point is your outcome metrics (sales or weight) are the result of certain behaviors. You can achieve weight loss through multiple behaviors, bulimia (bad) or a combination of eating less unhealthy foods and exercise (good).

One approach is based on unhealthy behavior to achieve a sometimes-false measure of health, the other is based on healthy behavior.

I know that if I want to lose weight in a healthy manner, I do not need to ever step on a scale.

If I measure the amount of exercise I get, the amount of alcohol I consume, and the number of desserts I eat, and those measurements trend in the right direction, the outcome of those behaviors will ultimately result in weight loss. I will not need to step on the scale. I will feel the results when I exercise and when I cinch my belt to hold up my pants.

Sales Behavioral Metrics vs. Outcome Metrics

Sales (bookings), revenues and profits are outcome metrics. Many people measure their success by such outcome metrics alone. Nothing wrong with that, if you also understand and pay attention to the personal and business behaviors that create those outcomes.

Outcome metrics like bookings, sales, and profits are dependent variables. Dependent (or antecedent) variables depend on performing the right independent behaviors. If you want revenue to increase, you need to do more of the right things and more of the productive behaviors that will ultimately result in the revenue outcomes you aspire to.

Healthy pre-revenue behaviors are called independent metrics, or independent variables. They depend on nothing except you doing them and knowing how to do them well.

In Figure 30 below every box that is lightly textured is an independent pre-sale behavior. Those are the independent variable behaviors you should perfect and measure. The outcome dependent variables that result are revenue and profit which are totally dependent on your ability to perform those other behaviors consistently well. These textured-box behaviors are the items you should strive to achieve and measure. If those are headed in the proper direction, revenue and profits will follow.

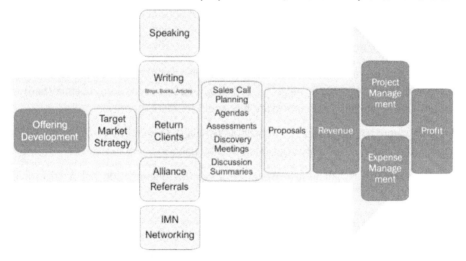

Figure 30: A Simplified High-Efficiency Sales Behavior Map

The key to success is assuring your team makes progress in identifying, monitoring, tracking closely, and dedicating their time to executing the right antecedent behaviors well.

Don't have the time to track things in that detail on a monthly basis?

Make the time. It is worth it to keep the team on track with the right antecedent behaviors.

Dealing with Slow Process Adoption

Occasionally, despite the best intentions of an EIC, implementation progress stalls. Over the years I have developed a rapid way of diagnosing the root cause of stalled efforts. Figure 31 illustrates a cascading chain of diagnostic levels which, when applied to a stalled progress situation, can be used to diagnose root cause.

I created it in the form of a small poster that clients might hang on the walls of their meeting or conference rooms for quick reference. It so happens that all the root causes begin with the letter "C".

Here are the 13 Cs of stalled progress:

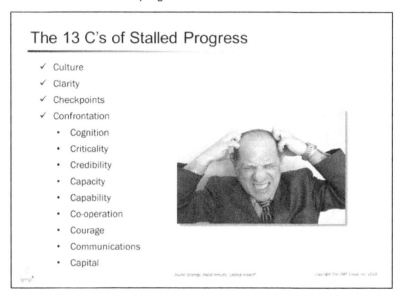

Figure 31: The 13 Cs of Stalled Progress

Culture: If the culture of an organization is dysfunctional, it is going to be difficult to accomplish anything. So, all issues of stalled progress that can be directly tagged to an organization's culture will point to the need to fix that problem first, and quickly.

Refer to your culture score from earlier in this chapter to determine if you will run into challenges in deployment.

Clarity: The team, its leader, and every individual on the team, must clearly understand their role, their objectives, the requirements against which to measure the quality of the achievement of their objectives and the dependencies related to them completing their objectives on time and to requirements.

Checkpoints: Frequent checkpoints assure that efforts do not proceed too far before they are checked to guarantee they are on track.

Confrontation: Any task that is drifting off track during a checkpoint review must be confronted and remedied immediately.

Confrontation is such an aggressive sounding word, but in this case, it simply means that deviations or delays once identified at a checkpoint, must be dealt with immediately. "Dealt with" does not mean screaming, shouting, cussing, or otherwise engaging in non-professional, abusive or threatening behavior. Instead, it simply means assertive and immediate collaborative problem diagnosis and attempting alternative approaches to resolve the stall.

The root causes of project delays will likely be found in the remaining eight items on this checklist.

Cognition: The individual team member, for whatever reason, may not know what they were supposed to accomplish, when it needs to be completed, why or how - and the dependency of other milestones on the accomplishment of their task.

Criticality: The individual did not understand the critical role that their accomplishment of a task plays in the ultimate success of the project.

Credibility: The individual did not *believe* their task was essential to the success of the project, and so gave it less than 100% effort.

Capacity: The individual does not have the time to complete their assigned tasks. This is often a result of poor or unrealistic priority setting.

Capability: The individual simply does not know how to accomplish what they have been asked to deliver. This may be attributed to inadequate training or inappropriate assignment delegation.

Cooperation: Completion of the task requires cooperation from another department or individual and repeated requests have been met with complacency, a lack of response and no sense of urgency.

Courage: The individual is not experienced in some form of the task that they are expected to accomplish. Fear of failure is holding back their effort. This is often related to capability, which in turn may be related to training or poor team formation.

Communication: The individual was not informed of some critical aspect of what they were being required to accomplish.

Capital: The individual needs authorization to purchase something critical to the project's progress and it has not been approved, or otherwise been delayed.

Overcoming barriers is essential to achieving outcomes. I liken the skills for quickly overcoming barriers to a pebble stuck under the front end of the wheel of a cart.

Have you ever been rolling your grocery cart down the aisle in a supermarket, and suddenly had it come to a skidding halt? If you are stubborn as I am, you may continue to push harder hoping that somehow the wheel of the cart will bump over the obstacle and release. That is, until you finally relent, move the cart backwards a few inches, kick whatever is jamming the wheel out of the way, and resume your shopping.

Consider the 13 barriers above as those little irritating objects that jam the wheels of progress.

It is a lot easier to remove the tiny object from in front of the cart's wheel, than lift the cart over the obstruction or continue to push against the resistance.

Post these 13 Cs in the meeting and conference rooms of any team you are working with. It will save you and the team a lot of time and anguish.

A Final Word Regarding Organizational Implementation

While understanding the sales process and training the team in its benefits and use will take time, so will its implementation. I strongly recommend the following guidelines:

- implement one technique at a time, in order of highest potential impact,

- reward those salespeople who implement the fastest,

- give credit and recognition to those who change and succeed,

- be firm in your resolve, and

- be patient.

*****

Part IV Appendices

Appendix A: Sales Process & Skills Organizational Effectiveness Assessment

Appendix B: Opportunity Qualification Rating Criteria

Appendix C: Market Strategy

Appendix D: New Business Development

Appendix A: Organizational Level Sales Process & Skills Effectiveness Assessment

Appendix A will provide a tool to the reader or EIC, with which to self-assess their organizational gaps in comparison to a high-performance Navigational Selling™ model.

The assessment requires the scoring of 30 descriptive situational statements against which to compare your current sales organization's effectiveness as compared to the Navigational Selling™ methodology. In this assessment, the performance bar is set high, so do not be discouraged if your scoring reveals significant gaps. It is meant to be a comparison to an ideal. Furthermore, not all gaps will need to be addressed immediately to realize performance improvement.

While this book is about sales, we recommend that gaps within the *Market Strategy* and *Culture* dimensions be addressed first. Small improvements in those dimensions can produce enormous benefit, even if the sales disciplines and behaviors remain less than perfect.

Taking the Assessment

Simply score the truth of each of the statements on a scale from 1 through 5, as they compare to the situation that exists within your current business. To have them compiled into a radar graph, as shown below in Figure 32, forward the raw scores to QMP1@qmpassociates.com and The QMP Group, Inc. will compile the response and send you the graphical results.

Organizational Level
Sales Process & Skills Effectiveness Assessment

Figure 32: Organizational Level Sales Process & Skills Assessment

Organizational-Level Sales Process & Skills Effectiveness Assessment Scoring

Instructions: On a scale of 1 through 5, with 5 being the highest score, rate the degree to which each statement accurately describes your current organizational sales effectiveness. Write in the score at the end of each statement.

1.   Commitment to Improvement:

Based on the current performance, and the strengths and weaknesses of our current sales approach, we know precisely what will be required to achieve meaningful improvement. That improvement plan is in place and incorporates process optimization changes, skills training, sales behavior modification, expectations-setting, increased accountability, and progress monitoring.

Score: ____

2.   A Performance-Driven Culture:

We consider ourselves a performance-driven organization. We judge ourselves as "Performance Driven" based on our commitment and adherence to the following cultural imperatives: data-driven investment decision-making, highly focused objectives, individual accountability & expectations, tracking of both behavioral and outcome metrics, repeated training, team alignment, collaboration, behavior-based reward systems, adherence to process discipline, and clear and unquestionable ethics.

Score: ____

3.   Teamwork:

Our organizational culture emphasizes teamwork, collaboration, and shared responsibility. Our reward system is team-based and explicitly recognizes selfless team players.

Score: ____

4.   Sound Market Strategies:

Each of the offerings we provide to clients has a sound market strategy. Each product and service market strategy clearly delineates: 1) a clear and validated, client-centered value quotient, 2) identification of the most lucrative target market segment and ideal client profile that will receive the highest value from it, 3) a strongly differentiated position vis-à-vis competitors, and 4) the most client-value-enhancing channel-to-market that should be used.

Score: ____

5.   Market Strategy Development Process:

We use a formal, documented, and proven process for developing sound market strategies for our products and services. No new product or service is introduced without rigorous vetting and client value market testing. This strategy development process is part of basic training for all new sales and marketing personnel.

Score: ____

6.   Use of Data and Market Intelligence Feedback:

Our product and service offering investment decisions are driven from market and client data derived from our sales team input, sales reports, client interviews and client issue research. No strategic investment is made without such data. Before a new product or service is launched into the market, it's client-centered value proposition is tested within its target market with potential clients that fit its ideal client profile.

Score: ____

7.   Ideal Client Profile:

A substantial list of prospect companies that match the ideal client profile of our offerings, and who face the challenges our product/service offerings address, has been created and shared with our sales force. In the past, clients that fit this profile, have been proven to receive high value from resolving those challenges with our offerings and we have case studies and testimonials as proof.

Score: ____

8.   Intra-Market Network Leverage:

We have mapped and know how to leverage the existing communications dynamic within the target markets our offerings are aimed at. We use the target market peer-to-peer networks, journals, and blogs read by EICs in those markets and participate in association events through *Thought Leadership*, memberships, and *Networking*. We have developed personal and professional relationships with the *Opinion Leaders* in those sectors associated with the kinds of challenges our offerings address. We focus substantial New Business Development effort in finding ways to leverage this network.

Score: ____

9.   Thought Leadership:

We do a good job of positioning our company and its products and services, through insightful *Thought Leadership* (articles, interviews, videos, talks, blogs, and white papers) communicated in on-line forums and through our target market Intra-Market Networks. Our *Thought Leadership* efforts have proven a productive source of highly qualified leads. As a result, technical and business leaders in our target markets consider us experts.

Score: ____

10. Sales Process Disciplines:

We adhere to a standard, yet flexible, set of sales process steps and disciplines. This sales process works well and supports the needs of the salesperson as they pre-qualify accounts and new opportunities, plan their sales calls, discover client needs and formulate winning proposals. In addition, each salesperson has a sales coach that provides guidance, advice, and strategic support to help them effectively navigate the selling process, formulate account strategies, and execute action plans.

Our sales process is essential basic training for all new and current employees who interact with clients.

Score: ___

11. Sales Skills:

The sales skills and behaviors we expect of our salespeople include independently finding new clients, qualifying new accounts and opportunities, questioning & listening, discovering client needs, discovering the client's decision process, identifying the key decision-makers and influencers, formulating solutions, and crafting winning proposals.   Within our overall sales team, I would rate these sales skills as excellent.

Score: ___

12. Sales Tools:

We have an excellent suite of sales process support tools to support our sales efforts. These tools include the use of on-line sales calls through Zoom, GoToMeeting, WebEx or equivalent, a customer relationship management (CRM) system to manage the sales pipeline and follow-up activities, a promotional e-mailing tool, technical webinars, participation in online networking forums, and access to a data base which enables researching targeted companies and individuals.

Score: ___

13. Account Targeting:

When identifying a target client that we want to penetrate, we dedicate a fair amount of time to researching their industry, challenges, news releases, website, news articles and key people within our networks that might offer a warm introduction. We make a strong effort to assure we have a good premise for contacting the target client and will be able to meaningfully relate our offerings to their needs.

Score: ___

14. Qualification Criteria:

We use a fairly strict set of criteria for determining whether an opportunity is "Qualified" before investing the effort to win it. Those criteria assure that; a) the client's needs are strong enough to warrant and compel a purchase by them, b) what they need is a good match for our capability, c) the value of solving their problem (or meeting their need) is significantly larger than the cost they will bear to buy and implement our solution and d) that there is a likely competitive advantage to our approach. Because of this qualification discipline, we rarely waste time on poorly qualified opportunities that we have a low probability of winning.

Score: ____

15. Leveraging Opportunity:

Our salespeople are excellent at identifying and communicating back to the home office the leverage that could accrue to our firm from key opportunities they have in their pipeline. We have an impressive track record of discovering and embracing these discoveries, as proven by the steady evolution of our offerings, the successful penetration of new target markets, and the steady growth of revenue and profit.

Score: ____

16. Sales Call Planning:

When our salespeople receive a lead, they follow good sales call planning disciplines. These disciplines include collaborating with the client to establish and objective and agenda and desired outcome for the upcoming meeting, requesting preliminary information about the client's challenge so they may prepare appropriately for the meeting, and suggesting participation by other key people within the client's organization who might be impacted by the challenge, have data to support its gravity and likely influence the ultimate decision.

Score: ____

17. Sales Call Homework:

Our salespeople use complementary preparation discipline for any new opportunity sales call. Collaborative preparation discipline comprises two parts. First, they ask the client to bring to the meeting any relevant data illustrating the challenge the client is facing, and secondly, our salesperson does some basic account and industry research to come up to speed on any current relevant information.

Score: ____

18. Relevance Preparation:

Our salespeople always tailor what materials they bring to a sales call based on the agenda, objectives, and nature of the client challenge to be discussed. The preparation includes collecting relevant case studies, testimonials, and references which validate delivered economic value.

Score: ____

19. Questioning & Listening Skills:

Our salespeople are trained to practice excellent Questioning & Listening skills. These skills enable our salespeople to ferret out key client information during a sales call, such as: the economic value they perceive of addressing their needs, the ultimate decision-maker, the key decision influencers, the personality styles and needs of all key people involved in the decision, the client decision-making process, the criteria by which the final decision will be made, and any critical timing or deadlines.

Score: ____

20. Assessments, Gaps & Implications:

Our sales team has a collection of client situation assessment tools, they can use in client Discovery to determine the magnitude of the client's challenges or performance gaps. There is one assessment tool per product and service offering. The questions in these assessments are designed to bring to light not only the gaps, but also the economic and other implications should those client gaps or challenges remain unresolved.

Score: ____

21. Discussion Summary:

Within 24 hours after each new major opportunity sales call, our salespeople prepare a summary of the key points discussed during the client meeting. The salesperson sends it to the client EIC to confirm the nature of the discussion, the details of what was discussed and any action items that may have been agreed to. This Discussion Summary is a useful mechanism by which to communicate and confirm with the client the details of their challenge and potential approaches to resolve them, as well as a communications tool for our internal team. The Discussion Summary document is attached to the opportunity within our CRM and sales pipeline management system.

Score: ____

22. Client Collaboration:

All product and service solutions offered to our clients are formally proposed only after extensive Discovery and close client collaboration to craft and tailor the solution to meet their unique and specific needs. While economic returns on the client's investment in our products and services can't be guaranteed, a mutual understanding of the magnitude of the expected improvement possible is established before the proposal is delivered. This open collaboration leads to a high win rate.

Score: ____

23. Proposing Creative Solutions:

The products and services we sell allow for creative, tailored solutions to be architected, depending on a client's unique set of needs and challenges. Our sales and sales support teams are skilled at formulating those creative solutions in a way to maximize value delivered to both the customer and our company. Due to the pricing flexibility this approach offers, this tailoring capability drives high profitability and keeps us away from price-war bidding and low-price competition.

Score: ____

24. Value Quotient:

We assure that a discussion of the customer value quotient is communicated in all of our proposals. Those sections of the proposal cover more than just the economic value quotient, including any applicable value contributors associated with emotional, social, political, and physical impacts as well.

Score: ____

25. Follow-Up:

To assure that our clients understand that we are ready to proactively serve their needs, we practice a disciplined program of current and past client follow-up. We keep all clients well-informed of our product and service developments, key personnel additions and any changes in strategy or policy. Such a program assures we can gain access to key decision makers upon request.

Score: ____

26. Winning:

We do not use tricky "closing techniques" to finalize a sale. We are aware of the research that revealed that using closing techniques with customers has a long-term negative impact on trust and the length of a business relationship: they are less likely to become a satisfied client, less likely re-buy, and less likely to refer others to us.

Score: ____

27. Account Management:

It is a primary goal of our business to develop collaborative, long term support strategies with our key clients. We have such strategic relationships with at least half of our current client base. Those strategies may include technology sharing, supply chain collaboration or joint-development relationships. Our efforts in this regard have allowed us to build a high degree of customer loyalty with our major clients. As a result, we are rarely surprised by client news.

Score: ___

28. Market Intelligence Feedback:

Our salespeople are required to produce monthly reports containing relevant market and sales intelligence. These reports are intended for feeding into our market strategy formulation process and must include relevant information concerning unique new client opportunities, extremely pleased clients (and why), market industry updates, competitive intelligence, offering/capability enhancement suggestions, and current account intelligence.

Score: ___

29. Sales Analytics:

We have a standard practice in our business of producing quarterly sales analytics reports for formal management review. These sales analytics reviews include analysis of sales by offering, target market, and region. The assigned analyst is required to dig into the data for anomalies that might provide hints of increased growth from specific industries or offerings. Much of the data the analyst gathers are extracted from our management system and reports. Analytics reviews must also incorporate information extracted from individual monthly sales reports.

Score: ___

30. Market & Competitive Analytics:

We have a standard practice in our business of producing market and competitive analytics reports for formal management review. These market & competitive analytics reviews include analysis of target market industry health and prognosis as well as competitive strengths and weaknesses. The assigned analyst is required to dig into the data for anomalies that might provide hints of increased growth from specific industries or offerings. Much of the data the analyst gathers are from our individual monthly sales reports, client and industry association phone interviews, and on-line information.

Score: ___

Appendix B: Opportunity Qualification Ratings

The following charts will assist the salesperson in consistently scoring the six qualification criteria for opportunities within their sales pipeline.

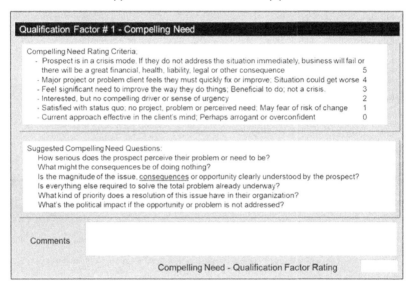

Figure 33: Qualification Factor # 1 - Compelling Need Rating Table

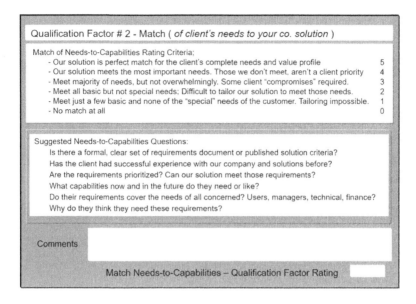

Figure 34: Qualification Factor # 2 – Match of Capabilities to Needs

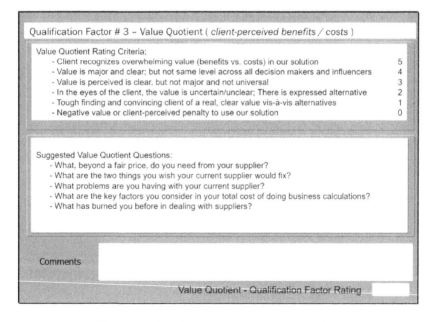

Figure 35: Qualification Factor # 3 – Value Quotient

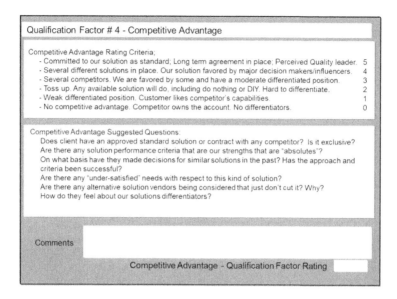

Qualification Factor # 4 - Competitive Advantage

Competitive Advantage Rating Criteria;
- Committed to our solution as standard; Long term agreement in place; Perceived Quality leader.   5
- Several different solutions in place. Our solution favored by major decision makers/influencers.   4
- Several competitors. We are favored by some and have a moderate differentiated position.   3
- Toss up. Any available solution will do, including do nothing or DIY. Hard to differentiate.   2
- Weak differentiated position. Customer likes competitor's capabilities.   1
- No competitive advantage. Competitor owns the account. No differentiators.   0

Competitive Advantage Suggested Questions:
Does client have an approved standard solution or contract with any competitor? Is it exclusive?
Are there any solution performance criteria that are our strengths that are "absolutes"?
On what basis have they made decisions for similar solutions in the past? Has the approach and criteria been successful?
Are there any "under-satisfied" needs with respect to this kind of solution?
Are there any alternative solution vendors being considered that just don't cut it? Why?
How do they feel about our solutions differentiators?

Comments

Competitive Advantage - Qualification Factor Rating

Figure 36: Qualification Factor # 4 - Competitive Advantage

Qualification Factor # 5 - Advocate

Advocate Rating Criteria;
- We have multiple politically powerful, high credibility Advocates with high I-A-A.   5
- An excellent Advocate and good stakeholder support for the concepts.   4
- A good Advocate with credibility. We have additional stakeholder work to do.   3
- Development of Advocate needs work. Stakeholder support is weak.   2
- No Advocate; no upper-level exposure; we are cold calling.   1
- A powerful, hard-over, antagonistic, anti-advocate exists.   0

Suggested Advocate Questions:
- Is there a key stakeholder who understands & is committed to our approach?
- Has the Advocate "adopted" our approach? Are they willing to promote it in their organization?
- Is the Advocate trusted in their own organization? Do we trust the Advocate?
- Do we believe that our Advocate will present our story well and with credibility?
- Does our Advocate allow us access to the other stakeholders at all levels?
- Is our Advocate committed to a partnership and collaborating with us to get the deal done?
- Do we know what the "wins" are for our Stakeholders? Can we deliver them?
- Does our Advocate have a key role in the decision-making process?

Comments

Advocate / Political Alignment - Qualification Factor Rating

Figure 37: Qualification Factor # 5 – Advocate

Qualification Factor # 6 - Leverage

Leverage Rating Criteria:
- Large initial revenue potential; follow-on opportunities; excellent reference account; strong intra-market network; industry leader — 5
- Large revenue opportunity; good reference account; some industry leverage — 4
- Medium revenue potential; average reference account — 3
- Low revenue potential; low growth; no industry momentum — 2
- Small revenue potential; no leverage or follow on — 1
- No long- term buy; no intra-market network power; no influence — 0

Suggested Leverage Questions:
- What growth is anticipated in the client's product/service? What is driving that growth?
- Are there follow on or other products/services in design that might use your capabilities?
- Is this opportunity indicative of an industry-wide opportunity?
- Is this client highly influential as a leader in their industry
- Is this a fragmented opportunity that can lead to a larger deal?
- What is the likely "stepping-stones" to turn this into a larger deal?
- Who are the key people that will help turn the deal into a bigger opportunity?

Comments

Leverage - Qualification Factor Rating

Figure 38: Qualification Factor # 6 – Leverage

Appendix C: Market Strategy

In this Appendix…

Good Market Strategy: The Biggest Factor in Sales Success

Market Strategy is not Tactical Marketing

Market Strategy: A Four-Part Construct

Assessing and Selecting the Most Lucrative Target Market

There is More to Strategy

Good Market Strategy: The Biggest Factor in Sales Success

We established at the beginning of Chapter 1, through the story of the Battle of Stalingrad in World War II, how important a wise strategy is to the success of either a battle or a business. Good strategies reward the firm, bad strategies penalize all the stakeholders – including clients. From the salesperson's perspective, even the best trained and conditioned sales soldier, becomes a casualty attempting to execute an unwise strategy.

Market Strategy is <u>not</u> Tactical Marketing

The differences between Market Strategy and Tactical Marketing are not subtle.

Tactical Marketing comprises a mixture of communications and promotional activities intended to stimulate client interest in the value your offerings can deliver to them. At its best, it delivers substantial quantities of new, pre-qualified client opportunities to the front-end of the sales pipeline. At its worst, unconnected and devoid of a sound market strategy, it wastes a lot of time and money.

A contemporary SMB2B Tactical Marketing plan will commonly comprise a mix of:

- a website,
- social media presence (LinkedIn, Facebook, Twitter, Instagram, et al),
- webinars,
- trade show participation,
- branding initiatives,
- advertising and promotional campaigns,
- e-promotions and marketing automation (to efficiently shepherd a prospective client through a series of messages depending on their expressed and implied interests, routed based on the response to previous communications),
- videos, and
- publicity & news releases.

This list is not comprehensive; there are many ways in which an SMB2B might invest, or waste, cash.

Unfocused, unclear, and untargeted Tactical Marketing can be expensive and produce low or no return, if not informed by a clear, sound Market Strategy. In contrast, formulating Market Strategy is inexpensive, requiring mostly brain energy, a small bit of focused research, a few phone calls, and an investment of your personal time.

Tactical Marketing requires orders of magnitude greater cash outlays than formulating Market Strategy.

A sound Market Strategy must precede Tactical Marketing initiatives to be productive.

In contrast, Market Strategy is a four-part construct comprising: 1) a lucrative target market focus, 2) an offering with a highly relevant, client-centered value quotient, 3) a differentiation that clients in that segment will perceive as market leading, and 4) a client value-enhancing channel-to-market.

Market Strategy establishes what market is worthy of your investments of time, energy, and cash.

Tactical Marketing considers what vehicles you will use to communicate your message of value, differentiation, service offerings and outcomes.

Crafting a Market Strategy: The Four-Part Construct

A *Market Strategy* must be crafted for each Offering. SMB2B's should consider their overall Market Strategy like a wall of bricks - each brick comprising and offering and its associated strategy. The mortar holding the bricks together is the firm's *Culture* and *Brand*.

What follows is an explanation of market strategy formulation at the *Offering* level. Offerings are what the salesperson is being expected to sell. A sales opportunity typically comprises one central offering to address one client main POG. That effort to sell that offering must be supported by a wise market strategy for that offering.

Part 1: A Lucrative Target Market Focus

The first, and most important decision an SMB2B must make in formulating a Market Strategy is the decision about what specific market segment of potential clients it can serve most effectively. Later in this Appendix we will suggest 13 target market segment attractiveness criteria that can be used to identify and select the best and most lucrative market available.

The recommendation to focus typically scares people because of some imagined fear that they will be missing too many opportunities if they focus too narrowly. To them, it seems counterintuitive that a narrower focus can generate faster and more profitable growth. Their faces, and sometimes their mouths, say, *"Are you nuts!? I do not have enough business now, and you want me to NARROW my efforts? I should be EXPANDING, not focusing."*

The truth is many times broadening an SMB2B's marketing and sales effort is not a cure for a stalled-sales situation. Focus is.

Let me ease the minds of those that might harbor the fear of missing out (FOMO) because of Focus.

Here is what focus does not mean. Focus does not mean you will reject, out of hand, some opportunity that appears from outside of the market focus you select. Bluebird opportunities are totally acceptable. Major distractions leading to a dilution of resources, a jumbling and misapplication of value messages, and an uncontrolled proliferation of offering variations are not. Focus simply means that an SMB2B will expend most of its resources (time, money, and energy) on the clients and target markets which receive the highest value-quotient from the firm's offerings.

The "Everybody Can Use It" Fallacy of New Offerings

When I ask clients who their new service is targeted to, they often respond with an enthusiastic, yet vague, *"Well, just about everyone can use it".* The false corollary is then, *"So, we ought to make everyone aware of it and try to sell it to anyone and everyone. Right?"*

Not so fast.

When they attempt to sell to anyone and everyone, they spread their attention, time, and investment very thin and develop no strong penetration and defensible position in any one market.

Why is a broad market attack unwise?

Because not every client receives the same level of value from your service. It makes sense that those who perceive the greatest value are more likely to buy it, pay more for it, be happier with it, tell others like themselves about it and return when they need more.

If you are launching a new business, product, or service, start with the highest value-received segment of customers first.

This desirable higher-client-value-received situation is most likely to exist in a focused sub-segment of the market. This will result in:

- faster market penetration,
- a higher market share,
- a stronger defensible position,
- the ability to charge higher prices or fees, and
- a more recognizable and valued brand.

A focused Market Strategy is more likely to achieve these outcomes, than a thinly spread, broad and expensive Tactical Marketing initiative.

So, while there may be a lot of truth in the statement *"Everyone can use it"*, it does not mean that every client will receive the same value or that you can be successful in attempting to sell it to everyone. You will be most successful, and get the greatest lift, from those segments and clients to which the Value Quotients delivers the highest impact.

Storytime: The Power of Market Focus Therapy

> I was once asked to help a Product Manager that had refused to focus. Her product's adoption into the market was so bad, it was about to be shut down by the CEO of the business. She spent all her time increasing distributors across the country because "… *everyone could use it*".
>
> With just a little historical sales analysis we found two current customers within one specific market, that had, unbeknownst to the manager, received enormous benefit from the product – a higher set of benefits than any other customer, in any other market the product had been sold to.
>
> With just a few phone calls and a visit to each of those customers we confirmed that the market they represented had all the characteristics of an attractive market focus opportunity, namely, a large number of potential clients facing the same challenge, a high tolerance for price premiums, and a regulatory requirement that would continue to drive demand.
>
> We re-focused their tactical marketing efforts, quickly tailoring the product's success stories and sales materials for that market and injected those stories into that market's intra-market network. Significantly increased sales activity developed quickly, with reduced, but more focused, tactical marketing efforts and expenses. In fact, we had discovered a *Value Vortex*™ – a largely unpenetrated segment of the market that had significant latent need and would receive huge value from the product.
>
> It was like being caught in a tornado. The market demand just sucked the product in.
>
> The largest single order from that market prior to focus was $20,000. After focus, within a year, the largest single order was over a million dollars. The number of customers in that segment purchasing product went from just the original 2 to over 150.
>
> Here is the real kicker. The average selling price increased by 4X, as customers in that market requested further market-specific product features.

Prior to that, the product manager had been peppering the management team for permission to drop price!

Moral of the Story: Market focus, driven by client-perceived value is much more effective than price reductions in achieving sales success.

End of story

This is only one of several similar situations in our archives. And while this is a product example, the point is valid for service offerings as well.

This story punctuates the mantra that you must constantly be on the lookout for what Peter Drucker has called "The Unexpected Success".

An unexpected success is a customer buying your product from some crazy, unexpected market that seems, well, weird. Constant vigilance and analysis of value-received will assure you do not miss something big. Use the 13 attractiveness criteria identified later in this Appendix to run the evaluation.

Part 2: A Distinct High-Value Quotient Offering

To achieve profitable growth, an SMB2B must develop and focus on those offerings that: a) will deliver compelling value quotients to address common POGs, b) are strongly supported by the firm's capabilities and strengths, c) can be leveraged to create and reinforce the form's perceived quality leadership position, and d) have been proven to deliver meaningful value to real clients.

Your product and service offerings and your delivery approach must provide a relevant and meaningful combination of Economic, Emotional, Physical, Political and Social value to clients that is uniquely tailored to their individual market circumstance.

Part 3: A Differentiated Positioning

Differentiation explains to clients why the products and services the firm is offering are *different and better* than competitors offering the same, similar or substitute offerings. Yet just being different is not enough. An offering must be better in some way that is substantive and meaningful to clients in its target markets. Its differentiation should add meaningful value to what it delivers.

A firm's corporate colors, logo and tag line are not valued differentiation in B2B markets. The firm's ability to make customer problems dissolve more quickly than the competition, because of some unique proven approach, is a meaningful substantive differentiation. Such differentiation contributes positively to the client's perception of the value quotient they are experiencing.

Part 4: A Client Value Enhancing Channel-to-Market

Channel-to-Market refers to the mechanics of how the firm will sell and deliver its offerings to prospective clients. Channel-to-Market has two critical considerations:

First, the channel must deliver highly differentiated and meaningful value to the client, thus enhancing the client's perception of the value quotient and differentiation of your offerings. In effect, the channel must enhance the client experience.

Secondly, the channel must embrace a broad view of the client relationship - from the client's first exposure, through to selection, delivery, configuration, and post-sale follow-up.

Thinking of a Channel-to-Market only from the selfish perspective of "getting the firm's name out there", getting products on the shelves, and "driving sales", flies in the face of wanting to establish a market leading perception of high quality, client-centeredness. Transparent, self-centered expectations of the value a channel-to-market is providing leaves an SMB2B vulnerable to competitors that deliver a better client-centered experience.

Market Strategy Summarized:

The four parts of a Market Strategy must be formulated for each offering, individually. Each market strategy then becomes the charted course for that offering.

A firm may, for different reasons, occasionally drift off-course along the way, driven by some unanticipated wind, but your primary course is to penetrate a specific target market. If formulated well individually, the combined offering market strategies will support each other – creating brand synergy.

Nothing in this explanation of the four ingredients of a market strategy has to do with Tactical Marketing.

Market Strategy is the "Thinking & Testing" before the detailed "Acting".

Tactical Marketing is the detailed "Acting" after the "Thinking & Testing".

Market Strategy can be 10X less expensive than Tactical Marketing and 10X more impactful.

Discovering the Most Lucrative Target Market

We start the description of how to assess and select the most lucrative target market with a story.

Storytime: Discovering the Gold Underneath Their Feet

> Several people approached me after I delivered a talk to a high-tech audience of about 100, sponsored by one of the large public accounting firms. The subject of the talk was "*Accelerating the Market Adoption of Your Innovation*".
>
> One pair of attendees, a CEO and CFO from the same firm, explained they had just launched an innovative piece of software that, in their words, "*just about any large company could benefit from.*" This software was easy to deploy and had the potential to provide enormous operational cost savings, while assuring regulatory compliance in any industry.
>
> They were feeling very frustrated. Sales had stalled since the product's launch two years ago. The senior management team was continually arguing amongst themselves about where to focus. They were burning through cash at a frightening pace and, at that rate, would need to find additional investment funding that would dilute the ownership of the original investors.
>
> Needless to say, they would not be pleased with that.
>
> **The Outcome:**
>
> Within ninety days of working with them, they had identified, assessed, and tested two promising markets. Both seemed to offer quick product adoption breakouts. One revealed a previously undiscovered, high potential market niche. The other was a bust.
>
> Within a couple of years, penetration in that high-potential market niche grew from just one client installation to more than 1,000 across the country!
>
> **How it came about:**
>
> Use of the market attractiveness assessment tool revealed two possible breakthrough markets. The team immediately jumped to testing those attractiveness and value-quotient hypotheses.
>
> Value validation testing with several clients in the first market proved that their initial client-value-delivered hypotheses were flat invalid. The compelling value that the team felt confident would excite clients in that first market turned out to be largely irrelevant to almost all they spoke with.
>
> On the other hand, testing of the hypothesis about the attractiveness of the firm's second market, concluded the opposite. The potential was big - and

real. The value the software would deliver to clients in that market was higher than any market the company had ever sold to.

After market value validity testing, the team agreed to focus. Bickering within the management team stopped. Each member of the management team signed covenants, agreeing to refocus marketing, sales, and new business development resources. The team launched a full-blown focused market initiative.

The adoption barriers dissolved, and the amount of marketing and development expense needed to achieve that breakthrough dropped significantly - assuring survival of the business and preserving owners' equity.

The truly remarkable part of this success story: At the time of value quotient validation testing, the company had only one customer in that market – but that one client was over-the-moon delighted with the value being delivered. That customer informed my client that there were 25,000 businesses like his across the U.S., all with the same problem needing to be solved!

Moral of the Story: Periodic sales analytics in a search for hidden client-received value can reveal potential breakthrough opportunities. Assessing those opportunities through a market attractiveness tool and validating its assumptions with some field testing can quickly supercharge growth.

End of story

Target Market Attractiveness Assessment Criteria

The market attractiveness assessment approach described in the following pages results in a first-cut look at the relative attractiveness of several different target markets a business might be considering. It evaluates a *Target Market* paired with an *Offering*, one matched pair at a time, ultimately revealing the most lucrative combinations to pursue.

A market segment can only be evaluated as attractive or unattractive based on the specific product or service offering it is paired with.

The market attractiveness criteria that follow provide a consistent method for evaluating and testing offerings and associated target markets, as matched pairs, using 13 attractiveness criteria. The prime objective of its use is to align your offerings with the markets to which those offerings will provide maximum client value.

Additionally, the tool provides a thought process through which to consider each of the four components essential to a sound market strategy: 1) a lucrative target market with momentum, 2) a compelling value quotient, 3) a differentiated market position, and 4) a channel-to-market.

Before you read and score the assessment criteria using the attractiveness factors below, please take note of the following three points:

- Your ratings need *not* be precise. First approximations will do for an initial analysis.

- Your assessment ratings and assumptions *must* be tested and validated with prospective clients in the target market before you commit to any major investment.

- The target market attractiveness assessment is used solely to point you in the best direction to investigate further. It should help you identify the highest probability of success match of target market and service for your business to offer.

To assess the attractiveness of a market-product (or offering) pair, follow the following steps:

1. Select one of your offerings,

2. Select a target market to which you believe that offering should provide high value to clients,

3. Rate each of the attractiveness factors on a scale of 1 to 10 for that offering-market combination,

4. Look for extremely low ratings to determine whether there are any deal-breakers, i.e., factor ratings that make the market highly unattractive and indicate they are not to be considered for focused efforts,

5. Run the same analysis for other offering-market pairs until one or two highly attractive combinations become apparent.

Remember these preliminary assessments need validation with field and client research before committing to any concentrated marketing and sales effort. In the following pages TMAF stands for Target Market Attractiveness Factor

TMAF 1: Market Momentum

Factor Definition: This factor rates the degree to which the market has some inherent momentum attributable to one or more market-specific conditions or circumstances, such as economics, demographics, regulatory requirements, or industry trends and deadlines.

TMAF 2: Compelling Need

Factor Definition: A measure of the strength and urgency of a specific common Problem, Opportunity, or Gap (POG) faced by members of this segment of the market. For example, the compelling need for security-screening devices for the airline industry after 9-11 terrorist attack in 2001 became acute. A compelling need may be driven by the need to save money, to remain competitive, to save time, diffuse a critical safety concern, or get a significant boost in productivity.

TMAF 3: Match

Factor Definition: To what degree is there a strong match of the compelling market need to your inherent capabilities, qualifications, and expertise to service that need? This capability-match rating is a judgement call on your part. If the match is not good, and only requires a modest affordable investment to fix, then it is acceptable to rate this factor higher, but make a note that an investment will be required. If the Match investment required is high, rate this lower.

Another consideration: It is possible to be led to believe that the match is good only to discover sometime down the road, during field-validity testing, that it is not.

TMAF 4: Profitability

Factor Definition: The degree to which engagements to improve the client's condition with the offering you are evaluating in this market will be profitable, now and in the future.

TMAF 5: Accessibility

Factor Definition: The degree to which you can gain access to the target market segment decision makers for the product or service under consideration. Access may be limited by trade barriers (if international), limited channel availability, long term engagement retainer contracts already in place with competitors, domination by a few large, well-established competitors or a high, prohibitive cost barrier to getting to the market. In other words, this factor assesses the degree of difficulty you might encounter reaching and meeting with ultimate EIC decision makers.

TMAF 6: The Number of Unfilled and Under-Satisfied Potential Clients

Factor Definition: This factor estimates market attractiveness based on the estimated total number of potential customers that could be facing the problem or challenge your service addresses. What percent have solutions installed and are happy with that solution? Entering and penetrating a target market when the market is saturated can still be accomplished, but it requires a fragmentation strategy. Such a fragmentation strategy will require either a laser focus on a highly under-satisfied sub-segment of the saturated market or launching a truly innovative product that taps into unmet latent needs.

TMAF 7: Utilization Rate

Factor Definition: Not all markets will utilize your product or service at the same rates. Factor 7 brings into the market attractiveness evaluation process; the number of repeat buys a client in a target market will make compared to selling the same product in another market.

For example: The rental car target market for automobile manufacturers is not as large as the market for selling cars to the general public. However, rental car companies will buy cars at many times the rate of the market of retired schoolteachers living in Florida. The rental car market segment will therefore merit a higher utilization factor rating.

TMAF 8: Intra-Market Network (IMN) aka the Market Ecosystem

Factor Definition: This factor rates the degree to which the target market sector has an internal network which can accelerate peer-to-peer information flow between EIC decision makers. IMN ecosystems typically comprise industry associations and journals, professional societies, social networks, government-sponsored groups, virtual industry groups, annual conferences, regional chapter meetings, opinion leaders, and the EIC decision makers of the clients you are targeting.

Intra-Market Networks are known to be an order of magnitude more effective than mass communications in disseminating information.

TMAF 9: Value Quotient

Factor Definition: The Value Quotient factor rates the extent to which client decision-makers and decision influencers in the market sector you are assessing will receive disproportionate value from meeting their challenges or compelling needs with your offerings, as compared to the total costs to them of your approach.

Value Quotient is a crucial pillar of the market strategy of any business and a crucial criterium in selecting target markets. It is discussed extensively in Chapter 5.

An Aside: Channel-to-Market adds to the Client Value Quotient through the Client Experience

The primary factor influencing the decision about an appropriate channel-to-market must be based on the degree of value it delivers, not to you, but rather to your clients. If a channel does not provide meaningful value to your clients, it is not a useful channel.

Think of that last statement in the context of books. Books deliver two primary types of value that buyers appreciate: entertainment and education – though they seem to also function as a popular backdrop for Zoom meetings these days.

In times past, books were distributed through one primary channel, the brick-and-mortar bookstore. Then technology and insight changed all that when Amazon launched a new way to provide additional differentiated value to books, namely the convenience of online ordering, quick delivery, audio versions, improved storage efficiency and portability using their Kindle and cellphone apps. The core client-relevant value of entertainment and education remained, but now additional value had been identified, delivered, and automated through the internet.

Channels that did not provide that value, withered. Whole bookstore chains went out of business.

The first law of Channel-to-Market:

The primary criteria by which a specific channel-to-market should be selected is the value it will provide to your customers or clients, not the role it may play in simply "getting your products or name out there".

When considering your channel-to-market, ask first what unfulfilled client value can be delivered by that channel. Enhancing the client experience must be the primary purpose of a channel-to-market. How well it delivers value is just as important. Different channels will deliver different types and levels of value to different market segments.

In rating this Target Market Attractiveness Factor remember to consider the contribution your channel contributes to client-perceived value and the client experience.

TMAF 10: RPQL Availability

Factor Definition: RPQL stands for **R**elative **P**erceived **Q**uality **L**eadership. This factor assesses the availability of such an RPQL position within the target markets and active competitors providing offerings like yours.

Marketing research published in the classic book on strategy, by Robert D. Buzzell and Bradley T. Gale, "*The PIMS Principles; Linking Strategy to Performance*", (The Free Press 1987), still holds true today. The primary finding from the massive amounts of strategic research compiled into that book; 3000 business units, 25 years of data, hundreds of data elements for each business, 450 companies, concludes:

"The single most important factor affecting a businesses' success is the relative perceived quality of its products and offerings compared to its competition."

The keys to long-term success are focus, specialization and becoming the de facto Relative Perceived Quality Leader (RPQL) in your field of specialization within your selected target markets. To achieve that position, you must be able to create and deliver a leading client experience with a compelling value quotient at its core.

Going head-to-head in a market against an established competitor that has both dominant market-share already and a well-established RPQL leadership position is expensive, extremely risky, and mostly doomed to failure. This category rating must recognize the extent to which an RPQL position is not established by any of the current competitors and is, therefore, open for exploitation.

TMAF 11: Competitive Turmoil

Factor Definition: The Competitive Turmoil factor evaluates the degree to which competitors are scrambling and fighting head-to-head to own a share of the market. Market size only matters to the extent you can find a profitable, defensible position within it. The odds are against any one competitor dominating a large market from inception.

Important to Note: This factor uses a reverse value rating. This means that the higher the competitive turmoil, the lower the attractiveness rating.

TMAF 12: Brand Leverage

Factor Definition: The Brand Leverage factor assesses the degree to which you can leverage your existing differentiated position, image, and reputation in the market under consideration with the product you are planning to introduce. For example, the Volvo brand is popularly understood to mean safety. That well-established brand reputation for safety could easily be leveraged into child car seats – but not coffee. There is excellent perception connection for the former, not so much for the latter.

Your core value proposition, differentiation, and client experience define your brand.

Your brand is the result of the customer experience you deliver, not the cause.

TMAF 13: Client Perceived Value of Your Differentiation

Factor Definition: This factor assesses the degree to which your proven and distinct differentiation is relevant to the target market segment under consideration. In an example from the auto world, car safety is a factor relevant to the family market, but perhaps not so much to the young, single, upper middle-class Gen Y.

Remember when you are trying to select your most attractive market...

... not every market receives the same magnitude and type of value from your product or service. It makes sense that those who perceive the greatest value are more likely to buy it, pay more for it, be happier with it, tell others like themselves about it and return when they need more. Always begin there.

Total Scores and Deal Breakers

A total score (the sum of all the ratings) is only useful if there are no "deal-breaker" ratings.

Deal-breaker categories are Momentum, Capabilities Match and Value Quotient, and for those business that do not have a lot of promotional money, the Intra-Market Network. After testing, if the scores in any of these factors are extremely low for a market segment, you should not waste time evaluating them further.

One of the most common mistakes users make is to look at Momentum and Compelling Need, while ignoring Capabilities Match. If a capabilities-to-compelling needs mismatch cannot be overcome quickly and affordably, leave it alone and go to your second-choice market. The appeal of the homerun under those circumstances is seductive and often leads to obsession and failure.

While Navigational Selling™ is a book about implementing a more effective sales process, it is important to note that clients who have implemented such a sales process, <u>and</u> developed a sound strategic market focus, found easier, longer-sustained, higher levels of success and profit.

*****

Appendix D: New Business Development

What Exactly is New Business Development?

New Business Development (NBD) is finding ways to generate steady and reliable sources of pre-qualified new business opportunities. New Business Development is the realm of non-linear approaches to growth.

It is "active", not passive. This means you must make the time to think about, identify, assess, plan, test, and execute NBD activities. It requires constant vigilance to avoid overlooking new sources of multiple opportunities that arise.

NBD is so closely tied to both selling and tactical marketing, and so broad in its definition and scope, that it is deserving of a book in its own right. To clarify how its key functions should be thought of and integrated into a SMB2B marketing & sales organization, it is included in Navigational Selling™ as this Appendix.

Because the NBD term in today's SMB2B world has no consistent definition across businesses, the roles and responsibilities of NBD may be indistinguishable from what an EIC might personally expect of either a Salesperson or a Tactical Marketer. The reality is that depending on how your SMB2B organization is structured, the placement and responsibility of the activities included in NBD is wherever _you_ decide to place them, and to whom you decide to assign the responsibilities for execution. There are no strict rules.

Figure 39 offers a map of the roles of Sales, New Business Development, Tactical Marketing and Market Strategy on a continuum.

Figure 39: Market Strategy to Sales Responsibility Continuum (redux)

Most SMB2B firms do not have the luxury of large staffs, so a disproportionate share of the activities shown in Figure 39 (to the left of the dashed line) will fall to the one role that most businesses _do_ have – the Salesperson. Everything to the right of the dashed line is outsourced or handled by someone else. Typically, in an SMB2B, a junior marketing person will handle Tactical Marketing activities, and the EIC the Market Strategy responsibilities.

In the smallest of firms, like a solo practitioner consultancy, there is no dashed line. All responsibilities fall on the shoulders of the solo practitioner, who, depending on the depth of their cash reserves, may contract out some of the activities within the tactical marketing realm.

What techniques work best for NBD?

Storytime: Many NBD Roads Lead to the Sales Pipeline

A few years ago, I participated in a meeting of 20 or so senior professional services salespeople to share best practices. One question posed to the group for discussion: "*What approach can you identify that has been the largest single factor responsible for your success in attracting _new_ clients?*"

As we passed the question around the room, the responses were all over the map. One person even said cold calling! That answer blew the rest of us away. Virtually no one likes to cold call.

Another identified their large personal network as the source of new client capture success, while another said he could attribute his success to his coach that regularly kicked his butt to "get out there and meet people", aka Networking. Another said a bit arrogantly, *"People simply like me"*, and another said it was their extensive production of Thought Leadership through articles and speaking on an international scale.

What did we learn from this collection of widely divergent approaches?

The two things the responses had in common were: 1) each individual leveraged their inherent talents and natural inclinations, and 2) no-one said anything about Tactical Marketing activity. Each individual used and leveraged the skills, talents and personality traits that were their strongest natural assets.

The salesperson that identified their personal network as the source of their success is an outgoing, gracious individual that never met a person they did not quickly befriend. He regularly circulated in both business and non-profit communities and rarely did anything alone. The individual that said "Thought Leadership" was truly a writer, and the one that said "speaking" was a person accustomed to being in front of crowds (as an entertainer) since childhood.

Wondering about the person that said cold calling?

Her business specialized in training inside salespeople to cold call.

Go figure.

Moral of the Story: Leverage who you are naturally, but do not depend on it as your only song.

End of story

There is no pat answer to capturing new clients. But know this: to continually generate new business a salesperson must do more than simply leverage their natural strengths.

Using the Popeye line, "*I am what I am.*", only cuts it in cartoons. The reality might be that your "natural abilities" cannot compete.

There are a large number of salespeople in the world. Many have great track records, great reputations, a clear focus, and a lot of sales experience. Others are dynamic public speakers that receive standing ovations. Some write insightful articles or have published a book. The most successful have great personal discipline, no fear of failure and incredible reserves of energy.

How will you compete?

In addition to understanding and leveraging your natural strengths, you must find ways to also leverage your most valuable asset – your time.

Efficiently executed NBD activities are required to make that happen. You must not only perform the right activities; you must execute them intelligently, efficiently and with skill. If you do, your success will be worth the effort. If you do not, you'll just waste a lot of time.

When it comes to NBD activities, it's more than just _what_ you do, it's _how well_ you do it that matters.

Sources of New Business Development Opportunities

Part 2 of this book detailed the Navigational Selling™ - the sales process steps for managing an opportunity once it is in a salesperson's pipeline. But getting opportunities to the front end of that pipeline is at least as much a challenge, and requires as much effort, as navigating them through to a win.

In this Appendix, we will discuss several approaches that a salesperson might use for efficiently generating streams of new business opportunities. These NBD approaches should be well within the capabilities of a journeyman salesperson. They are:

- intelligently and efficiently *Networking*,

- building a small army of highly respected *Referral Sources*,

- crafting *Alliances*,

- target Account Research, and

- Thought Leadership.

Each of these activities should be within the realm of a salesperson's capability to execute on their own. I say this because I know hundreds of solo-practitioner consultants and single-salesperson SMB2B firms that execute them successfully.

Networking

If there is one thing that SMB2B salespeople do inefficiently, if they do it at all, it is networking. The objectives of networking fall into two categories: *Meeting the right People* and *Market Intelligence Gathering*.

The immediate objectives of the *Meeting People* category may be obvious:

- meeting EIC decision makers and decision influencers with POGs who could become clients,

- meeting potential Alliance partners who could refer clients to you, and

- meeting influential others within the network that might provide Referrals.

The *Market Intelligence Gathering* objective is too often not given equal importance. It comprises:

- to learn about the *common issues facing potential clients* within a target market,

- to learn about the *communications dynamics of a target market*, and

- to discover a target market's most *respected and trusted Opinion Leaders*.

Given the dual sets of objectives, the salesperson should select and focus their networking time primarily on those industry and networking events that are part of their most lucrative target market infrastructure. This focus will likely be more productive than a scattershot approach. Don't let the FOMO monster control your life and drive you to attempt to be everywhere.

Focus!

The Simple Rules of Networking

There are only a few rules for networking:

Rule 1: Focus Your Networking Time and Investments by striving, first, to network within your most lucrative target market ecosystem.

Rule 2: Create your honest, succinct, and impressive *"What do you do?"* response.

Rule 3: Build your *Referral Network* with *Opinion Leaders* in your target market ecosystem who fit the 4 criteria for importance. Be efficient when networking for coffee. Always use an agreed agenda and if the person with whom you are meeting is not an Opinion Leader, only meet with potential referral sources who are otherwise well-networked with EICs.

Rule 4: Network from the front of the room whenever possible, aka be the guest speaker (covered a bit later in this Appendix). If you are not the speaker, network only at venues that attract the types of professionals that are potential decision makers or Referral Sources that can provide qualified introductions to EICs.

Rule 1: Focus Your Networking Time and Investments

Appendix C, Market Strategy, discussed the process for assessing and selecting the best target markets for your offerings. We provided 13 criteria against which to evaluate any combination of offering and target market. One of those is the degree to which a market has a robust *Intra-Market Network* or *Market Ecosystem*. We use those two terms interchangeably.

An Intra-Market Network or Market Ecosystem comprises the formal and informal communication and influence infrastructure that operates between decision makers, decision influencers, opinion leaders, and peers within a target market.

Mapping the Intra-Market Network or Market Ecosystem

The communications and influence infrastructure in a target market comprises:

- *Venues:* Where participants and members of the market segment meet to discuss common challenges and exchange best business practices,

- *Vehicles:* What they read, view, listen to, or otherwise use as their sources of information,

- *Opinion Leaders:* Those individuals within the network with the highest degree of influence in the identification, communication, promotion, and adoption of innovation, based on their position of trust within the network, their experience, expertise, and reputation,

- *Primary Referral Sources:* Folks who are trusted advisors to economic decision makers in the network, and

- *Executives in Charge (EICs):* Those executives that hold ultimate economic decision-making authority to approve a purchase of the offerings you provide.

Understanding the mechanics of your target market's Intra-Market Network is like having a chart to help you navigate a previously unfamiliar bay. See Figure 40.

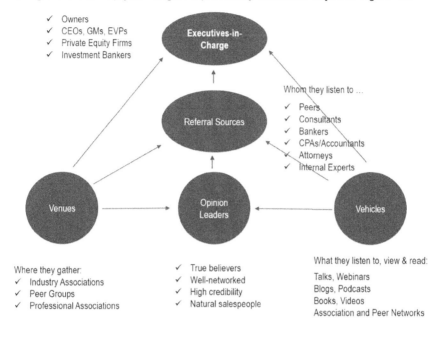

Figure 40: A Target Market Intra-Market Network (IMN)

Networking within the Intra-Market Network of your most lucrative target market with your best service offering (the offering that provides the highest value quotient to clients) is efficient and profitable.

The Parts of the Intra-Market Network

EICs: The Most Important People

Referring to Figure 40, at the top of the IMN hierarchy are the people who make the ultimate decisions to invest in your offerings. They are the EICs, the ultimate economic authority within the organizations you wish to serve. While they may consider inputs from committees or high-credibility influencers within their sphere of control, they ultimately approve and sign the contract.

Resting the next level down within the Intra-Market Network are the Referral Sources. Referral Sources are the people that EICs listen to. They trust them to recommend people and investments to help the EIC meet the challenges and fix the problems in their organizations. An EIC's referral sources may reside inside or outside the company and organization the EIC manages.

EICs typically listen to people they trust highly. This can range from their CFO (the Financial Manager inside the organization), to a technical specialist, to bankers, lawyers, or a peer from another organization outside the firm.

As a salesperson, if you are focused on a specific industry, you must chart and learn its market ecosystem before sailing its waters. You must get to know the opinion leaders, trusted referral sources, technical specialists, the industry's national association team, event planners and whether there are regional chapter events in which you can network.

The Venues & Vehicles

The two remaining parts of an industry ecosystem are the Venues (where all those people who live and work within the IMN ecosystem hang out to share and learn), and the Vehicles (the content and journals they read, the videos they view or the podcasts to which they listen to stay informed).

Do Not Attempt Sail the Seas of a Target Market Without a Current Chart

Making the time to chart your target market IMN is a must. Of course, you do not need to do it all at once before engaging with it. But If you are going to spend the effort, time, and money to participate and network in an IMN ecosystem, there is not a more productive activity than charting it and building a plan accordingly.

IMN ecosystems are fluid and evolve over time. Consider the following factors likely to change:

- the target market's industry association leadership changes periodically,

- the communications vehicles and formats change, (on-line forums, e-zines and virtual meeting formats have grown immensely vis-à-vis hard copy magazines and regional face-to-face meetings),

- the extensive adoption of webinars and Zoom meetings have replaced once-a-year, in-person conferences,

- membership rolls change,

- mergers and acquisitions change accessibility and decision makers, and

- industry-specific issues, such as economics, regulations and technology trends can change quickly.

In early March 2020, I attended a conference of regional small business CEOs (my target market decision makers) and sat at a large round table listening as they shared their most pressing problems. At that time, their most common concern was finding enough qualified talent.

Three weeks later, the Covid-19 Corona virus hit hard. Their problem focus changed almost overnight. As of this writing, with the end of the pandemic economy in the US less than a year ahead, the search for qualified talent has already come to the top of their to-do lists again.

Charting and keeping your IMN ecosystem information current through networking is a key objective of New Business Development activities.

Rule 2: What do you do? Handling the Most Common Question You Will Hear While Networking

"*What do you do?*" is the most common question salespeople get asked at a networking event when they meet someone new. Go to a networking meeting, approach someone you have never met before and strike up a conversation. Odds are that shortly after you exchange names and share a quick handshake, the person you are speaking with will ask you this question.

"What do you do?"

Don't immediately respond with the words, I'm a Salesperson – or I sell (fill in the blank). Instead, briefly state what you do in terms of the people you help and what you help them with. Quickly cite an example. Then return the question.

There are several versions of dialogue that may ensue. Only one is effective.

Bad Dialogue 1: The Pulling Teeth Exchange

Them: "Pleasure to meet you. So, what do you do?"

You: "I'm a Salesperson"

Them: "What kind of selling do you do?"

You: "Accounting Software and Services."

Them: "Any specialty?"

You: "Taxes and Negotiations with the IRS."

Them: "Interesting."

You: "Sometimes."

Them: (silence)

Likely Outcomes: The dialogue has reached a dead-end.

There are only so many questions a person is willing to ask, and so much time they are willing to engage, to give you a chance to impress them – particularly if there is no payoff by you asking them what they do in return.

In the pulling-teeth scenario, awkward silences fill the space between you both. The other person is noticeably shifting their weight from one leg to the other, furtively looking around the room for an escape route - unless the other person is also a Salesperson with no networking and conversational skills - in which case this is a safe, yet unrewarding situation for both of you.

Even an exchange of business cards is unproductive. Neither of you have built any base for *Credibility* or *Trust*. No meaningful impression has been made.

Since a referral is a transfer of Trust, without the other person knowing and trusting you, no referral will ever ensue in either direction.

Bad Dialogue 2: The Burst Damn Approach

Them: "What do you do?"

You: "I sell Tax Accounting services. For the last 25 years my firm has been helping clients fix tax problems. You would not believe how many tax-troubled businesses there are in this area? Some of them are in this room!", (as you look around slyly). "It's amazing how many highly placed business executives know so little about accounting and taxes…. Blah, blah, blah…"

You proceed with ten minutes of an uninterrupted barrage of info and "ain't-it-awfuls" about you, your offerings, your clients (a real ethical no-no), your professional credits, your golf handicap, your vacation travel, and your kids - especially the one attending State that earned a 4.0 in her first semester and is there on a full ride scholarship for being on the chess team.

Them: (looking over your shoulder for an escape route), "Excuse me I think I need a refill.", or "I think I see a client who has been evading me for the last 5 years."

At which point they leave your presence with an insincere, "*Nice to meet you.*"

Likely Outcome: The conversation abruptly ends as they run - even before you have had time to regale them with your fishing stories and cell phone photos. They avoid you the rest of the evening and for the next millennium.

Good Dialogue: The Gentle, Succinct Hook (using my own example)

Them: *"What do you do?"*

Me: *"My firm repairs Marketing & Sales Engines for small-to-midsized B2B firms. We're sort of mechanics. We diagnose - then repair the parts of the engine that are not functioning as they should be. We've been able to find hidden opportunities for growth which, in some cases, have doubled a client's business in relatively short amounts of time."*

Them: *"That's interesting. Tell me more."*

I then hand them a business card which has our hierarchical marketing & sales engine model printed on the back. Pointing to the engine, I say.

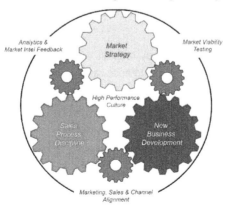

> Me: *"Every organization has some form of a marketing & sales engine at work in their business - whether they recognize it as such or not. We have a diagnostic tool that assesses a client's engine and based on the results, we customize programs to repair, replace or tune-up any of the engine gears that are not working. Just like your car mechanic."*
>
> *"How about you? What do you do?"*
>
> Them: *"Thanks for asking, I'm ...."*

With this less-than 60 second explanation you have: a) been clear about what you do, b) used a clear, easy-to-understand example/model of the service you company provides, and c) punctuated that explanation with some proven results.

If they persist questioning or say, *"What you explained is intriguing. Tell me more."* , then you must also make the next level of your answer as easy to understand – but just as succinct.

> Me: *"Most people are familiar with the process of bringing their car in to a dealer for service. The first thing the service attendant does is plug it in for a diagnosis. Repair recommendations follow the diagnosis. So that's what we do, we have suite of proprietary diagnostic tools that lets us immediately discover their needs and tailor a program to tune up their engine."*
>
> *"Now tell me what you do."*

If you can get your initial *"What do you do"* response across clearly in less than 60 seconds, you have done well. If you can get your point across in 60 seconds and elicit information about them in the next 10 minutes, (because they trust that you are not putting the arm on them in some kind of a high-pressure sales dialogue), then you have hit a home run.

Likely Outcome: They get it. They respect you. They appreciate that you respect them. They appreciate your succinctness and willingness to quickly move the conversation to ask about and listen to them. They then proceed to answer your questions - which is what you really want to happen so that you might discover potential opportunities.

You get to discover more. Of the two, talking and discovering, the latter is more valuable.

The point is, when you are asked the *"What do you do?"* question, you must be succinct and be prepared to quickly, and clearly, describe what it is you do. You must communicate in a way that paints a picture in a concise, easy-to-understand way.

You have only seconds to capture their interest in a way that they can relate and understand.

By the time you walk away from this succinct give and take, you should be able to determine:

- Is this person a potential client decision maker or decision-influencer?

- Is this person a potential alliance partner or referral source?

- Is this person a potential service provider (accountant, lawyer, IT professional, etc.)?

- Is this person someone with whom I would like some other kind of business or personal relationship?

If you have not determined that in a few minutes, you have wasted your encounter.

Two final points need to be made about face-to-face, 1-on-1 networking:

First, when answering the question, *"What do you do?"*, be succinct. Leave them with an accurate, yet simple picture of what you do and who you are. No need to paint the Sistine Chapel.

Second, when listening, ask a lot of questions.

Rule 3: Referral Sources: Building a Loyal and Productive Cadre

Building and maintaining a collegial cadre of well-respected people within a target market ecosystem is a wise and crucial component of your NBD activities. Such a cadre can feed opportunities to you on an ongoing basis.

Storytime: The Enormous Power of Referrals

The power of referrals was never brought home to me more than when, being an analytic type, I decided to trace every single client engagement I had been requested to propose, both losses and wins. The data spanned more than ten years of my business and scores of individual clients.

I discovered, if I included the opportunities to speak and write, I could trace more than 90% of my opportunities to two original referral source advocates – one in Dallas, Texas and the other in Portland, Oregon. Those two powerfully connected believers in me and what I did, ultimately led to thousands of contacts and 30 years of consulting engagements.

Moral of the Story: Some referral sources will be much more productive than others. Learn to figure out who they are, maintain a trusted relationship, and appreciate them.

End of story

Opinion Leaders

Among Referral Sources exists a special class of referrer, the Opinion Leader.

Just because you know someone – doesn't make them a referral source. The best Referral Sources are Opinion Leaders with the following characteristics:

- *Rabid Believers:* This is the degree to which they are a true believer in you, your firm, your offerings, and the value they deliver. Since referrals are a transfer of trust, the Opinion Leader must have substantive reasons to recommend you and believe you will perform well for the person to whom he recommends you - or else their Opinion Leader credibility will be compromised.

- *Well-Connected:* They are highly respected and networked with individuals at the right levels in your target clients' organizations - executives that have the power to approve a contract with you for an engagement. Opinion Leaders should be well-networked within the industry you are targeting. Introverts need not apply. Typically, at industry events you can pick out the Opinion Leaders by observing who in the room appears to be "holding court" with small groups of other attendees paying rapt attention.

- *High In-Network Credibility:* They are highly trusted and credible in the IMN. When they speak, the people in the network who know them listen. Rabid belief in your capabilities and being well-networked are insufficient to determine if you have a good opinion leader on your side. Their opinion must bring high credibility with it.

- *Natural Salespeople:* They are willing to enthusiastically recommend you and your offerings to people whom they know might benefit. The previous factors are important, but useless unless the Opinion Leader is a natural salesperson who wishes to connect people and help folks. Introverts who are True Believers in you and your expertise, are well-networked, and have high credibility, are useless if they never have the courage to speak up and make recommendations.

Storytime: Missing an Important Ingredient

I once hired someone to help with business development who had three of the four criteria – they were a true believer in the QMP Methodology, well-networked, and a natural salesperson.

Shortly after they began representing my firm, I received a call from one of my former clients whom they had contacted. That former client cautioned me that the approach my new rep was taking was abrasive. He informed me that while the person who was now representing me was well-known and a frequent participant in industry events, they had no credibility. The hard-sell, pushy, aggressive approach being used was rapidly damaging my client-experience reputation in the market.

After bringing this feedback to my rep's attention, and asking for adjustments, nothing changed. We parted ways quickly.

Moral of the Story 1: Opinion Leaders must have all four ingredients to be of value to both you and your clients.

Moral of the Story 2: Some communications to an IMN ecosystem are not always better than none.

End of story

An Opinion Leader has significant influence and broad reach within the IMN ecosystem. That power to influence reaches across many organizations, regions, and levels. Typically, that influence is based on some network-recognized specialty, position, expertise, or experience.

Within an IMN ecosystem, trusted influence flows upwards from opinion leaders through Referral Sources, to EICs – the ultimate economic decision makers.

If you can win the trust of an Opinion Leader you have achieved a great milestone. An Opinion Leader that is one of your Referral Sources has immense influence and referral power throughout an ecosystem.

Caution: A referral puts both the referrer and the client you were referred to, at modest reputational risk. Your collegial cadre of Referral Sources needs to be maintained and nurtured. The best way to accomplish that is by delivering great client experiences for the people to whom they refer you.

Making a referral is an act and transfer of trust. Just one poor client experience with someone a primary referral source introduced you to, will destroy future trust between you and that referral source forever.

One-on-One Meetings with Referral Sources

I meet a lot of salespeople that seem to be on an endless merry-go-round of meetings with other salespeople just like themselves that are desperately seeking referrals and opportunities. They drink a lot of coffee and warm a lot of chairs at popular coffee houses.

Most of those meetings are non-productive. They are typically representative of a mindset that equates activity with progress.

Think about it. They drive 30 minutes in traffic, meet for an hour, drive 30 minutes back and have burned 2 hours during which they could have done something way more productive, like crafting or refining their networking *"What do you do?"* response.

Here are a few suggestions for deciding whether to schedule a referral source coffee meeting and, if you do, making them productive.

- Meet only with people you know that have been successful and have established trusted connections with EICs and Opinion Leaders within your target markets.
- Do not agree to meet without a pre-agreed Agenda and Objective.

Here is a suggested agenda for meeting someone for the first time that you hope will become a Referral Source.

- Personal Introductions and Background Sharing - 10 minutes
- Overview of their Business (offerings, value quotient, differentiation, business challenges) - 15 minutes
- Overview of your business (same topics) – 15 minutes
- Synergy Discussion - 10 minutes
- Next Steps (as appropriate) – 5 minutes

Listen, ask, and record the details of the conversation for summary. Share the podium. Listen more than you talk. Be succinct. Have your answer to the *"What do you do?"* question prepared. Make your differentiation clear and have your value quotient supported by compelling case studies and testimonials. Exchange business cards. Agree to connect on LinkedIn.

Share case studies and your most impressive results delivered to clients - but be sure not to exchange client proprietary information.

Just like meeting a stranger at a networking event, it shouldn't take long for you to impress them with what your firm does, how it's done, and the kinds of great results your clients have realized.

After you meet, send a thank you message via email, recapping the topics discussed, opportunities for synergy and mutual actions agreed to. If this is a worthwhile Referral Source you will know it after your discussion and their response to your discussion summary.

Worthwhile referral sources should be captured in your CRM and follow-ups scheduled every 6 months.

LinkedIn

LinkedIn cuts across so many aspects of Networking it is difficult to enumerate all the places it can help. Let me mention just a few:

- discovering people (by name title and location) who work for a firm that may be a target prospect or a current opportunity in your pipeline,
- a place to post, and keep current, your own *"What do you do?"* information,
- a place to post news updates and Thought Leadership blogs,
- a mechanism to discover if, and where, people have moved to,
- a place to discover industry association events,
- a place to search for warm introductions from those you know and trust, to other people you would like to get to know.

LinkedIn has become a place for business professionals. More so than Facebook and Twitter, it has stayed relatively clear of being usurped and infected by either caustic political dialogue or photos of the family cat. It is an invaluable tool for finding people who are executives (EICs), specialists, potential referral sources and people who believe in you and would be willing to offer a warm referral to a potential target person with whom they are connected,

Any networking plan that does not include LinkedIn is missing an important NBD enabler.

Rule 4: Thought Leadership - Network from the Front of the Room

The *Intra-Market Network* is the viral neurological system through which the peer-to-peer communication of relevant ideas and breakthrough insights happens within a target market segment. If you wish to gain traction in building your, or your firm's perceived leadership reputation in a market, you must plant the seeds of wisdom from your insights directly into this ecosystem so it can be sucked into the natural communication vortex that already exists.

Planting Beneficial Insight Viruses in the Intra-Market Network Ecosystem

There are several ways to inject your insight viruses into an Intra-Market Network ecosystem. The most productive are written pieces (articles, blogs, and books) and speaking (speeches, talks and webinars).

As a salesperson, you and your firm must be perceived as experts. So even if you, or the experts in your firm, do not currently write or speak, you had better collectively learn – and become good at it.

To punctuate the importance of being perceived as an expert, research has identified where management executives go to find the help they need. They do not await a cold call from a product or service provider. They do not try to remember the most charming person they met at a networking mixer.

The two primary ways executives search for solutions to their problems are by asking trusted peers and advisors whom they should call to help with a specific problem (Referrals) and by discovering smart and dynamic solutions through insightful writings and talks (Thought Leadership).

EICs do not review Facebook in search of solutions to their POGs. What they do is ask peers and colleagues and listen to or read material from Thought Leaders. They only search the web and LinkedIn after exhausting those first two activities.

Be prepared to speak and write - or encourage the specialists in your firm to do it. It's important!

Thought Leadership - Articles

Publishing insights in industry journals builds your reputation as an expert – differentiating you in the eyes of your target market decision makers.

Articles published in professional and industry journals (most online these days) seem to be the last living space of good editors and editorial guidelines. Most journals have an editorial policy stating the format, length, and content of the kinds of written pieces that appeal to their readership. Those guidelines can be obtained by contacting the editor or reading the front of the journal where the chief editorial contact is listed.

I consider blogs published on LinkedIn or your own website, as un-editor-ized (not really a word) content - since a LinkedIn-employed editor will not review content before publication of the piece. If you publish your ideas through your website or on LinkedIn, there are no strict guidelines for number of words, accuracy of grammar, topics, or style. No one but you, approves the article, the content, or topic you select. Your ability to publish on LinkedIn, your website and some community forums is typically editor-and-guideline free.

The lack of an editor or pre-publication review is not always good.

Some communities do have a reviewer to preview your work prior to publication, to assure it meets the community standards. Vistage is an example.

I typically publish blogs in the Vistage manufacturing community. Submittal, review, and publication can take a month. Vistage also has other topic-specific communities, such as Family Business, Diversity, Construction, Deals, Global Business, Healthcare and more.

Upon the publication of a post, it is immediately announced via email to all community members – numbering in the thousands in some communities. It is a great way to establish yourself as a thought leader among peers and executives. Vistage membership exceeds 23,000 executives worldwide – the majority of them EICs. All have access to these community network publications.

Because of readers' short attention spans, you should make your points quickly and keep your posts to less than 1500 words. Many bloggers recommend around 600 words. I try to limit mine to 1,000. Remember it is a blog not a book. Make a few insightful points quickly.

As a tip to attract readers, in addition to an intriguing topic and title, you might consider adding the read time required to get through the article. A four-minute read time is a reasonable investment for a reader to gain an insight that may help them their whole career.

The Math of Blogs Posted on LinkedIn

Let us assume you have 900 contacts on LinkedIn. If you have been selective with whom you connect with, perhaps 50% or more might be folks in a position to either recommend or engage you to consult with them. If each of those people you have in your stable of connections have, on average, 200 unique connections (links to people with whom you are not both connected), the multiplier potential of your blog post is incredible. In this case, 900 X 50% x 200 = 90,000 potential reader impressions.

That would require half of your contacts to "share" the blog post. That would be extremely rare. But even if you get only 10 shares the multiplier is large, 900 contacts x 50% relevance rate x 10 shares = 4,500 impressions.

My recommendation: If you wish to be considered a true thought leader to achieve a reputation in wisdom and insights in your field, publish frequently in the relevant on-line communities. It will greatly increase your favorable exposure to a larger audience.

Thought Leadership – Talks

You must constantly seek the opportunity to share your insights through *Talks* in the Venues associated with your offerings' target markets.

Some venues do not allow service providers, such as salespeople, to be speakers. Meeting planners are too concerned that the talk will turn into a poorly disguised sales pitch. This venue restriction is not absolute however, and one way to work around it, (and I have done this before), is to offer to be a panel moderator for three industry executives EICs on a key challenge facing the industry.

Thought Leadership – Videos

Videos are a combinations of Talks and Blog Posts. They combine the brevity of a four-minute blog post, with the visual power of an informal personal conversation. The same material and insights of the blog post can be re-purposed as the raw material for the video.

Blog posts and articles (published on LinkedIn, Vistage, or other virtual venues), Videos (published in Vimeo or YouTube) and live, in-person talks at industry forums provide highly multiplicative opportunities to communicate the value you and your firm provide.

Alliances

Alliances are informal or formal agreements between salespeople of complementary products or services. These alliances are intended to:

- support one another in a client engagement, as appropriate to everyone's expertise,

- be a mutual referral source, as well as a responsive and responsible referral receiver,

- act as a sounding board for confidential discussions of client issues (with a signed mutual confidentiality agreement in place),

- share best business practices in selling (tools, techniques, insights),

- test new ideas before you take them public, and

- if the alliance associates are comfortable with it, provide a safe place for personal or business confidential discussions.

Forming trusted alliances with highly skilled salespeople or service providers with capabilities complementary to your own, requires face-to-face discussions that build trust and reveal mutually beneficial synergy.

Over time, vetting and building a stable of trusted, respected, and highly qualified salespeople and providers of complementary products and services through mutually beneficial alliances, will reinforce your reputation as a strategic resource, thus building your perceived value with clients.

Alliances should be reinforced with mutual, signed confidentiality agreements so that client situations can be discussed openly for the benefit of the client.

Most business-to-business firms have similar organizational structures. They typically have separate departments for each of their major business functions, such as operations, sales, accounting, marketing, quality, and human resources. No matter your specialty, if you are delivering product or services offerings to a client, you will inevitably encounter or be informed of issues, needs, and challenges within departments that are not within your firm's specialty or the scope of your engagement.

In this situation, the first rule is to inform the person who has been identified as your counterpart within your client's organization (typically the EIC) of your awareness of their problem.

The second rule is to not allow scope creep to trap you into attempting to fix a problem that is *not* within your specialty and skill set or is outside of the scope of your firm's contracted-for offering. The temptation to do this can be overwhelming, for example, for consultants. Most salespeople and consultants are natural problem-solvers and when they see a problem, they feel compelled to try to fix it.

The larger the salesperson's firm, the less likely the salesperson, in offering solutions, will wander too far afield of the firm's core offerings. Offerings in larger firms are typically more tightly defined, priced, and limited.

The third rule is to put yourself in a position to offer the client a referral to a high-quality, proven resource that you believe has the capabilities to resolve the issue you identified. Thus, the power of developing a good stable of alliances with providers of complementary products and services, is in a way a valuable differentiator.

Your imperative is to address the client's POG within the scope of your offerings and contract. When you have identified another POG outside of that scope, it is most appropriate to politely offer your observations and your perspective of the business impact of the problem on not only your engagement objectives, but also its impact on the overall health of their business. That approach prepares the ground for a referral recommendation if asked by the client.

Target Market Industry Research

To be relevant, you must know and understand the challenges the decision makers within your target market are facing. You must be able to frame your product and service offerings in the vocabulary, context, and current challenges of that market.

This means approaching a new target market requires some research. There are several approaches that enable you to accomplish that research quickly.

Call the National Association for the Industry

Typically, the Membership Chair or National President of the association is well versed in the challenges facing the industry and the association's membership. They will likely be able to answer any question you have regarding industry challenges, or at minimum, refer you to some prominent member or staff person in the organization who can answer the question.

Join the Target Market's National Association

Every target market I can think of has at least one national association. They typically make their membership list available to members only.

Google the Question

A simple Google search of, "*The biggest challenges facing the (fill in the blank) Industry in 2020*' will likely produce a collection of articles or blogs on that subject. Here is a tiny sampling of what I found on the multiple pages that appeared when I did that for the Ceramics Industry.

- Insights into the World Ceramic Tiles Market (2019 – 2024) www.prnewswire.com
- Ceramic Tiles Market 2020: Top Countries Data, Global ... www.marketwatch.com
- Fine Ceramic Market 2020 Global Industry Analysis, www.nbc-2.com
- Track 1: Industry Trends & Applications: Ceramics Expo www.ceramicsexpousa.com

Caution: You will find when conducting a Google search of such a question there will be a lot of market data regarding the market size. Don't' be distracted. You are not looking for market size data. You are looking for common issues and challenges faced by target clients, so that when you talk to prospects you can relate through a relevant premise.

Call Any Firm in the Industry

Ask for the operations manager, CEO, or marketing executive. Tell them you are a marketing professional researching the issues and challenges that are demanding their attention these days.

From the earliest days in my career, I have always been amazed at the amount of information people are willing to share if your inquiry is sincere and honest.

So, be honest. There is no need to be coy.

Let them know you are exploring a service you'd like to approach the market with and are simply trying to validate the industry's specific challenges so you can tailor and frame those offerings and their benefits in the right context.

That beginning will inevitably elicit the question, *"What kind of offering is it?"*

After that, the conversation has begun, but be cautious of the trap this presents.

Caution: Do *not* turn this conversation into a hard sell or push. Use the opportunity for its expressed purpose - to gather issues information to allow you to prepare your offerings appropriately to fit the market terrain. Otherwise, you have destroyed your credibility and trust with this person. You must not bait and switch from your stated purpose.

For some salespeople, patience is difficult. Please remember, there is no better way to turn off, shut down, and destroy trust, than a hard sales push poorly disguised as sincere issues exploration. There will be plenty of time for selling after you have created a compelling value-quotient and market-specific story. What you what to accomplish at this point is the collection of information. This is your opportunity to get that information.

Do not become distracted.

Connect with Someone on LinkedIn that Works for the Company or in the industry

Through LinkedIn, connect and begin a conversation with someone who works in the industry. Use the same approach as #4 above.

Target Account Research

There are several ways to accomplish the identification of specific clients to target in your target market.

Find the NAICS Code and Use Your Library's Online Databases

NAICS stands for the North American Industry Classification System. It is the standard used by Federal statistical agencies to classify all registered businesses. Its intent is to provide a standard mechanism by which to enable industry data to be collected, analyzed, and published. Each individual NAICS code corresponds to an industry, product, or service type.

The way to discover the NAICS code for your target market is simple. Go to Google and type in "What is the NAICS code for the ceramics industry?" Here is what you will find.

NAICS Code 327110:

Definition of **NAICS Code** 327110. This **industry** comprises establishments primarily engaged in shaping, molding, glazing, and firing **pottery**, **ceramics**, plumbing fixtures, and electrical supplies made entirely or partly of clay or other **ceramic** materials. Apr 17 2016

NAICS Code 327110
Definition | Illustrative Examples | Cross Reference

Class C des

Figure 41: NAICS Code Google Inquiry

Next, log in to your library's online Reference USA (RefUSA) Data Base. My local library, and many other county-affiliated libraries offer a free data base service called Reference USA or something similar. It is accessible on-line if you have a library card.

If you log in to the RefUSA data base and use this NAICS code, you will see a list of entities that have registered themselves as participants in the ceramics industry. You can sort your data base inquiry by company size in revenue, number of employees and geographic region. The data revealed can be extensive.

For purposes of this book, I logged into my library and searched for a randomly selected target market (ceramic parts) in a randomly selected, metropolitan area in the Midwest. I discovered an interesting ceramics firm and was amazed at the extensive amount of data available.

That company's RefUSA filing included the following information:

- website,
- phone number,
- address,
- name of Executive-in-Charge (EIC),
- other NAICS codes the company is involved in,
- parent company name,
- number of employees,

- annual sales for 10 years,

- ranges of expenditures in key areas like advertising, telecommunications, technology, utilities, payroll, legal expenses and more, and amazingly

- the names of 14 members of the management staff and their roles.

For the purposes of generating a list of target clients, this method is a bit more work than joining an association. The list of companies generated from this approach is extensive and requires culling. Some companies listed are only peripherally associated with the NAICS code of interest. So, it takes some sorting and thrashing to find the wheat.

On the other hand, when you find an ideal target client, the company specific data can be comprehensive and very revealing.

Go to the Firm's Website

When perusing the website look for the names of the Management Team and read the News releases. The names of the key executives may be different than the RefUSA list. The website will typically provide more current information on the key people and events impacting your specific target.

Use LinkedIn to Discover More About the Key People at the Firm

Once you have the names of the management team, particularly those with the titles that typically engage your service, you can check to see if they are participating on LinkedIn by either searching the database or using LinkedIn navigator, an enhanced research feature. You can also simply type in the name of the company, and it will provide you the number and names of the employees that work in that company who also have profiles on LinkedIn.

Since LinkedIn also informs you of the people with whom you are linked, that are also linked with your target individual, you can determine who might be the best mutual connection you might request a warm introduction of.

New Business Development (NBD) Summary

In this Appendix we have briefly described NBD activities and how they differ from, and complement, the "In-the-Pipeline" sales activities covered in Part 2 of Navigational Selling™.

Where the responsibilities for NBD activities are assigned, varies from company to company. But even a single sole proprietor salesperson can execute them, if they have the will and understand their enormous value.

*****

Afterword

Navigational Selling™ was written in an attempt to help SMB2B businesses improve their probability of achieving growth, long-term success, and value enhancement. It has intentionally explored the bigger picture, interconnectedness, and dependencies of marketing and sales-related business processes.

For some it will appear to have attempted to cover too much detail. I can accept that observation. It has merit.

In response, I will only say, it covers a lot of ground and involves a lot of detail because there is a lot that a responsible EIC needs to understand to make sound decisions and invest wisely. There are many stakeholders (employees, families, suppliers, clients, and the communities in which they live) whose well-being and futures depend on that understanding and decision making.

From others, it may receive criticism for its repetition. That too was intended. Few if any business professionals I have encountered in my long career have eidetic memories and repetition helps. As stated in the Notes to Readers at the front of this book, "*If it's repeated, it's important*".

In my long consulting career, so few EICs and Marketing & Sales executives have demonstrated an in-depth, empirical science-based understanding of how it all works together that I felt it important to leave no stone unturned.

For various reasons, (luck, good guesses, technology, overwhelming positive market momentum), many of those EICs achieved degrees of success, without such an understanding. I do not begrudge that success.

While I am delighted for their achievements and proud to have them as friends, I reserve the right to ponder the question, *"How much more would they have achieved if they did have that knowledge?"*

For those to whom this book will be helpful, please accept it book as a humble offer of knowledge. For those EICs and salespeople who have been successful to their satisfaction and believe that slogging through these pages is not worth the effort, I sincerely wish you continued good fortune.

*****

Glossary of Terms

Absolute Honesty	A cultural imperative that requires direct, open, and honest communication between employees and up-and-down in the organization.
Accountability	A cultural imperative that holds individual responsible for doing what they say they will and doing what they are required to do to perform their role in a professional, effective, and efficient manner.
Account Management	The activity of servicing a current customer and keeping current with what is happening within their business.
Account Pre-Qualification	The act of researching firms within your primary target markets, that are not current clients, to determine the likelihood that they may be experiencing the kinds of POGS your offerings address.
Advocate	An individual within a client organization that has high affinity for your solution or approach and is willing to promote it within the client organization.
Affinity	The degree to which any buy or influencer at a prospective client is attracted to your service offering.
Alignment	A cultural imperative that requires that all company and channel employees execute their roles and responsibilities in close coordination, as a team, and consistent with the strategic objectives of the firm.
Alliance	A formal or informal arrangement with other Salespeople of complementary products and service whom you trust. Such an arrangement may comprise a formal mutual confidentiality agreement, complementary offerings, working arrangements as a sub-contractor to one another, mutual marketing efforts, co-authors, bidirectional referrals, peer support group participation and/or partnering in the development of intellectual property and thought leadership.
Applicability	The degree to which a client prospect EIC believes your firm's approach and offering is well-suited to address their POG.

ASS	Action Sans Strategy: Action taken in pursuit of a sales opportunity without adequate analysis and strategizing.
Assessments	Assessments are diagnostic tools that assist both the salesperson and the client Executive-in-Charge determine what areas of their business (process, skills, culture, etc.) have performance deficiencies. Assessments using the client's own scoring help the client acknowledge the need for action.
Analyzer	A personality type of buyer who requires a great deal of information and comparisons before making a recommendation or decision to buy.
Authority	The economic and organizational power needed to decide to buy something.
B2B	Business-to-Business, wherein a business buys goods and services for the purpose of improving their business operations.
Barrier	A barrier is a roadblock the client is experiencing in making progress on achievement of some important initiative they are undertaking. The client has recognized this roadblock is of such a nature that that they will not be able to overcome it themselves. Therefore, the client has decided to seek and engage outside help to resolve it.
Behavioral Metrics	Behavioral metrics are measurements of the independent salesperson's behaviors that will produce the desired outcome metrics (dependent metric).
BMMDI	(Boss-Made-Me-Do-It); A type of client employee that provides minimal commitment and support for a consulting engagement or project, only to the extent their boss pushes or monitors their progress.
Brand	An SMB2B firm's Brand is the meaning its reputation conjures in the minds of its clients. That Brand reputation is the result of the collective clients' experiences in transacting business with the firm. A winning Brand cannot be built on bad client experiences, and a good brand can be destroyed by bad client experiences. Relative Perceived Quality Leadership (RPQL) in client experience compared to the firm's competitors will lead to leadership market share and Brand reputation.
Challenge	A barrier the client perceives as preventing them from achieving some outcome, objective, or goal.

Coaching

Coaching is the act of assisting an employee through both business and personal challenges. Coaches assist employees navigate the road to achieve both their personal and business goals, by listening, offering sage and experienced advice, and the emotional support needed to see the employee through tough times.

Compelling Need (opportunity-related)

Compelling Need is an opportunity qualification factor that rates the degree to which a challenge or problem faced by a client is critical, needing to be addressed immediately or soon, or there will be significant consequence for not doing so. Regulatory compliance, safety considerations or the need to meet bank covenants are just a few examples of needs that fall into a high Compelling Needs category.

Compelling Need (target market attractiveness related)

Compelling need is also a factor used in assessing the attractiveness of target markets. In that case Compelling Need relates to the degree to which, across a large swatch of client in the market, there is a common issues, problem or challenge that can be serviced by your offering.

Copyright

The exclusive right of the creator to make copies of an original written work or other creation. Copyright permissions can be granted by the creator to other users for a fee. (See License)

Decision Influencer

Any individual within the client organization who will exert influence over the buying decision. Influencers do not wield ultimate authority, meaning they cannot provide the ultimate yes, but can contribute a qualified "no". These are often technical people or other specialists.

Decision Maker

An individual within a client's organization with the final authority to legally commit and bind a client organization to a consulting engagement.

Decision Making

The cultural characteristic demonstrated by data-based decision making, clear authority and a sense-of-urgency.

Deliverable

"Deliverable" is the generic term for something you promise the client will receive from doing business with you. Deliverables can take several forms – they are not limited to distinct defined products or services. The accomplishment of an objective, the achievement of a milestone, the realization of a measurable goal, or the arrival at a desired outcome can also be considered deliverables.

Dependent Variables — Measurable metrics that are dependent on specific behavioral variables for their achievement.

Differentiation — The market-relevant capability or unique characteristic of the consulting service you provide that makes it stand out among all other similar offerings offered to the market.

Director — A manager in a client organization that exhibits authoritative and assertive behaviors in unilateral decision making and management style.

Discovery — The second step in the CNP consulting sales process which is intended exclusively for fact-finding and extracting from the client team all the information needed to formulate a winning proposal.

Discussion Summary — A message sent the client EIC within 24 hours of a discovery meeting, that summarizes the discussion and key points of the meeting and captures any mutually agreed, follow-on action items.

Economic Value — A clear economic value quotient calculation (benefits/costs) of customer-received economic benefits divided by economic costs associated with implementing the Salesperson's recommendation.

Ego — A salesperson's self-esteem. A strong Ego enables a salesperson to focus on the client and their POG first, without anxiety that their own success may be at risk. The stronger the Ego, the higher the likelihood of a win-win outcome.

Emotional Value — A qualitative value quotient calculation (benefits/costs) of customer-received emotional benefits divided by emotional costs associated with implementing the Salesperson's recommendation.

Empathy — The ability of the salesperson to understand and feel the client's discomfort associated with their need to resolve their Problem, Opportunity, or Gap (POG).

Energizer — An emotive individual in a prospective client organization whose sees their role as to generate excitement and enthusiasm. That enthusiasm is often the extent of their commitment. Their enthusiasm can be misinterpreted by the Salesperson as commitment.

Ethics	A cultural imperative that establishes the guiding principles (interpersonal, legal, moral, and business-related) by which employees will conduct themselves.
Expectations Setting	In the cultural context Expectations Setting is the degree to which individual and group-level objectives, behaviors, and ethics are clearly communicated and universally established within the organization.
Fair-Elastic Pricing	Price setting based on the magnitude of the value to be received by the client. As the perceived value increases so do the prices proposed.
Fair-Fee Setting	The act of setting consulting fees based on a mutual understanding of the value to be received by the client.
Focus	Closely related to alignment, focus is the clear common understanding of which target market, ideal clients, value quotients and differentiated characteristics are driving the market strategy of an offering.
GDP	Gross Domestic Product: The total value of goods and offerings in the US economy comprising = private consumer spending + gross investment + government investment + government spending + (the value of exports – the value of imports).
Goal	A Goal is an objective that is distinct, quantified, specific, and time bound. The accomplishment of a Goal is confirmed if the stated and measurable success criteria and conditions have been achieved. Let's say, "Reduce operating expenses by 10% in the coming fiscal year 2022, as compared to 2021."
Goal Setting	In the corporate cultural context, Goal Setting is the degree to which quantifiable objectives are commonly established and used against which to measure progress.
Harmonizer	A personality type within a client's organization whose primary concern in engaging with a Salesperson is to preserve the harmony and stability of the team involved in its evaluation purchase and execution. Harmonizers will be satisfied with less-than-optimal functional solutions if the key players in the organization have had their say and agree.
Ideal Client Profile	Ideal client profiles describe the client problems whose resolution will provide client significant value, but also describe the personality

types of clients and client cultural characteristics that will likely embrace your offerings and approach. Ideal client profiles are specific to each offering.

Independent Variables   Measurable behavioral metrics that are _not_ dependent on any other behavioral variables for their achievement.

Industrial Production Index

The measure of all industrial B2B business activity in the economy.

Intra-Market Network   The communication and influence structure within a target market, comprising its Venues (where members meet), Vehicles (what they read), its Opinion Leaders, Primary Referral Sources and the Economic Decision Makers associated with the offerings you provide.

Influencer   The specific individual within a client's organization that for some reason, has the ability and willingness to advise and promote an idea or course of action to a person of equal or higher stature and authority.

Influence   The ability to advise and promote an idea or course of action to a person of equal or higher stature within a society, peer group, organization, or business.

Intellectual Property   Any work or invention that is the result of creativity, such as a tool, manuscript, or design, to which one has rights, and for which one may apply for a patent, copyright, or trademark.

Key Process Discipline   The documentation and consistent adherence to the key operating processes of the firm. Changes to key processes must undergo a formal test and approval process to assure a) changes do not cause more harm than good and b) quality is maintained.

Law of Imbalanced Value   All cash that accrues to your consulting , does so based on a client's perception and belief that they will receive greater economic, emotional, physical, political and/or social value, than the economic, emotional, physical, political, and social costs associated with deploying a service.

License   A contract which allows a person to use the intellectual property of another in exchange for a usage fee.

Lipotage	Lipotage® is the act of expressing support of an initiative or idea in public while sabotaging the idea in private conversations through criticism, negative comments, or other counter-productive behaviors.
Market Ecosystem	(See Intra-Market Network)
Market Positioning	A conceptual way of capturing a comparative perception of value in the minds of your target market decision makers.
Match	Match is the second opportunity qualification factor which rates the degree to which your service offering precisely meets the challenges presented by that client's Compelling Need. It is insufficient to believe that your offering is a good match to their problem. The client's perspective is the only perspective that has meaning in determining the Match rating.
Measurements & Metrics	The use of quantifiable assessments of progress regarding a) adherence to positive desired behaviors, b) business process effectiveness, and c) individual and corporate goals.
Mentoring	(See Coaching)
Metric(s)	Metrics are measurements that are tracked to assess level of performance.
Milestone	A milestone is the clearly identifiable completion or accomplishment of an essential step on the path to achieving the client's Objective or a Goal.
Navigational Selling	A sales process methodology which recognizes the role of the salesperson similar to that of the Navigator of a ship, planning and advising the client of the best approach to journey from where they are to where they want to be.
Navigator Mindset	The Navigator Mindset is characterized by a primary focus on achieving the client's goals through a win-win solution, a priority to listen over talk, a motivational imperative to help - not hype, and a drive to build trust over "closing at all costs."
NBD or New Business Development	Activities within a consulting or other business aimed at finding, opening, and developing new sources of multiple opportunities.

Those activities can include networking. venue identification, vehicle identification, thought leadership, distribution channel development, licensing, franchising, and alliance development.

Objective
A non-quantified, generalized goal the business wished to achieve. It may be expressed by the generalized statement, such as, "*We want to achieve continuous growth.*"

Objectively Targeted Solution (OTS)

A solution offered to a client that exclusively addresses what the expert salesperson believes is needed to solve the client's problem, overcome the client's barriers, or avail themselves of an opportunity, based on thorough Discovery. An OTS purposely eliminates anything the client wants that is deemed by the expert as superfluous, potentially harmful, or counterproductive.

Offering
An offering is what an SMB2B firm sells. It can be either a product, a service, or a combination of both.

Open Communications
A critical component of a culture of Absolute Honesty. "Open Communications" encourages the direct and clear communication between employees, upwards, peer-to-peer and downwards within the organization. "Open Communications" depends on good listening skills, data-based conversations, and a fear-free environment.

Opinion Leader
An individual within a target market ecosystem (intra-market network) that is considered by others in that target market as an expert in a certain area of knowledge or experience. Opinion leaders are, both informally and formally, expected to provide guidance to others in that market and are key nodes of communication and influence for the spread of helpful ideas and concepts.

Opportunist
A prospective client decision maker or influencer that is looking for a "deal' to such an extent that the deal becomes more important that the consulting service or the outcome delivered.

Opportunity Qualification
Opportunity Qualification refers to specific needs within any type of account, (new or existing), for the sale of one or more of your firm's offerings. Not all opportunities that arise in discussions with a pre-qualified account will be attractive or appropriate to attempt to win.

Opportunity
The word Opportunity has two meanings in the context of Navigational Selling, one from the salesperson's perspective and the second from the client's perspective.

From a salesperson's perspective: An opportunity is a specific chance to sell a product or service that will assist a specific client solve a problem, overcome a barrier, or avail themselves of an opportunity to improve their situation. Clients are likely to be well aware of a problem or a barrier to achieving their objectives, but not certain how to overcome them.

From a client's perspective: An opportunity is a path to make significant progress toward a goal or outcome. Typically, a client may not be aware of such a path. For example: A client may perceive your offering as an opportunity to open up a new market that will double sales. In this case the client views the offering as opening up this opportunity, in contrast to seeing the offering as a way to solve a problem or overcome a barrier.

Outcome	An Outcome is a future state. Outcomes can be tangible (let's say a product or service successfully delivered), or intangible-emotional (for example, specific problem-related stress relief).
Outcome Metrics	Measurements of the ultimate results of sales efforts, such as, bookings, revenue, and commissions.
Ownership	The degree to which responsibilities for achieving objectives and goals is clearly established within individual employee responsibilities. Ownership also applies to decision-making, including financial levels of signatory approval, scope of purview, and the limits of any legal authority to commit the firm to contractual obligations.
Physical Value	A qualitative or quantitative value quotient calculation (benefits/costs) of customer-received physical benefits divided by physical costs associated with implementing the Salesperson's recommendation.
POG	A client's Problem, Opportunity, or Gap.
Political Value	A qualitative or quantitative value quotient calculation (benefits/costs) of customer-received political benefits divided by political costs associated with implementing the Salesperson's recommendation.
Premise	A credible, logical, and valid benefit a key client decision-maker or decision-influencer within a target account might receive from speaking with you. Premises must always be formulated from the

primary perspective of their relevance and benefit to the specific client with whom you will be speaking.

Primary Referral Source (PRS)

A Primary Referral Source (PRS) is a well-networked colleague or client who believes strongly in your capabilities and therefore acts as a source of referrals for new opportunities.

Problem

A difficulty faced by the client, which because of its complexity, is beyond their capability to the client to quickly resolve without help.

Proposal

A formal documented offer to provide a consulting service to a client.

Quality

In its strictest definition, Quality means meeting the client's needs. A perception of Quality is only valid from the client's perspective.

RPQL

Relative Perceived Quality Leadership is a perception in the mind of a client and market as to the benefits of a service compared to other similar offerings offered to that client or market.

Robinson-Patman

Legislation which was put in place to assure fairness in pricing and competition. Suppliers may not charge any of their customers (that might compete with one another) different prices without reason. The act applies to products and not services.

SGO

A Sincerely Growth Oriented potential client decision maker or influencer whose primary consideration in evaluating and buying a consulting service is its ability to accelerate the growth of their business.

SMB2B

Small-to-Midsized Business-to-Business. Typically considered those businesses with less than 500 employees. For purposes of Navigational Selling™ we are considering firms with annual revenues in the range of $1M to $300M.

SAP Sheet

SAP is an acronym for Strategy-and-Action-Planning. A Sap sheet is single page document (or screen) which displays all relevant opportunity information, used to formulate strategies and action plans.

Scrum Board

A visible method of tracking progress by stage.

Sense of Urgency	A cultural characteristic which can be observed by the intensity and speed with which challenges are met, decisions made, barriers overcome, and results achieved.
Social Media	Mechanisms and vehicles used to communicate between members within your target market ecosystem. Examples include Facebook, LinkedIn, Twitter, Instagram and more.
Social Value	A qualitative or quantitative value quotient calculation (benefits/costs) of customer-received social benefits divided by social costs associated with implementing the Salesperson's recommendation.
Socket	A potential company in which a consulting service can be applied and provide value.
Statement of Work	Primarily used in the context of proposals, a Statement of Work describes the kinds of services the salesperson's firm will be performing for the client. It includes the expert stand-alone services that will be delivered by the seller (engineering or technical expertise, diagnostics, analysis, design, etc.) and the services surrounding the tangible product deliverables (tailoring, configuration, installation, integration, testing, training, etc.).
Strategic Marketing	The activities associated with selecting the most lucrative markets to approach, defining, and designing what offerings to offer to that market, testing its client-perceived value, deciding how to price it and through what channel to sell it.
StuMP	A prospective client personality type characterized by an unwillingness to buy consulting offerings, even though the need may be critical.
Tactical Marketing	Expenditures made to execute a communications plan aimed at a specific target market. Typical tactical marketing expenditures include website, email promotions, tradeshows, advertising, printed fliers, branding, social media, logo, and tag line development and more.

Target Market Attractiveness Factor

See TMAF.

Taker	A client who wished to steal and use, without a licensing arrangement, a Salesperson's intellectual property in the form of tools, and trademarked or copyrighted materials.
Teamwork	The degree to which employees work effectively in groups to achieve goals and objectives.
Thought Leadership	Thought Leadership is the group of activities associated with sharing and spreading relevant insights concerning some aspect of the client challenges that your offerings address. It comprises articles, blogs, webinars, talks, and whitepapers produced by an expert in the field (one of your most knowledgeable, and experienced employees), delivered to groups of client decision makers and decision influencers within the intra-market network.
TMAF	Target Market Attractiveness Factor, used when evaluating the relative attractiveness of several different product-market combinations.
Trademark	A recognized and exclusive right to use, copy, license or sell a self-conceived and documented written or creative work.
Training	Employee instruction in key business process. Training must always be followed by deployment, checkpoints to assure positive impact and periodic re-training.
TT	Terribly Troubled client executives. TTs typically need to act quickly to fix some compelling business problem and make decisions fast.
Value Vortex™	A value vortex is a market need that is so compelling for clients, that when matched with a high-customer value received service offering will be swept up by accelerating demand. Think of what happens when object get too close to a tornado.
Venue	A gathering a place or event for the key people in a target market. These typically comprise tradeshows, industry conferences, national and regional association meetings, and networking events.
Vehicle	Within a market ecosystem, a vehicle is an accessible source of information that members of that community commonly use to find news and information. Typically, vehicles encompass both web-based and physical journals, blogs, videos, webinars, seminars, books, and other published material sources.

Value Quotient

The ratio of benefits received by the client divided by the costs to the client involved in buying and executing a consulting engagement. For a service to provide meaningful value the benefits must significantly outweigh the costs.

Value Quotient (Qualification)

The client Value Quotient qualification factor rates the long-term value that will be realized by the client, of acquiring and using your solution to fix their problem or meet their challenge, compared to the costs borne by the client of implementing that solution. The Client Value Quotient is both a subconscious and conscious calculation in the mind of the client. It comprises both, the five perceived benefits (economic, emotional, physical, political, and social) divided by the five perceived costs (economic, emotional, physical, political, and social).

Value Quotient Clarification

The communication and explanation by the salesperson to the client of the magnitude of the Value Quotient that will be realized by the client from the Offering and Proposal.

Vision

A Vision is a situational Outcome desired by the client that incorporates both tangible and significant emotional-intangible elements. Visions are effective in selling and garnering client enthusiasm and buy-in - but hard-to-define and prove delivery of as a promised Outcome.

*****

Table of Figures

****

Index

*****

About the Author

Jerry Vieira, CMC is a Certified Management Consultant and President & Founder of The QMP Group, Inc., a Portland, OR based Market Strategy and Marketing & Sales Transformation consulting firm that works with small-to-midsized businesses-to-business firms across the U.S. He is the author of two books, The Consultancy Navigator® and Navigational Selling™.

In addition, Jerry is the sole creator and developer of the QMP Marketing & Sales Organizational Transformation Program, the QMP Marketing & Sales Engine™ model, the IOEA™ family of tailorable Individual & Organizational Effectiveness Assessments, and numerous other strategic marketing, business development, sales and organizational culture change training programs and tools.

He is an Engineer, Market Strategist, Salesperson, Business Owner, Public Speaker, Business Coach, Author, Musician/Composer, Dad, Granddad, and Fisherman. Since founding The QMP Group in 1990, Jerry has helped hundreds of companies and trained, coached, and influenced over a thousand individuals, from CEOs to field salespeople.

Raised on the East Coast, Jerry earned a Bachelor's in Electrical Engineering from Manhattan College, an MBA from the University of Rhode Island and a Bachelor's in Music from Portland State University, where he studied trumpet, composition and arranging.

He has a U.S. patent and two books to his name, as well as dozens of original musical compositions. He spends his work time consulting, coaching, and writing. His spare time is spent hacking away at any piano within reach, and fishing in the bays, rivers and along the shores of the Oregon coast.

*****

Made in the USA
Middletown, DE
25 February 2022